L. Nguyen

the family cookbook: **french**

the family cookbook

by Alvin Kerr

Special Consultant:

James Beard

Illustrations

by Helen Federico

Photography

by Irwin Horowitz

A Ridge Press Book | Holt, Rinehart and Winston | New York

RIDGE PRESS:
Editor-in-Chief: Jerry Mason
Editor: Adolph Suehsdorf
Art Director: Albert Squillace
Project Art Director: Harry Brocke
Project Editor: Barbara Hoffbeck
Associate Editor: Ruth Birnkrant
Associate Editor: Moira Duggan
Art Associate: Mark Liebergall
Art Associate: David Namias
Art Production: Doris Mullane

RA

RESTAURANT ASSOCIATES:
Project Director: Alan Reyburn
Supervising Chef, Restaurant Associates: Josef Renggli
Executive Chef, Four Seasons: Maurice Chantreau

Courtesy of BLOOMINGDALE'S, New York, in lending
objects for photographic still lifes is gratefully acknowledged.

Prepared and produced by The Ridge Press, Inc. Published in the
United States of America in 1973 by Holt, Rinehart and Winston, Inc., Publishers,
383 Madison Avenue, New York, New York 10017, U.S.A. Published
simultaneously in Canada by Holt, Rinehart and Winston of Canada, Limited.
Library of Congress Catalog Card Number: 72-78136
ISBN: 0-03-001401-8
Printed and bound in Italy by Mondadori, Verona.

contents

introduction

In all the world there are only two really great cuisines: the Chinese and the French. China's was created first, untold centuries ago, and is judged to be the greater—when executed by superb chefs. It is the most complicated cuisine; it uses ingredients no other employs; and it is distinctive in that, for the most part, it is *cuisine à la minute.*

In time, other remarkable styles of cooking evolved: Indian, which never has been superlative but always has been interesting, and Persian, which was extraordinarily fine when this sophisticated civilization was at its height. (As someone has remarked, the Persians cooked rice as intricately as they designed their buildings and detailed their miniatures.)

Rome marked the climax of the *hautes cuisines* of antiquity. It far exceeded Greece, both in the complexity and decadence of its cooking. Thereafter, the art of the kitchen declined. Not until the heyday of Venice in the sixteenth century did it revive as a concern of men of sensibility. Venetian cooks were brilliant and were invigorated by the period's voyages of discovery which brought home new foods and new methods of preparation.

By the Late-Renaissance, there was evidence in France of what now are known as *la cuisine simple* and *la cuisine bourgeoise,* two of the three dimensions of classic French cooking. It remained only for

Catherine de Medici, as she went forth to become queen of France, to take with her the Venetian chefs and Venetian finesse which would provide the foundation for the third dimension—*la grande cuisine.*

In the subsequent four centuries, France refined each of these dimensions and conferred them on the world. *La cuisine simple* is, indeed, utterly, utterly simple—the most basic food prepared in the most casual fashion, yet nonetheless flavorful, interesting, memorable. It requires a deft hand in cooking and the skillful addition of appropriate seasoning but none of the flourishes found in more advanced studies of the culinary art. This is family cooking by and for the family that loves food. I am afraid that it does not thrive today so well as it once did.

La cuisine bourgeoise generally is the French cooking most people are familiar with. For our acquaintance with it Americans are indebted to early disciples of French cooking, particularly Eliza Leslie, who in 1832 published her translation of a recipe book containing many great French dishes—the first such book to appear in America. In the 1840's and 50's the country was further educated by a touring chef named Pierre Blot. *La cuisine bourgeoise* is best known for such marvelous dishes as Boeuf à la Bourguignonne, Coq au Vin, Gigot d'Agneau Béarnaise, and Gigot Bretonne. It includes fruit tarts and the wonderfully sweet rice combinations which are the sophisticated cousins of our rice puddings. These are relatively uncomplicated dishes to which loving care and subtle seasoning have been added. Some of them are numbered among the great dishes.

La grande cuisine is almost mythical these days. It embraces the supreme creations of the supreme chefs, the self-expression they indulged when they wished to show off for royalty, for notable palates, for celebrated occasions. It is a cuisine which involves intricate saucings, garnitures, and *pièces montées,* the elaborate designs of chefs who had had architectural training. This is a cuisine which has all but disappeared. We simply are no longer blessed with a sufficiency of trained superchefs, who never were numerous, but who arose with surprising frequency in France.

This does not mean that the great cuisine of France is dead. It is flourishing both in France and in America, where it is striven after as the ultimate achievement. French cooking is considered to be mental cooking—meaning careful planning, careful buying, and minute attention to detail. Yet it should not be any more difficult for the average cook than any other school of cookery, and I feel that one of the things that Alvin Kerr has accomplished in *The Family Cookbook: French* is to erase people's fears that certain dishes are too much for them to undertake. Such dishes as a Breast of Duckling with Pepper

Sauce, for example, or a Lemon Carrot Casserole, or a Custard with Fresh Salmon, or a fine soufflé are no more exacting than making a Devil's Food Cake with Fudge Icing, or a perfect Fried Chicken with Cream Gravy. They merely require fresh approaches. It is this newness of approach and an evident delight in creating a repertoire of international cookery that has inspired this very well-planned cookbook.

Each French cookbook is a variation on classic themes. Each author has his own particular way of expressing an established recipe in the French tradition. Alvin Kerr is a cook and a teacher of cooking whose food I have eaten over a period of thirty-five years. His infinite care in the kitchen, his "cooking hands," which are excellent and fascinating to watch, and his exceedingly sensitive palate have helped to create in this book an authoritative gospel of French family cooking.

I find the recipes in *The Family Cookbook: French* pleasantly various, knowledgeable in their conception, charmingly presented, and simple to follow. The author has worked in concert with the master chefs of Restaurant Associates to achieve this happy result. I am quite sure you will find that this volume of French cooking according to Alvin Kerr has a most active and vital place on your cookbook shelf.

—James Beard

Filet
Anchois
PASTE

1 | hors-d'oeuvres and canapés

As its name suggests, the hors-d'oeuvre is an extra, a prelude to the planned meal. As such, it must not be alien to the other offerings at the table but should complement them, even as the sauce, the vegetables, and other accompaniments complement the main course and relate to it. A quiche rich with eggs would be ill-suited to a meal that is planned to culminate in a soufflé. While a light meal can agreeably accommodate an hors d'oeuvre of substance, a lusty main course could hardly support an equally hearty introduction.

A large assortment of hors-d'oeuvres, *hors-d'oeuvre variées,* is appropriate for buffet presentation, less so for a first course at a family table. It may, and occasionally does, provide the entire main course at luncheon, if the cook is inclined to such elaborate preparation for the midday meal. Cold hors-d'oeuvres, of simple preparation, are usually a midday offering. The whetting of the appetite is an important aspect of the hors-d'oeuvre course, so take extra care in presenting and garnishing these dishes attractively.

Steamed Clams | Praires à la Vapeur

1 small onion, sliced
½ cup water
6 dozen soft-shell clams
Melted butter

In a large kettle heat the onion in the water. Add the clams, cover the kettle tightly, and let the clams steam 10 to 12 minutes until the shells open. Discard any clams that do not open. Strain the broth through several thicknesses of cheesecloth (to strain out any sand and bits of shell there may be in the broth). Reheat the broth. Serve the clams with individual portions of the broth and melted butter. This recipe provides 6 servings.

Clams in Aspic | Praires en Gelée

18 Steamed Clams (above)
¼ pound cooked crabmeat
1¼ cups broth of steamed clams, strained
1 envelope (1 Tbl) unflavored gelatine
1 cup Chicken Broth (page 53 or canned)

Remove the clams from the shells. Separate the shells and reserve 24 perfect halves. Discard the rest. Put the clams and crabmeat together through the fine blade of a food chopper and rub the ground mixture through a fine sieve. Strain ¾ cup of the clam broth into a saucepan and heat it. Soften the gelatine in ¼ cup of the chicken broth and dissolve it in the hot clam broth. Stir in the remaining chicken broth. Pour 1 cup of the gelatine mixture into a shallow pan and cool and chill it in the refrigerator until it gels firmly. In a mixing bowl combine the remaining gelatine liquid and the remaining clam broth, and blend in the clam-crabmeat mixture. Chill that mixture until it begins to gel, and whip it lightly with a fork. Fill the reserved shells with this aspic and chill them until the fillings are set. Finely dice the clear aspic and sprinkle it equally over the filled shells. Apportion the shells for 6 servings of 4 each.

Fillets of Mackerel in White Wine | Maquereaux au Vin Blanc

1 large onion, thinly sliced
1 small branch dried fennel
2 bay leaves
¼ tsp dried sage
1 tsp salt
4 peppercorns
3 cups dry white wine
6 thin slices unpeeled lemon
6 thin slices unpeeled orange
2 pounds fillets of mackerel
1 medium tomato, cut into 6 slices
Sprigs of parsley

Preheat oven to 350 degrees. In a saucepan combine the onion slices, separated into rings, the fennel, bay leaves, sage, salt, peppercorns, and wine. Bring the liquid to a boil and cook over high heat until the wine is reduced to about 2 cups. Arrange ½ the slices of lemon and orange in a lightly buttered enamel-coated or heat-proof glass baking pan and place the fish over them. Do not overlap the fillets. Cover them with the slices of tomato and the remaining slices of lemon and orange, and pour over them the hot wine mixture. Set the pan in the preheated oven and cook for 20 minutes or just until the fillets are tender. Do not overcook them. Let them cool in the cooking liquid. Transfer the fillets to a serving platter and strain over them just enough of the cooking liquid to cover them. Chill before serving. Reserve a few of the lemon and orange slices. Discard the remainder. Decorate the serving platter with the reserved slices and sprigs of parsley. This recipe provides 6 servings.

Steamed Mussels | Moules à la Marinière

4 quarts mussels (see Note)
1 cup moderately dry white wine
¼ cup water
2 Tbl butter
2 stalks celery, finely chopped
1 medium onion, finely chopped
4 sprigs parsley
1 small clove garlic, crushed
½ bay leaf
¼ tsp thyme
⅛ tsp pepper
Salt
2 Tbl finely chopped parsley

Scrub the mussels and, with a sharp knife, scrape off the beards. Set

the mussels in a pan of barely tepid water for a few minutes, during which time they will rid themselves of any sand. Rinse them in fresh cool water and drain them. In a large deep saucepan over high heat cook together, at boil for 2 minutes, all of the remaining ingredients except the salt and chopped parsley. Remove and discard the garlic and bay leaf. Add the cleaned mussels, cover the pan securely, and continue cooking, shaking the pan frequently, for 6 minutes or until the shells open. If any have not opened after 10 minutes, remove and discard them. Season the broth with salt to taste, if needed. Apportion the opened mussels into soup plates to provide 6 servings and strain the broth equally over them. Sprinkle each serving with a little of the chopped parsley. Serve with warm crusty French Bread.
NOTE: In some areas mussels are sold by the pound. A quart of mussels is the equivalent of about 2 pounds.

Variation:

Strain the broth, blend into it ¼ cup Fish Velouté Sauce (page 145) and a few drops of strained lemon juice, and pour over the mussels.

Fried Mussels | Moules Frites

3 quarts mussels
1 small onion, finely chopped
1 stalk celery, finely chopped
2 sprigs parsley
2 cups water
¼ cup bland cooking oil
1 Tbl olive oil
Juice of 1 lemon, strained
1 Tbl finely chopped parsley
2 cups sifted flour
¼ tsp salt
1½ cups light beer
2 dashes Tabasco
2 egg whites, stiffly beaten
Additional flour for dredging
Oil for deep frying
Fried Parsley (page 185)
Lemon wedges

Clean the mussels (see Steamed Mussels, above). Combine the onion, celery, sprigs of parsley, and water in a large saucepan and bring the liquid to a boil. Add the mussels, cover the pan securely, and cook, shaking the pan frequently, for 6 minutes or until the shells open. If any have not opened after 10 minutes remove and discard them. Drain the mussels and shell them.

A brilliant first course is this layered mousse of ham, subtly blended with herbs and wines, and set in a ring of cherry tomatoes (page 33).

In a mixing bowl combine 3 tablespoons of the bland oil, the olive oil, lemon juice, and chopped parsley. Add the mussels and let marinate for 30 minutes, turning them frequently. Drain them and pat dry between sheets of paper toweling. In another bowl prepare a smooth batter by thoroughly combining the flour, salt, beer, Tabasco, and the remaining bland oil. Fold in the beaten egg whites. Dredge the mussels lightly with flour and coat them well with the batter. Fry in deep hot oil (360 degrees) to a golden brown, 3 to 5 minutes. Drain quickly on paper toweling and serve at once garnished with fried parsley and lemon wedges. This recipe provides 8 servings as a first course or 6 as a light entrée.

Mussels with Snail Butter | Moules au Beurre d'Escargot

2 quarts Steamed Mussels (page 15)
Snail Butter (page 168)
1 cup fine soft bread crumbs

Drain the steamed mussels, reserving the strained broth, if desired, for other uses; it is not needed for this recipe. (The broth can be kept under normal refrigeration for about 1 week or frozen for about 3 months.) Shell the mussels, reserving half of each shell. Spread ½ teaspoon of the prepared butter in each half shell, place a mussel on it, and cover evenly with more butter. Sprinkle the tops lightly with the bread crumbs. Arrange the filled shells in a shallow baking pan and chill them in the refrigerator for several hours or overnight to blend the flavors.

Preheat oven to 350 degrees and bake the mussels in it for 5 minutes or until the crumbs are lightly browned and the butter is bubbling. This recipe provides 6 servings of 10 to 12 mussels each.

Oysters Mignonnette | Huîtres Mignonnette

36 oysters
⅓ cup white vinegar
1 Tbl very finely chopped shallots
4 tsp coarsely ground white pepper
½ tsp lemon juice
¼ tsp salt

In a Provençale version of the pizza, fresh tomato filling is latticed with zesty anchovies and dotted with succulent black olives (page 41).

Shuck the oysters, or have the fish market open them for you, reserving half of each shell. Arrange the oysters on the half shells in 6 individual serving plates. In a mixing bowl thoroughly combine the vinegar, shallots, pepper, lemon juice, and salt. Pour ½ teaspoon of the sauce over each oyster or pass the sauce separately.

Soufflé Roll with Fresh Salmon | Roulade de Soufflé au Saumon

1½ pounds fresh salmon, in 1 piece
Poaching Broth (page 57)
½ cup finely grated seeded cucumber, drained
Hollandaise Sauce (page 150)
¼ cup butter
½ cup flour
½ tsp salt
2 cups milk, scalded
4 eggs, separated
1 Tbl fine dry bread crumbs

Poach the salmon in the broth at simmer for 12 minutes or just until it is tender when pierced with the tines of a fork. Drain it, remove the skin and bones, and flake the fish coarsely. Combine it with the grated cucumber and blend in ⅓ cup of the Hollandaise sauce or just enough to bind the mixture firmly. Keep it warm. Reserve the remaining sauce.

Preheat oven to 325 degrees. In the top pan of a double-boiler heat the butter and blend in the flour and salt. Cook this roux for 2 minutes, stirring constantly so that it does not brown. Vigorously whisk in the hot milk to produce a smooth, very thick sauce. Set the pan over simmering water and cook the sauce for 5 minutes, stirring frequently. It will thin considerably. Remove pan from over water and beat the egg yolks into the sauce. Let the mixture cool.

Oil a shallow 11 X 15-inch baking pan, such as a jelly-roll pan, with bland cooking oil. Do not use butter (it will burn). Line the pan with waxed paper, oil it lightly also, and sprinkle it with the bread crumbs. Beat the egg whites until they are stiff but not dry, and fold them into the cooled yolk mixture. Spread the batter evenly in the prepared pan and bake it in the preheated oven for 30 minutes or until the top is well browned. Invert it onto lightly buttered waxed paper and peel off the baking paper. Spread with the prepared salmon and roll it down the length, using the under paper as a guide. Transfer the roll, seam side down, onto a warm serving platter. Serve the roll with the remaining Hollandaise sauce passed separately. Serves 8 as an hors-d'oeuvre or 6 as a light entrée.

Glazed Scallops and Mushrooms | Coquilles Saint-Jacques

4 scallions, white parts, thinly sliced
5 Tbl butter
1½ cups medium-dry white wine
½ cup water
½ tsp salt
⅛ tsp white pepper
1 pound scallops
½ pound mushrooms, sliced
2 Tbl flour
2 egg yolks
1 cup heavy cream
1 tsp strained lemon juice
2 Tbl grated Parmesan cheese
2 Tbl fine white bread crumbs

In a saucepan gently sauté the scallions in 1 tablespoon of the butter. Add the wine, water, salt, and pepper, and cook at simmer for 10 minutes. If sea scallops are used, halve or quarter them. Use bay scallops whole. Add them and the mushrooms to the wine broth and cook for 5 minutes or just until the scallops are tender. Do not overcook. Drain them and the mushrooms, reserving cooking liquid, and put them in 6 buttered scallop shells or individual heat-proof serving dishes.

If the cooking liquid is in excess of 1 cup reduce it in the saucepan over high heat to that quantity. In another saucepan heat 2 tablespoons of the remaining butter. Blend in the flour and cook gently, without browning, for 2 minutes. Add the reserved cooking liquid gradually, stirring constantly to produce a smooth sauce. Remove pan from heat.

In a mixing bowl thoroughly combine the egg yolks and cream, and stir the mixture vigorously, a little at a time, into the sauce. Add the lemon juice. Pour the sauce equally over the scallops and mushrooms and sprinkle each serving with 2 teaspoons of the cheese and bread crumbs combined. Dot each with 1 teaspoon of the remaining butter, cut into small bits, and brown lightly under a hot broiler. Serve at once.

Seafood Mousse | Mousse de Fruits de Mer

6 ounces fillet of haddock
½ pound uncooked lobster meat
¼ pound small shrimp, shelled & de-veined
¼ pound scallops
¾ tsp salt
¼ tsp white pepper
⅛ tsp ground coriander
3 egg whites
2½ cups heavy cream
1½ cups Tomato Cream Sauce (page 145)

Finely grind the seafood all together, and blend in the salt, pepper, and coriander. Beat in 1 of the egg whites and force the mixture through a fine sieve or reduce it to a paste in an electric blender. Add the remaining egg whites, 1 at a time, working them in thoroughly with a wooden spoon. Chill the mixture in the refrigerator for 2 hours.

Preheat oven to 350 degrees. Remove the fish mixture from the refrigerator and vigorously beat the cream into it, a little at a time, to produce a paste the consistency of stiffly whipped cream. Spread the mixture evenly in a well-buttered 6-cup ring mold and cover it with buttered foil. Set the mold in a pan of hot water in the preheated oven and bake for 25 minutes, or until the mousse begins to shrink from the sides of the pan and a table knife inserted in the center of the mousse can be withdrawn clean. Let the mousse rest for 2 to 3 minutes before unmolding it onto a warm serving platter. Fill the center of the mold with the sauce. Serve hot. This recipe provides 6 servings.

Chilled Seafood Rémoulade | Fruits de mer Rémoulade

36 medium-size shrimp, shelled & de-veined
Rémoulade Sauce (page 159)

Poach the shrimp at simmer in lightly salted water for 3 minutes. Let them cool in the liquid.

Apportion shrimp or other seafood (see Note) in individual serving dishes to provide 6 servings, or combine a sufficient quantity of each seafood to provide servings of similar size. Dress each equally with the sauce.

NOTE: Three quarts of Steamed Mussels (page 15), shelled, or the cooked meat of three 1-pound lobsters cut into bite-size pieces may be substituted for the shrimp.

Glazed Shrimp | Gratin de Crevettes

48 large shrimp (about 3 pounds)
8 Tbl unsalted butter
2 Tbl cognac
2 shallots, finely chopped
1 clove garlic, finely chopped
3 large ripe tomatoes, peeled, seeded & coarsely chopped
1 tsp chopped fresh tarragon (or ¼ tsp crumbled dried tarragon)
½ cup Béchamel Sauce (page 144)
Salt & pepper
⅓ cup heavy cream, whipped

Shell and de-vein the shrimp. In a large skillet heat 6 tablespoons of the butter and in it briskly sauté the shrimp for 3 minutes or just until they turn pink. Sprinkle them with the cognac and set the spirit ablaze. When the flame expires remove the shrimp, leaving the remaining butter in the skillet. Distribute 36 of the shrimp equally among 6 individual gratin or heat-proof serving dishes. Finely chop the remaining 12 shrimp and reduce them to a paste, along with the drippings in the skillet, either in a blender or by forcing them through a fine sieve.

Heat the remaining butter in the skillet and in it lightly sauté the shallots and garlic without letting them brown. Add the tomatoes and tarragon, cover the skillet, and cook for 20 minutes or until the tomatoes are reduced to a thick paste. Blend in the béchamel sauce and prepared shrimp paste. Add salt and pepper to taste and let the mixture heat through. Remove pan from heat and stir in the whipped cream. Pour the sauce equally over the shrimp in the gratin dishes and brown lightly under a hot broiler. Serve at once.

Snails | Escargots

3 dozen large snails
1 cup coarse salt
2 cups cool water
1 Tbl baking soda
4 cups Poaching Broth (page 57)

Fresh, live snails sometimes appear in American markets and may be used in a number of recipes. Precook as directed here for 6 servings. (For procedures with canned snails, see Note.)

Scrub the shells clean and scrape out the chalky covering over the opening of the shell. Place the shells in a large enamel-coated kettle. Dissolve the salt in the 2 cups of cool water and pour the liquid over the snails. Use a cover that will admit air into the kettle (a cake rack is ideal), and fit it on securely. Let the snails remain so in a cool place (not in the refrigerator) overnight. Drain the snails and rinse them thoroughly in several changes of water until they are no longer sticky. Return them to the kettle, now washed, and cover them with boiling water. Cook at gentle boil for 15 minutes. Drain again and when cool enough to handle take the snails from the shells. Discard any that do not come out easily. With a sharp knife cut off the black ends. Replace the shells only in the kettle and cover them with cool water in which the baking soda has been dissolved. Boil the shells for 30 minutes. Drain, rinse, dry them, and set them aside. In a large saucepan heat the poaching broth. Add the shelled snails and cook them, covered, at simmer for 3 hours. Let them cool in the broth. Drain them and prepare as required in specific recipes.

NOTE: Most snails consumed in the United States come from France—in cans, usually with a separate container of shells. Canned snails are precooked and need only heating in Poaching Broth, 1 cup for each 3 dozen snails, along with the cooking liquid in which they are packed, before preparing them Burgundy Style (below), Chablis Style (page 26), or as desired.

Snails Burgundy Style | Escargots à la Bourguignonne

Snail Butter (page 168)
36 snail shells
36 canned snails, heated & drained, or fresh snails, precooked (above)

Place 1 teaspoon of the snail butter in each shell and set a snail in it. Cover each snail with more of the butter (about 2 teaspoons), sealing in the snail completely. These may be prepared a few hours in advance and kept under refrigeration. Remove them 30 minutes before serving time.

Preheat oven to 425 degrees. Arrange the prepared snails in a baking pan in a bed of coarse salt, to keep them upright, or, preferably, in special snail pans (*escargotières*), and heat them in the preheated oven until the butter in the shells melts and is bubbling. (Or the snails, without the shells, may be placed in individual heat-proof serving dishes with the butter and heated in the same way.) Remove the shells carefully, so as not to spill the butter, and apportion the snails for 6 servings with crusty French Bread.

Snails Chablis Style | Escargots à la Chablisienne

36 canned snails, heated, or fresh snails, precooked (page 24)
2 shallots, finely chopped
1 Tbl butter
1 cup Chablis
2 tsp Demi-Glaze (page 56 or see Note)
Salt & pepper
36 snail shells
1½ cups Snail Butter (page 168)

Drain the snails and let them cool. In a saucepan cook the shallots in the butter until they are soft but not brown. Add the wine and reduce it over high heat to ¾ cup. Dissolve the demi-glaze in it and season with salt and pepper to taste. Let the mixture cool completely. Pour 1 teaspoon of the seasoned Chablis into each shell and place a snail in it. Cover each with snail butter (about 2 teaspoons), sealing in the snail completely. If the snails are not to be served immediately keep them in the refrigerator until 30 minutes before they are to be served.

Preheat oven to 425 degrees. Arrange the prepared snails in a baking pan in a bed of coarse salt to keep the shells upright or in special snail pans (*escargotières*), and heat them in the preheated oven until the butter in the shells melts and is bubbling. (Or the snails, without the shells, may be placed in individual heat-proof serving dishes, covered with the Chablis mixture and snail butter, and heated in the same way.) Remove the shells carefully, so as not to spill the butter. This recipe provides 6 servings.

NOTE: If you do not have demi-glaze, you may substitute the following: In a small saucepan melt 1 tablespoon of butter, blend in 1 teaspoon flour, and let it brown slightly. Stir in 1 tablespoon of canned beef broth and cook, stirring, until it is very thick.

Burgundian Cheese Puff | Gougère

½ cup milk
¼ cup water
3 Tbl unsalted butter, cut in small pieces
1 tsp salt
⅛ tsp white pepper
¾ cup sifted flour
4 eggs
¾ cup finely diced Gruyère cheese
2 tsp heavy cream

Preheat oven to 375 degrees. In a saucepan combine the milk, water, butter, salt, and pepper, and bring the mixture to a full boil over low heat. When the butter is melted, add the flour all at once and stir vigorously until the resulting paste clears the sides of the pan and is formed into a ball. Remove pan from heat and thoroughly beat in 3 of the eggs, 1 at a time. Continue beating for a minute or two longer until the paste is smooth and glossy. Reserve 2 tablespoons of the cheese and stir the remainder into the paste. Blend in the cream. Using a soup spoon with a rounded bowl, scoop out large spheres and arrange them on a lightly buttered baking sheet, adjoining them so as to make a circle about 8 inches in diameter. Top each of those spheres with another one, using all of the remaining paste. Flatten the tops slightly and brush them with the remaining egg, beaten. Gently press the reserved cheese into the tops and sides.

Bake in the preheated oven for 45 minutes or until the pastry is well puffed, golden brown, and crusty. Caution! A *gougère* rises completely and browns well during the first 20 minutes of baking. Seen through the glass door of an oven, the pastry will seem to be already done. It is not. Opening the door even partially during that time can cause the pastry to collapse. Wait at least 15 minutes longer. Test by tapping the top lightly. If the crust is firm, the *gougère* is ready. Turn off the heat. Pierce the sides of the pastry in several places with the tines of a fork and let the *gougère* remain in the slackening oven for 10 minutes longer. Serve warm, separating the segments to provide 6 to 8 servings as a first course or as accompaniment to the meal's final glass of red wine.

Roquefort and Avocado Mousse | Mousse Verte

2 envelopes (2 Tbl) unflavored gelatine
¼ cup strained lemon juice
¼ cup strained orange juice
1 cup boiling-hot Chicken Broth (page 53 or canned)
6 ounces Roquefort cheese
2 ripe avocados
2 tsp finely chopped parsley
2 tsp grated onion
Salt & white pepper
Sprigs of parsley

Soften the gelatine in the lemon juice and orange juice combined, and dissolve it in the hot chicken broth. Let the mixture cool. Force the cheese through a fine sieve. Peel, seed, and mash the avocados smoothly. Stir the cheese, avocados, parsley, onion, and salt and pepper to taste into the gelatine mixture, blending them in well. Spread the mixture evenly in a 1-quart mold rinsed in ice-cold water and thoroughly drained. Chill in the refrigerator until the mousse is firm. Unmold it onto a chilled serving platter and garnish with sprigs of parsley. This quantity of mousse is sufficient for 6 servings.

Éclairs with Red Caviar Butter | Éclairs au Caviar Rouge

Cream Puff Paste
for Hors-d'Oeuvres (page 227)
1 cup unsalted butter
⅔ cup red caviar
½ tsp finely grated lemon rind
½ tsp strained lemon juice

Preheat oven to 400 degrees. Using a pastry bag fitted with a very large plain tube, pipe onto a buttered baking sheet 12 éclairs of the paste, each 3 inches long, 1 inch wide, and mounded about ¾-inch

high. Bake them in the preheated oven for 25 minutes or until they are delicately browned and dry. Turn off the oven. Pierce the sides of the éclairs with the tines of a fork and let them remain in the oven for 10 minutes longer. Remove them and cool them on a rack in a place free from drafts. Too much breeze may cause them to collapse. When the éclairs are cool, cut a small slit in the side of each.

In a mixing bowl thoroughly combine the butter, caviar, and lemon rind and juice. Again with a pastry bag, but fitted with a smaller plain tube, fill the éclairs equally, piping in the butter through the slits in the sides. Chill briefly before serving. This recipe provides 12 servings.

Filled Bread Shells | Croustades de Pain de Mie

6 slices 2-day-old white bread, 1½ inches thick
Bland cooking oil for deep frying
½ pound lean boiled ham, finely ground
2 Tbl thick Béchamel Sauce (page 144)
1 egg, lightly beaten
Salt & pepper
Filling (see below)

Trim the slices into 3-inch squares and with a narrow sharp knife cut a 2-inch square 1 inch deep into each, leaving a ½-inch border around the slice. To prevent cutting too deeply, wind a strip of adhesive tape around the blade of the knife 1 inch from the point to use as a guide. In a fryer or deep saucepan heat oil for deep frying to 350 degrees and in it fry the slices as many at a time as the pan can accommodate until they are lightly browned. Drain them on paper toweling. When they are cool enough to handle, carefully lift out the scored square from the top of each slice and scoop out the crumbs, taking care not to break the walls. In a mixing bowl work to a paste the ham, béchamel sauce, egg, and salt and pepper to taste. Line the sides and bottom of each well in the bread slices with the mixture. Set the croustades on a baking sheet in a slow oven (225 degrees) for a few minutes until the linings are firm.

Fill the croustades with one of the following: Glazed Shrimp (page 23); Piquant Meat Cakes (page 130); Fondue (page 213) and

chopped ham; Hard-Cooked Eggs with Artichoke Hearts and Chicken Livers (page 76); Chicken Livers with Orange (page 108); Sweetbreads in Cream (page 124).
NOTE: Miniature Patty Shells (page 233) may be filled in much the same way and served as cocktail snacks. Larger patty shells (page 230) are suitable for first course hors-d'oeuvres.

Eggs in Aspic | Oeufs en Gelée

6 Poached Eggs (page 81)
1 envelope (1 Tbl) unflavored gelatine
2 cups Clarified Chicken Broth (page 54 or canned)
2 Tbl Madeira wine
Fresh tarragon or parsley
3 thin slices ham (about 2 ounces)
6 lettuce leaves

Trim each egg as directed in the recipe to fit a ½-cup-capacity oval mold (the classic dish for eggs in aspic), and let the eggs cool completely. Soften the gelatine in ¼ cup of the broth. In a saucepan combine the remaining broth and the Madeira. Heat the mixture, dissolve the softened gelatine in it, and let the broth cool. Pour 2 tablespoons of it into each mold and chill in the refrigerator until it sets firmly. Arrange 2 leaves of fresh tarragon or tiny sprigs of parsley on the aspic. Dribble a few drops of the broth over each decoration and chill to secure it. Place an egg in each mold and pour in just enough broth to cover it. Chill again to set. Cut the ham into 6 ovals to fit the tops and arrange them over the eggs. Cover with a final spoonful or two of the broth and chill until firm. Unmold the eggs onto lettuce leaves in a chilled serving dish for 6 servings.

Hors-d'Oeuvre Omelettes | Omelettes Hors-d'Oeuvre

9 large eggs
1 Tbl cool water
½ tsp salt
⅛ tsp white pepper
3 Tbl butter

In a mixing bowl combine the eggs, water, and seasonings, and beat with a fork until the ingredients are well blended. Prepare French-style omelettes as directed in the basic recipe (page 77), using ½ cup of the egg mixture for each of 6 omelettes. Cook each in 1½ teaspoons butter heated in a 5-inch skillet. The 6 omelettes should take no longer than 5 minutes to prepare. Slit them as directed and fill them equally with one of the suggested combinations below or as desired.

Filling 1:

6 ounces red caviar
¼ cup sour cream
1 tsp finely chopped chives
½ tsp lemon juice

Combine all ingredients and fill hot omelettes with the chilled mixture.

Filling 2:

¾ cup Fresh-Tomato Purée (page 160)
⅛ tsp dried tarragon, pulverized
Salt to taste
2 strips crisply cooked bacon, crumbled

In a saucepan combine and heat the purée, tarragon, and salt. Add the bacon.

Filling 3:

12 Steamed Clams (page 14), shelled & finely chopped
⅓ cup Creamed Spinach (page 195)
¼ tsp finely grated lemon rind
Salt to taste

Combine all ingredients in a saucepan and heat without boiling.

Filling 4:

¾ cup tiny onions
2 Tbl butter
¼ cup Chicken Broth (page 53 or canned)
2 Tbl heavy cream
1 Tbl grated Parmesan cheese

In a saucepan lightly brown the onions in the butter. Add the broth and cook, covered, at simmer until onions are tender. Stir in the cream and cheese, and heat through.

Filling 5:

12 chicken livers, split
2 scallions, white parts only, thinly sliced
2 Tbl butter
Salt & pepper
⅓ cup Chicken Velouté Sauce (page 145)
¼ tsp curry powder

In a skillet sauté the chicken livers and scallions in the butter. Season with salt and pepper to taste. Stir in the sauce seasoned with the curry powder and continue cooking until the livers are cooked through.

A Variety of Stuffed Eggs | Oeufs Farcis

9 Hard-Cooked Eggs (page 75)
¼ cup Mayonnaise (page 156)
3 Tbl unsalted butter
¼ tsp Dijon-type mustard
2 tsp anchovy paste
½ tsp finely grated lemon rind
1 Tbl thick Fresh-Tomato Purée (page 160)
⅛ tsp ground coriander
¼ tsp salt
1 Tbl Roquefort cheese
½ tsp finely chopped dill
½ tsp dry sherry
Lettuce leaves

Shell the eggs, cut them in half crosswise, and trim off a thin slice of the white from each half to provide stable bases. Carefully remove the yolks, reserving the whites intact, and force the yolks through a fine sieve into a mixing bowl. Blend into them the mayonnaise, butter, and mustard to produce a smooth paste. Divide this into 3 equal parts. Blend into 1 part the anchovy paste and lemon rind, into the second the tomato purée, coriander, and salt, and into the third the cheese, dill, and sherry. Using a pastry bag fitted with a decorative tube, pipe each of the prepared yolk mixtures into 6 halves of the egg whites. Chill until the fillings are firm. Serve on lettuce leaves. This recipe provides 6 servings.

Eggs in Tapénade Sauce | Oeufs en Tapénade

24 pitted large black olives
¼ cup capers
8 anchovy fillets
1 cup drained canned tuna fish
10 hard-cooked eggs, shelled
¼ cup olive oil
¼ tsp Dijon-type mustard
1 tsp lemon juice
1 tsp cognac
Salt & pepper

Finely chop, all together, the olives, capers, anchovies, tuna fish, and the yolks of 4 of the eggs. Reserve the 4 egg whites. Force the mixture through a fine sieve into a mixing bowl and with a wooden spoon work it to a smooth paste or reduce it to a paste in an electric blender. Beat or blend in, a few drops at a time, just enough of the olive oil to produce a sauce the consistency of mayonnaise. Stir into it the mustard, lemon juice, cognac, and salt and pepper to taste, and spread it evenly in a shallow hors-d'oeuvre serving dish. Cut the remaining eggs into halves lengthwise and arrange them cut sides up in the sauce. Finely chop the reserved egg whites and sprinkle them around the eggs. Chill slightly before serving. Serves 6.

Parsleyed Mousse of Ham | Mousse au Jambon Persillée

¾ pound boiled ham, finely ground
2 Tbl port wine
2 Tbl Fresh-Tomato Purée (page 160)
½ tsp paprika
⅛ tsp white pepper
4 tsp unflavored gelatine (1 envelope plus 1 tsp)
1½ cups Chicken Broth (page 53 or canned)
2 eggs, separated
1 cup heavy cream
3 Tbl dry white wine
1 Tbl white wine vinegar
1 Tbl chopped chives
½ cup finely chopped parsley
Salt & black pepper
Cherry tomatoes, sliced
Sprigs of parsley

In a mixing bowl combine the ham, port wine, tomato purée, paprika, and white pepper, and work the mixture to a smooth paste with a wooden spoon or reduce it to a paste in an electric blender. Soften 3 teaspoons of the gelatine (1 envelope) in ¼ cup of the chicken broth. In the top pan of a double-boiler thoroughly combine the egg yolks, ¾ cup of the chicken broth, and ¼ cup of the cream. Set the pan over simmering water and cook the mixture, stirring constantly, until it coats the spoon. Remove pan from over water. Stir in the softened gelatine and, when it is dissolved, blend in the ham paste. Let the mixture cool and fold in the remaining cream, lightly whipped, and the egg whites, beaten until stiff but not dry. Set the mousse aside for the moment, but do not let it become firm. If it begins to set, beat it vigorously with a whisk.

In a small bowl soften the remaining gelatine in the white wine and vinegar combined. In a saucepan heat the remaining chicken broth and dissolve the softened gelatine in it. Stir in the chives and parsley. Season with salt and black pepper to taste. Let the mixture cool, and chill it until it begins to gel. Immediately beat it with a whisk until the aspic and herbs are combined (the herbs settle to the bottom before the broth gels). Spread ⅓ of the mixture evenly over the bottom of a 1½-quart loaf pan rinsed in ice-cold water and drained. Chill that layer in the refrigerator until it is firm. Cover it with ½ the ham mousse and chill until it is firm. Continue so, in turn, with ½ of the remaining parsley mixture, all of the remaining mousse, and the rest of the parsley mixture, allowing each layer to gel firmly before adding the next. When the entire loaf is firm, unmold it onto a chilled serving platter and garnish it with the sliced cherry tomatoes and sprigs of parsley. Cut the loaf into thick slices to provide 6 to 8 servings. *(See photograph, page 17.)*

Ham and Custard Tartlets | Quiches Lorraine

Short Plain Pastry (page 236)
¼ pound cooked ham, thinly sliced
2 cups heavy cream
⅓ cup milk
2 whole eggs
1 egg yolk
½ tsp salt
⅛ tsp white pepper
Few grains nutmeg

Preheat oven to 375 degrees. Roll the pastry ⅛-inch thick and with it line 6 individual tartlet pans each 4 inches in diameter and 1 inch deep. Line the pastry with foil and fill with dried peas to keep the pastry in place during the preliminary baking. Bake in the preheated oven for about 8 minutes or just until the shells are firm. Remove the peas and foil, and let the shells cool in the pans. Reduce oven heat to 350 degrees.

Cut the ham into short, very narrow strips and distribute them equally in the pastry shells. In a mixing bowl thoroughly combine the remaining ingredients and pour the mixture equally into the shells. They should be no more than ¾ full. Bake them at the re-

duced temperature for 20 minutes, or until the shells are well browned and the fillings are puffed, golden brown, and firm. Serve warm.

Pâté Specialty of the House | Pâté Maison Kerr

¾ pound lean beef
½ pound lean veal
½ pound moderately fat pork
1 clove garlic, finely chopped
1 tsp salt
¼ tsp pepper
¼ tsp dried basil
⅛ tsp thyme
Few grains nutmeg
2 Tbl cognac
2 eggs
¾ pound fat bacon, thinly sliced
¼-pound slice lean ham, about ¼-inch thick
Sprigs of watercress

Preheat oven to 350 degrees. Finely grind the beef, veal, and pork together, and blend in the garlic and seasonings. Gently heat the cognac and set it ablaze. Stifle the flame and stir the cognac into the meat, along with the eggs, well beaten. Line a 1½-quart loaf pan with the slices of bacon, allowing the slices to overlap the edges of the pan about 2 inches on all sides. Spread ½ the meat mixture evenly in the prepared pan. Cut the ham into ¼-inch wide sticks and arrange them, slightly separated, along the length of the pan. Cover with the remaining meat mixture and fold the overhanging bacon over it. Cover the pan securely with foil and set it in a pan of hot water in the preheated oven. Bake for 2½ hours. Remove the foil and continue baking for 30 minutes longer or until the pâté is well browned. Remove pan from oven. Set another pan of the same size bottom side down on the pâté. Set a heavy object on the pan and let it weight the pâté until it is cool. Chill the pâté, unmold it into a serving platter, and decorate the platter with sprigs of watercress. Serve with *cornichons,* French sour gherkins. This recipe will serve 8 to 12.

Chicken Liver Pâté with Cognac | Pâté au Cognac

12 Tbl unsalted butter
1½ pounds chicken livers
1 medium onion, finely chopped
¼ cup Chicken Broth (page 53 or canned), heated
1 Tbl Worcestershire sauce
1 tsp curry powder
1 tsp salt
½ tsp paprika
⅛ tsp pepper
2 Tbl cognac

In a skillet heat 2 tablespoons of the butter and in it lightly brown the chicken livers and onion together. Stir in the hot chicken broth and simmer for 5 minutes or until the livers are cooked through. Transfer the mixture, along with any remaining juices, to the container of an electric blender. Add the remaining ingredients, except the butter, and blend at high speed for 15 seconds. Add 8 tablespoons of the remaining butter, a little at a time, and continue to blend until it is incorporated. Lacking a blender, the mixture may be forced through a fine sieve and worked to a smooth paste in a bowl with a wooden spoon. Spread the pâté evenly in a serving bowl and pour over it the remaining 2 tablespoons butter, melted. Chill for 2 hours or until the pâté is firm. Serve with squares of white toast. This quantity of pâté is sufficient for 6 servings.

Pork Pâté | Rillettes

4 pounds boned lean loin of pork
3 pounds leaf lard
1¼ cups boiling water
4 tsp salt
¼ tsp pepper
¼ tsp ground allspice
2 truffles, finely chopped (optional)

Preheat oven to 300 degrees. Cut the pork into very thin slices. Heat the lard in a large heavy casserole and brown the pork in it slowly. Stir in the hot water and seasonings. Cover the casserole and transfer it to the preheated oven. Cook the pork so for 3 hours or until the liquid has entirely evaporated and the meat is very soft. Drain off but reserve the fat. Work the meat to a smooth paste with a wooden spoon. Blend the truffles into the mixture and pack it into a heat-proof serving bowl. Heat the reserved fat and pour it over the pork, filling the bowl. Cool and chill thoroughly. Remove the fat and serve the rillettes with squares of toast. Rillettes, well covered, can be kept under refrigeration for several weeks. This recipe provides 6 servings.

Sausage in Pastry | Saucisson en Croûte

1 large spicy sausage, such as kielbasa (about 1½ pounds)
Flour for dredging
Flaky Pastry (page 235)
1 egg, beaten

Trim off the ends of the sausage and remove the protective casing. Cut the sausage into 2 lengths of equal size and dredge each with flour, coating them lightly but completely. Preheat oven to 375 degrees.

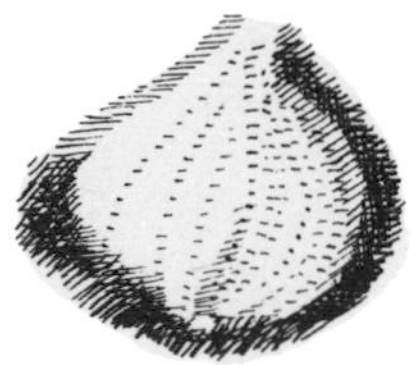

Divide the pastry into 2 portions and roll each into a rectangle 6 inches by 9 inches. Wrap each length of sausage in a rectangle of the pastry, rolling it down the length and folding the sides of the pastry over it. Brush the end with cool water and press it to the body of the pastry to secure it. Brush the rolls with beaten egg and place them on a greased baking sheet. Bake them in the preheated oven for 20 minutes. Slide a cool baking sheet under the hot one and continue baking for 15 minutes longer or until the pastry is well browned. Cool the rolls somewhat, but serve them warm, cut into generous slices and, if desired, with an accompaniment of Tomato Sauce (page 161). This recipe provides 6 to 8 servings.

Celeriac with Mustard Dressing | Céleri-Rave Moutarde

1 pound celeriac
3 cups plus 3 Tbl water
1¼ tsp salt
Juice of 1 lemon
3 Tbl white wine vinegar
¼ cup Dijon-type mustard
2 Tbl Mayonnaise (page 156)
⅛ tsp white pepper
6 Tbl olive oil

Peel the celeriac, slice them very thinly, and cut the slices into short, very narrow strips. In a saucepan season 3 cups of the water with 1 tsp of the salt and the lemon juice. Bring the liquid to a boil and in it blanch the strips of the celery roots for 1 minute. Drain them and plunge them immediately into ice-cold water. Drain the strips again and dry them thoroughly between sheets of paper toweling. Transfer them to a mixing bowl and set aside for the moment in the refrigerator.

In a saucepan heat together the remaining water and the wine vinegar, and stir in the mustard, mayonnaise, white pepper, and remaining salt. Remove pan from heat and vigorously beat in the olive oil, a few drops at a time, to produce a smooth thick dressing. Let it cool and stir it into the chilled celeriac. Let the mixture season in the refrigerator for 1 hour. Serve it chilled. Serves 6.

NOTE: Celeriac is also known as celery root and knob celery.

Stuffed Mushrooms | Champignons Farcis

36 medium-size mushrooms
¾ cup unsalted butter
½ cup finely ground cooked veal
2 Tbl finely chopped parsley
2 shallots, finely chopped
1 large clove garlic, finely chopped
½ tsp finely grated lemon rind
Salt to taste
2–3 dashes Tabasco

Preheat oven to 325 degrees. Gently rinse and thoroughly dry the mushrooms. Remove the stems, chop them very finely, and cook them in a skillet in ¼ cup of the butter until they are quite dry. Cool the stems and combine them with the remaining ingredients to produce a well-blended butter. Fill the mushroom caps equally with the mixture and arrange them filled sides up on a buttered baking sheet. Set the sheet in the preheated oven and let it remain until the mushrooms are warmed through and the filling is bubbling. This quantity is sufficient for 6 servings.

Raw Mushrooms with French Dressing | Champignons Crus Vinaigrette

½ cup French Dressing (page 163)
1½ pounds medium-size fresh mushrooms

Prepare vinaigrette sauce as directed in the recipe but substitute unflavored white wine vinegar for the red.

Wash the mushrooms lightly in cool water and dry them thoroughly. Trim off the stems flush with the caps. Reserve the stems for other uses (soups, sauces, etc.). Slice the mushroom caps down through the tops and place the slices in a salad bowl. Gently toss them with the French dressing. Serve chilled, on lettuce leaves if desired. This recipe provides 6 servings.

Cucumbers in Cream | Concombres à la Crème

3 large cucumbers
1 tsp salt
1⅓ cups sour cream
⅔ cup heavy sweet cream
Salt & white pepper
1 tsp chopped fresh dill (or ¼ tsp dried dill weed)

Peel the cucumbers, cut them in half lengthwise, and scoop out the seeds. Cut the halves crosswise into slices about ⅛-inch thick. Put them in a glass bowl, sprinkle them with the teaspoon of salt, and let them steep under refrigeration for 30 minutes. Drain the cucumbers and gently squeeze out a little more of their liquid. The slices should remain quite crisp. Return them to the bowl. Combine the sour and sweet creams and season the mixture with salt and white pepper to taste. Stir it into the cucumbers along with the chopped dill. Chill well. This recipe provides 6 servings.

Pimientos with Anchovies | Poivrons aux Anchois

9 large fresh or canned sweet red peppers
Piquant Poaching Broth (page 57)
18 anchovy fillets

Cut the fresh peppers in half, trim off the stems, and remove the white pulp. Cook the peppers in the poaching broth at a gentle boil for 15 minutes. Drain the cooked peppers, reserving the broth. In a saucepan over high heat reduce the broth to ¾ cup and pour it over the peppers. Cool and chill them in the broth. Drain the peppers completely and arrange the halves in a chilled serving platter with an anchovy fillet placed diagonally over each. Chill briefly before serving. This recipe will provide 6 servings.

Canned pimientos, drained, need only be marinated for several hours in the reduced poaching broth. Drain the peppers completely before garnishing with the anchovies.

A French Pizza | Pissaladière

1 deep 9-inch Short Plain Pastry shell (page 236)
6 large ripe tomatoes (2½ pounds)
2 Tbl butter
1 clove garlic
4 large sweet onions (2 pounds)
¼ cup olive oil
¼ tsp dried rosemary
1 tsp salt
¼ tsp white pepper
2 Tbl grated Parmesan cheese
12 anchovy fillets
12 pitted black olives

Partially bake the pastry shell as directed in the recipe and set it aside to cool. Peel, seed, and chop the tomatoes. Heat the butter in a saucepan and in it slowly cook the tomatoes to a thick paste. Peel and crush the garlic. Thinly slice the onions. Brown the garlic gently in a skillet with 3 tablespoons of the oil. Remove and discard it. Add the onions and sprinkle them with the rosemary, salt, and pepper. Cook, covered, for 30 minutes or until onions are tender but not browned. Drain well. Preheat oven to 375 degrees.

Sprinkle the prepared pastry shell with the grated cheese and spread the onions over it. Cover evenly with the tomato paste. Split the anchovies and olives lengthwise. Arrange the anchovy strips over the tomato paste in a lattice of 1¼-inch squares, and place an olive half in each. Brush the top lightly with a little of the remaining oil. Bake the tart in the preheated oven for 20 minutes or until the pastry is well browned and the filling is bubbling hot. Brush the top lightly again with the oil and let the tart rest for 10 minutes before cutting it to provide 6 to 8 servings. *(See photograph, page 18.)*

Potatoes in Vinegar and Oil | Pommes de Terre Vinaigrette

2 pounds boiling potatoes
2 cups Beef Broth (page 52 or canned)
1¾ tsp salt
½ cup dry white wine
½ tsp Dijon-type mustard
2 Tbl white wine vinegar
⅛ tsp white pepper
6 Tbl olive oil
1 Tbl chopped fresh chervil (or ½ tsp crumbled dried chervil)
1 Tbl finely chopped parsley

Cook the potatoes, unpeeled, just until they are tender in the broth and as much cool water as needed to cover them, seasoning the liquid with 1½ teaspoons of the salt. Drain the potatoes and when they are cool enough to handle (they should still be warm), peel and cut them into slices about ⅛-inch thick. Arrange the slices in a rather deep platter, taking care not to break them, and pour the wine over them. Let them absorb as much of the wine as they will and drain off the remainder. In a small mixing bowl dissolve the mustard and remaining salt in the vinegar and add the pepper. Beat in the oil a little at a time until the mixture is emulsified. Blend in the herbs. Pour the dressing over the potatoes and baste several times. Serve the potatoes warm or chilled as one of the dishes of a variety of hors-d'oeuvres.

Radishes with Lemon Butter | Radis au Beurre de Citron

30 large globe radishes with stems
⅔ cup Lemon Butter (page 167)

Wash and thoroughly dry the radishes. Trim off the roots and any bruised edges of the stems, but leave the greens otherwise intact. Split the radishes lengthwise to provide 60 halves each with part of the green stem. Using a pastry bag fitted with a star tube, pipe a rosette of lemon butter onto the cut surface of each radish half, covering it completely. Chill the radishes until the butter is firm. Serve them with squares of dark bread. This recipe will provide 6 servings.

Spinach Dumplings | Pâte Cuite aux Épinards

1 pound young spinach
¾ cup unflavored Boursin cheese
1 tsp milk
3 Tbl butter, melted
⅛ tsp nutmeg
Salt & pepper
3 Tbl flour
3 Tbl grated Parmesan cheese
2 eggs
Flour for dredging
Chicken Broth (page 53 or canned)
Additional grated Parmesan cheese

Thoroughly wash the spinach and drain it well. Cook it in a saucepan over low heat for 3 minutes with just the water that clings to the leaves. Drain the greens, pressing out as much of the liquid as possible, and chop finely. Return the spinach to the saucepan and combine with it the Boursin cheese, milk, 1 tablespoon of the melted butter, the nutmeg, and salt and pepper to taste. Cook the mixture over low heat, stirring constantly for 5 minutes. Remove pan from heat and blend in the flour and grated cheese. Beat in the eggs. Transfer the batter to a bowl and chill it, covered, in the refrigerator for several hours or overnight.

Preheat oven to 325 degrees. Form the chilled batter into small rolls, about 1 X 2 inches, and dredge them lightly with flour. In a large saucepan over low heat bring the chicken broth to bare simmer and in it poach the spinach rolls a few at a time for 5 minutes, or just until they rise to the surface of the broth and are moderately firm. Drain them carefully and arrange them in a well-buttered baking dish. Dribble the remaining butter over them and sprinkle with the grated cheese. Bake in the preheated oven for 5 minutes or until the dumplings are heated through. Serve at once. Serves 6.

Tomatoes in Cream | Tomates à la Crème

6 medium tomatoes (about 2 pounds)
¾ cup heavy cream
½ cup milk
2 thin slices cooked ham (about 2 ounces), finely ground
Dash of Tabasco
Salt to taste
1 Tbl tomato paste
1 Tbl finely chopped parsley

Peel the tomatoes and trim out the stem ends. In a large skillet combine the cream, milk, ham, and Tabasco, and cook at simmer for 5 minutes, stirring frequently. Add salt, if needed, and stir in the tomato paste. Arrange the tomatoes stem sides down in the cream and continue cooking for 15 minutes, basting frequently. The tomatoes should be just partially cooked and still quite firm, but heated through. Serve them hot, 1 to a serving, with equal quantities of the sauce and sprinklings of the chopped parsley.

Chilled Piquant Vegetables | Légumes à la Grecque

Vegetable of choice (see below)
Piquant Poaching Broth (page 57)

Although designated, even in France, as Greek-style, these hors-d'oeuvre vegetables are stanchly French.

Prepare the vegetable as directed below and cook it in the piquant poaching broth the indicated length of time. Drain the cooked vegetable, reserving the broth, and transfer it to a serving dish. In a saucepan over high heat, reduce the broth to ¾ cup and pour it over the vegetable in the serving dish. Let the vegetable cool and chill it in the broth. Each is sufficient for 6 servings.

Celeriac | Céleri-Rave

1½ pounds celeriac
3 cups water
½ tsp salt
Juice of ½ lemon

Wash and peel the roots and cut them into slices ¼-inch thick. In a saucepan bring the water to boil with the salt and lemon juice. Add the sliced roots and blanch them for 5 minutes. Drain them and complete the cooking at simmer in the piquant poaching broth specified in the basic recipe until the slices are tender, about 10 minutes longer. Proceed as directed in the basic recipe.

Leeks | Poireaux

18 leeks

Trim off the roots and dark green stalks. Cook the leeks in the piquant poaching broth specified in the basic recipe at simmer for 20 minutes or just until they are tender. Do not overcook. Proceed as directed in the basic recipe.

Mushrooms | Champignons

1½ pounds button mushrooms

Trim the mushrooms and wash them lightly in cool water. Cook them in the piquant poaching broth specified in the basic recipe at simmer for 10 minutes. Proceed as directed in the basic recipe.

Artichokes | Artichauts

60 tiny artichokes
Juice of 1 lemon
Salt

Trim and wash the artichokes as directed in the Artichoke recipe (page 172). Place them in a saucepan. Cover them with boiling water combined with the lemon juice and 1 teaspoon salt for each 4 cups water. Cook at simmer for 10 minutes. Drain and complete the cooking in the poaching broth specified in the basic recipe for 10 minutes or until artichokes are tender. Proceed as directed in the basic recipe.

Raw Vegetables | Crudités

Cauliflower
Hearts of celery
Radishes
Green beans
Cherry tomatoes
Fennel
Celeriac (celery root)
Green onions

Provide 4 or 5 different raw vegetables, such as those listed above. Wash and trim them, and cut into bite-size pieces. Marinate the vegetables in French Dressing (page 163) or serve them just chilled with Roquefort Cheese Dipping Sauce (page 164).

Cheese and Anchovy Canapés | Canapés de Fromage et d'Anchois

6 slices white bread, toasted
3 Tbl butter
¾ cup Petit Suisse or other cream cheese
2 Tbl anchovy paste

Trim the toast and butter the slices while they are still warm. Spread each with 2 tablespoons of the cheese and cover with a film of the anchovy paste, using about a teaspoon for each slice. Serve as a first course canapé, 1 to a serving, or cut the prepared slices each into 4 squares or triangles and serve as cocktail snacks.

Gruyère Cheese Pâté | Pâté de Fromage à la Bière

1 pound Gruyère cheese
1 Tbl bland cooking oil
1 Tbl Worcestershire sauce
1 tsp lemon juice
1 clove garlic, put through a press
1½ tsp dry mustard
½ tsp paprika
½ tsp salt
1¼ cups light beer
1 egg white
Squares of dark bread

Finely grate the cheese into a mixing bowl. Add the oil, Worcestershire sauce, lemon juice, garlic, mustard, paprika, and salt. Work the mixture with a wooden spoon, adding the beer a little at a time, to produce a smooth paste. Stiffly beat the egg white and stir it into the paste. Chill until firm. Serve as a spread with squares of dark bread.

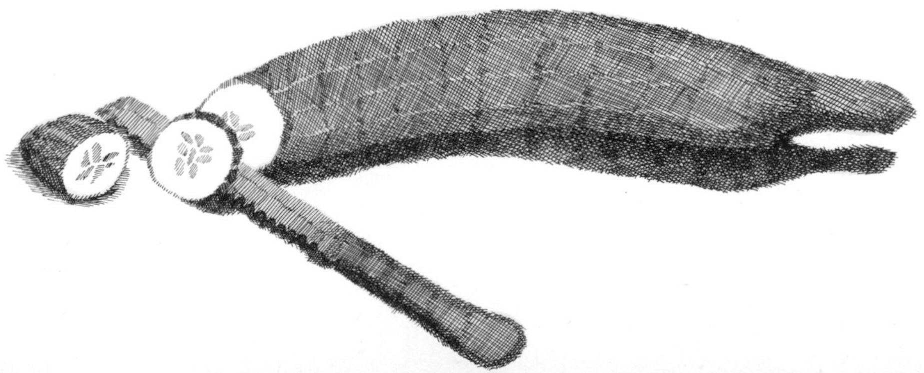

Cheese Straws | Paillettes de Fromage

Flaky Pastry (page 235)
3 ounces Gervais cheese, softened (see Note)
Dash of Tabasco
1 egg, beaten
Salt

Preheat oven to 375 degrees. Roll the prepared pastry into a rectangle ⅛-inch thick. Season the cheese with the Tabasco and spread it evenly over ½ the rectangle. Fold the other half of the rectangle over it. Press the halves together to secure them and cut into 3-inch lengths, each ½-inch wide. Arrange the strips on a lightly buttered baking sheet and brush them lightly with beaten egg and sprinkle them with salt. Bake in the preheated oven 12 minutes or until the straws are well puffed and nicely browned. Serve slightly warm or cool as cocktail snacks.

NOTE: Gervais, a double-cream French cheese of refreshingly sour flavor, is available in shops which specialize in cheese. If unavailable, 3 ounces cream cheese with 1 teaspoon sour cream and ⅛ teaspoon salt plus the indicated Tabasco may be substituted.

Carrot Rounds | Carottes en Rondelles

6 young carrots
1 cup Chicken Broth (page 53 or canned), heated
2 Tbl white wine vinegar
⅓ cup olive oil
¼ tsp dried chervil
Salt & white pepper
1 Tbl finely chopped parsley

Peel the carrots and cut them into rounds about ¾-inch thick. Spread them in a single layer in a skillet and pour over them the hot broth. Cook, covered, over medium heat for 5 minutes. Drain the carrots, leaving the remaining broth in the skillet, and place them in a mixing bowl. Reduce the broth over high heat to ¼ cup and let it cool. Combine with it the vinegar, oil, chervil, and salt and white pepper to taste, and pour the mixture over the carrots in the bowl. Let the carrots steep so in the refrigerator for 2 hours, turning them from time to time so that they become uniformly seasoned with the marinade. Drain them, sprinkle with the parsley, and serve chilled, with accompanying toothpicks, as cocktail snacks.

Stuffed Raw Mushrooms | Champignons Crus Farcis

36 medium-size mushrooms
¼ pound Roquefort cheese
½ pound cream cheese, softened
2 tsp finely chopped fresh dill (or ¼ tsp dried dill weed)
2 Tbl cognac
1 Tbl heavy cream

Clean the mushrooms by wiping them with damp paper toweling and dry them well. Carefully remove the stems, leaving the hollow caps intact. Reserve the stems for other uses. Force the Roquefort cheese through a fine sieve into a mixing bowl and blend into it the cream cheese, dill, cognac and, cream. Using a pastry bag fitted with a large star tube, pipe the mixture equally into the mushroom caps. Chill the caps in the refrigerator until the fillings are firm. Serve with cocktails.

Smoked Salmon Canapés | Canapés de Saumon Fumé

6 slices white bread
3 Tbl butter
¾ pound smoked salmon, thinly sliced
⅓ cup sour cream
2 tsp finely chopped fresh dill (or ¼ tsp dried dill weed)
Salt & white pepper
4 scallions, white parts only, thinly sliced

Brown the bread on both sides in the butter in a skillet or toast the slices and butter them while they are still warm. Trim off the crust, and cover the slices evenly with the salmon. Combine the sour cream and dill and season to taste with salt, cautiously (the salmon may provide enough salt), and pepper. Spread 1 tablespoon of the mixture over each slice of bread and sprinkle equally with the scallions.

Shrimp Canapés | Canapés aux Crevettes

36 medium-size shrimp, shelled & de-veined
6 slices day-old white bread
3 Tbl butter
¼ cup Shrimp Butter (page 168)
½ cup Béchamel Sauce (page 144)
1 Tbl tomato paste
3 Tbl fine soft bread crumbs

Poach the shrimp at simmer in lightly salted water for 3 to 4 minutes. Drain them.

Trim the crust from the slices of bread and brown them, a few at a time, on both sides in the butter heated in a skillet. In a mixing bowl blend 2 tablespoons of the shrimp butter in ¼ cup of the béchamel sauce. Spread the mixture evenly over the browned bread. Cut the shrimp in half lengthwise and arrange 12 halves, slightly overlapping, on each slice. Cover evenly with 1 tablespoon of tomato paste and the remaining shrimp butter and béchamel sauce, combined. Sprinkle the slices equally with the bread crumbs and brown them lightly in a very hot oven. Apportion the canapés 1 to a serving.

Shrimp Toast | Canapés Chinois

6 slices day-old white bread
½ pound raw shrimp, shelled & de-veined
¼ pound boiled ham
4 water chestnuts
4 scallions, white & lighter green parts
1 Tbl cornstarch
1 Tbl flour
1 tsp salt
¼ tsp dry mustard
¼ tsp sugar
1 egg, lightly beaten
Bland cooking oil for deep frying

Preheat oven to 200 degrees. Trim the slices of bread, place them on a rack in the preheated oven, and let them dry partially without browning. They should not be crisp. Put the shrimp and ham together through the fine blade of a food chopper. Very finely chop the water chestnuts and scallions and combine them in a mixing bowl with the ground shrimp and ham. Blend in the cornstarch, flour, salt, dry mustard, and sugar, and stir in the egg. Spread the slices of bread evenly with the mixture and cut them in half.

In a fryer or deep saucepan heat the oil to 375 degrees and in it fry the prepared slices of bread, a few at a time, first shrimp sides down, then turned, until both sides are golden brown. Drain quickly on paper toweling and serve immediately, 2 halves to a serving. The prepared slices of bread may be cut into quarters. Fried so, they may be served as cocktail canapés.

2 | soups and stocks

Homemade soup, once considered the basis of the French national diet, seems to be rapidly disappearing from city tables, probably a victim of the fast pace of modern life and the shrinking size of urban kitchens. The *petite marmite,* long the revered and inexhaustible wellspring of homemade soup, has been removed from its place at the back of the stove and relegated to ignominy on the storage shelf. To help hasten its return, we have set down here what we hope will prove to be irresistibly tempting recipes for broths—the *fonds de cuisine*—and the beautiful soups they make possible.

Imagine sitting down to such elegancies of the soup kettle as the essence of celery and tomato, the consommé with noodles fine as angel's hair, the lusty soups of cabbage and onion, the leek-and-potato soup called *potage Parmentier* (after a man who loved potatoes), and its famous derivation, vichyssoise.

Let these not become just memories. Bring back the *petite marmite* to its well-loved function! *Vive la bonne soupe!*

Broths | Fonds

Fonds, properly *fonds de cuisine,* translate for all practical purposes as broths, but they are considerably more than that. They are the flavor of France, the essence of the mainstays of the French repast. Nobody can deny the superiority of broths made at home, but not every household can devote itself to preparing large quantities of those nectars, much less find space to store them. And small quantities are quickly depleted. When they are, and time is also of the essence, canned beef and chicken broths, simmered for a little while with carrot, celery, onion, and an herb bouquet of thyme, bay leaf, and parsley, provide satisfactory substitutes. Clam juice, straight from the bottle, can serve as adequate replacement for fish broth.

Homemade broths, as well as unused portions of the commercial preparations, should be stored in a refrigerator or freezer. Under normal refrigeration they can be kept for about 2 weeks, but must be reheated to boiling every 3 days to prevent deterioration. Homemade preparations can be frozen for longer storage, in which case periodic reheating is not necessary.

Salt and pepper are omitted from the basic preparations which follow to prevent intensification of seasoning when reduction of the broth is required in other recipes in which they may be used.

Beef Broth | Fond Brun de Boeuf

4 pounds shin beef (see Note)
2 pounds beef bones, cut in short lengths
1 pound veal knucklebone, cracked
2 carrots, peeled & sliced
2 stalks celery, sliced
2 medium onions, sliced
5 quarts boiling-hot water
Bouquet Garni (see Glossary)

Preheat oven to 425 degrees. Place the meat, bones, and vegetables in a baking pan in the preheated oven and roast them for 45 minutes, turning the pieces frequently so that they brown evenly and well. Transfer the ingredients to a large kettle on top of stove. Set the baking pan on top of stove over moderate heat. Pour some of the hot water into it and stir up the brown cooking glaze at the bottom of the pan. Pour this liquid along with the remaining hot water over the ingredients in the kettle and bring it to a boil over low heat. Add the bouquet garni. Continue cooking with the kettle partially covered at simmer for 3 hours, and with the kettle uncovered for 30 minutes longer.

Strain the broth, cool it, clarify it if necessary (page 54), and store it in the refrigerator or in a freezer. Use the approximately 3 quarts of broth as required for specific recipes.

NOTE: If you keep a "stock pile" of meat trimmings or leftovers and chicken gizzards, necks, and backs in the refrigerator or freezer, substitute these, without browning, for part of the beef.

Chicken Broth | Fond de Volaille

5 pounds stewing chicken (see Note)
1 pound veal knucklebone, cracked
2 carrots, peeled & sliced
2 stalks celery, sliced
2 medium onions, sliced
Bouquet Garni (see Glossary)
5 quarts boiling-hot water

Combine all ingredients in a large kettle without browning them and cook, partially covered, at simmer for 3 hours. Continue cooking with the kettle uncovered for 30 minutes longer. If only a whole chicken is used, remove it from the broth when it is tender, after about 2 hours of cooking. Bone the chicken, reserving the meat under refrigeration until required. Return the bones to the broth and continue cooking for 1½ hours. This recipe provides about 3 quarts of white chicken broth.

NOTE: You may substitute an equal amount of chicken gizzards, necks, and backs for the whole chicken.

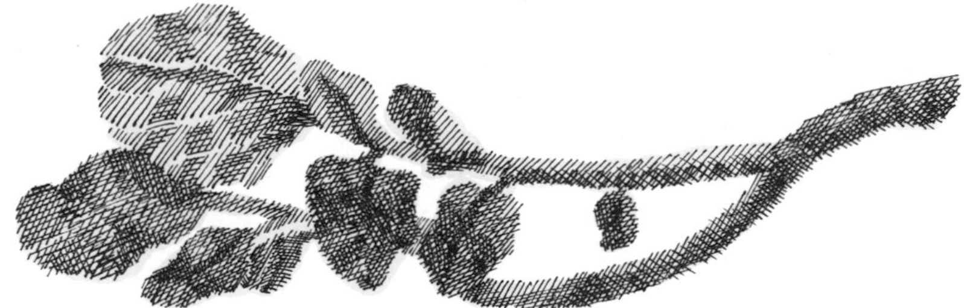

Fish Broth | Fumet de Poisson

3 pounds fish and/or shellfish, plus fish bones & trimmings
1 stalk celery, sliced
1 carrot, peeled & sliced
1 medium onion, sliced
1 medium tomato, cored & chopped
Bouquet Garni (see Glossary)
½ cup white wine
3½ quarts water

Thoroughly wash the fish, bones, and trimmings, and combine them in a large saucepan with the remaining ingredients. Bring the liquid to a gentle boil and skim it. Continue cooking, uncovered, at simmer for 1 hour. Strain the broth through a sieve lined with a fine cloth wrung out in cold water. This recipe provides about 3 quarts of fish broth for use as required in specific recipes. This broth, too, may be refrigerated or frozen. If kept under normal refrigeration it should be reheated to boiling every 2 days. If it is to be stored for longer than 1 week, it should be kept in a freezer.

To Clarify Broth |

3 quarts strained Beef, Chicken, or Fish Broth (above)
5 egg whites, lightly beaten

Skim the broth of all fat. The broth cannot be properly clarified unless it is completely fat free. Chill the broth in a bowl in the refrigerator, if necessary, to solidify any remaining bits of fat and remove them. Pour the de-greased broth into a large kettle and spread the beaten egg whites over it. Set the pan over low heat and bring the broth to a simmer, beating constantly with a whisk backward and forward across the bottom of the pan. The broth will not clear well if it is stirred in a circle. When the mixture begins to boil, remove pan from heat until the boiling subsides. Heat the mixture again to a simmer, without beating, and turn off heat. Let the mixture settle for 10 minutes.

Line a sieve with a closely woven cloth (such as a piece of bed sheeting) wrung out in cold water, and set it over a deep bowl. Pour the mixture into it very gently and let the liquid take its time to seep through. Discard the egg whites.

Clarifying takes its toll of the broth, but it leaves 2 quarts of clear consommé, sufficient for 6 servings as soup or as required for specific recipes. If it is to be served as soup, season the consommé with salt to taste.

Jellied Consommé | Consommé en Gelée

Consommé prepared from any of the preceding recipes for broth should gel sufficiently to serve as a jellied soup. Test for consistency by pouring a little of the consommé into a saucer and chilling it in the refrigerator. The resulting jelly should be soft. If a slightly firmer jelly is desired (it should not be stiff), it may be made so by softening 1 envelope unflavored gelatine (1 tablespoon) in ¼ cup of the cool liquid consommé and dissolving it in 4 cups of the soup, heated. Increase the gelatine proportionately for each additional 4 cups of the consommé. Chill the soup in the refrigerator until it is gelled.

Aspic | Gelée

Jellied consommé, somewhat firmer than for soup, for glazing and molding foods is generally called aspic, although properly that designation should be reserved for the glazed or molded food itself. Sufficiently firm jellies can be made by dissolving 1 envelope unflavored gelatine (1 tablespoon), softened in ¼ cup cool liquid consommé, in 3 cups of the heated soup. The preparation should be used almost immediately it cools. It will begin to set very quickly thereafter. Directions for its use are given in specific recipes.

Meat Glazes | Glaces de Viande

Demi-Glaze | Demi-Glace

A demi-glaze is a broth, usually beef, reduced to the consistency of a double-thick brown sauce. Prepare the broth as directed in the recipe (Beef Broth, page 52). Strain the resulting 3 quarts into another saucepan and skim off the fat. Continue cooking for another 2 hours, over low heat, or until the broth is reduced to 1 quart. Cool the demi-glaze and store it in a covered container in the refrigerator or a freezer. Even under just normal refrigeration, it can be kept for several weeks. Use to enrich soups, sauces, and stews, or as required in specific recipes.

Full Glaze | Glace de Viande

Strain the demi-glaze into a smaller saucepan and continue cooking in progressively smaller saucepans as the glaze is reduced, after about 1 hour, to slightly less than 1 pint. Cooled, the glaze will be firm enough to require cutting with a knife. Use, in smaller amounts, as directed for demi-glaze and store in the same way. Full glaze can be dissolved in boiling-hot water to produce rich broth, thereby completing the circle.

Poaching Broth | Court-Bouillon

1 stalk celery
1 carrot
1 medium onion
4 cups water
Bouquet Garni (see Glossary)
4 peppercorns
⅛ tsp salt
2 cups dry white wine
1 Tbl white wine vinegar

Coarsely chop the vegetables and combine them in a saucepan with the water, bouquet garni, peppercorns, and salt. Bring the liquid to a boil and cook, covered, over medium heat for 30 minutes. If the liquid is in excess of 2 cups, continue cooking until it is reduced to that amount. Add the wine and vinegar, and cook, uncovered, for 2 minutes.

This recipe provides 4 cups poaching broth with which to poach fish or shellfish or to use as required in specific recipes. Strained, it can be kept under normal refrigeration for 1 week to 10 days or in a freezer for several months.

Piquant Poaching Broth | Court-Bouillon Piquant

3 cups water
¼ cup olive oil
¼ cup lemon juice
2 Tbl dry white wine
1 stalk celery
1 medium onion
1 small tomato
¼ tsp dried chervil
6 peppercorns
¼ tsp salt

Combine the ingredients in a saucepan and cook them, covered, at simmer for 40 minutes. If the liquid is in excess of 2 cups continue cooking, uncovered, until it is reduced to that amount. Strain the broth and use it as required for specific recipes.

Consommé with Fine Noodles | Consommé aux Cheveux d'Ange

1½ cups Homemade Fine Noodles (page 200)
2 quarts Clarified Chicken Broth (page 54 or canned)

In a saucepan over moderate heat bring lightly salted water to a rolling boil. Add the noodles a few at a time so as not to stop the boiling and cook them for just 2 minutes. Drain the noodles and cook them in the broth for 1 to 2 minutes longer. Apportion the consommé and noodles to provide 6 servings.

Consommé with Spring Vegetables | Consommé Printanier

2 quarts Clarified Chicken Broth (page 54 or canned)
¼ cup fine julienne of young carrots
¼ cup fine julienne of young turnips
¼ cup fresh young peas
¼ cup green beans, cut diagonally into thin slices
12 tiny fresh asparagus tips
Salt & pepper
12 leaves fresh chervil or parsley

Bring the clarified chicken broth to a boil in a large saucepan over moderate heat. Add the vegetables and cook them, uncovered, for 10 minutes or just until they are tender. Do not overcook. Season with salt and pepper, and cook for 1 minute longer. Float 2 leaves fresh chervil or parsley over each of the 6 servings provided by this recipe. Serve the soup hot. *(See photograph, page 68.)*

Consommé Madrid Style | Consommé à la Madrilène

5 cups Clarified Chicken Broth (page 54 or canned)
3 cups Clarified Beef Broth (page 54 or canned)
1 cup Fresh-Tomato Purée (page 160 or see Note)
Salt & white pepper
1 large ripe tomato, peeled, seeded & chopped

In a saucepan combine the broths and purée, and cook the mixture for 1 hour. Season it with salt and white pepper to taste and apportion it hot to provide 6 servings, or cool the consommé and serve it garnished with the chopped tomato.

NOTE: Two cups canned tomatoes with the juice, sieved to remove the seeds, may be substituted for the Fresh-Tomato Purée.

Jellied Consommé Madrid Style |
Consommé à la Madrilène en Gelée

2 envelopes (2 Tbl) unflavored gelatine
8 cups cool Consommé Madrid Style (above)
1 Tbl strained lemon juice
1 Tbl finely chopped parsley

Soften the gelatine in ½ cup of the cool consommé. In a saucepan heat the remaining consommé and dissolve the softened gelatine in it. Stir in the lemon juice. Cool the consommé and chill until it gels. Apportion the jellied consommé among 6 chilled soup cups and sprinkle each with ½ teaspoon of the chopped parsley.

Essence of Celery and Tomato | Consommé de Céleri et Tomate

1 bunch celery with leaves
6 large ripe tomatoes (about 2½ pounds)
3 quarts water
Salt

Separate the celery stalks, wash them thoroughly, and cut them into thin slices. Core and chop the tomatoes. Combine the vegetables (including the celery leaves) in a large saucepan with the water. Cook for 2 hours or until the vegetables are very soft and the broth is reduced. Strain the broth into a mixing bowl through several thicknesses of cheesecloth, pressing the vegetables to extract all the juice. Discard the pulp. Season the broth with salt to taste, and clarify it if necessary as directed (page 54). Serve the essence hot, apportioned for 6 servings with, if desired, Tiny Puffs (page 227).

Fish Soup | Bouillabaisse

2 medium onions, coarsely chopped
¼ cup olive oil
4 cloves garlic, mashed to a paste
4 medium tomatoes, cored & coarsely chopped
2 quarts strained Fish Broth (page 54) or bottled clam juice
1 quart water
⅛ tsp dried fennel
1 bay leaf
¼ tsp powdered saffron
¼ tsp pepper
1 Tbl coarse salt
Fish trimmings from the following fish ingredients
2 pounds red snapper, cleaned
1 pound haddock, cleaned
1 pound eel, skinned & cleaned
2 1-pound lobsters
French Bread
1 quart (about 2 pounds) mussels, scrubbed clean & bearded

Any preparation made in the United States from native fish and called bouillabaisse is a fraud. The fish for a true bouillabaisse swim only in the waters around Marseille and rarely stray farther a-sea than Toulon. For that reason the bouillabaisse here is designated as Fish Soup, although it may not even be that. Even the Marseillais are of two minds concerning their own preparation, frequently insisting that it is less *potage* than piscatorial *pot-au-feu.* Whatever it is, here it is, with one hundred percent American fish, but with a method of preparation authentically French.

In a large saucepan cook the onions in the olive oil over low heat for 5 minutes or just until they begin to soften. Add the garlic and tomatoes, and cook 5 minutes longer. Pour in the fish broth and water, and add the herbs, seasonings, and fish trimmings, if any. Increase the heat to moderate and cook the ingredients, uncovered, for 20 minutes. Strain the broth into a large kettle.

Cut the fish and eel crosswise into slices 2 inches thick. Split the lobsters and remove the sacs and intestinal tubes. Cut off the claws. Cut 6 thick slices of the bread and dry them out in a moderate oven. Do not let them brown. Return the kettle to high heat and bring the broth back to a boil. Add the haddock, eel, and lobsters, and cook, uncovered, for 5 minutes. Add the red snapper and mussels, and continue cooking 5 minutes longer or until the fish are tender and the mussel shells open. Discard any shells that do not open.

Place a slice of the dried bread in each of 6 soup plates and apportion the fish and broth among them.

Shrimp Bisque | Bisque de Crevettes

2 cups Fish Broth (page 54) or bottled clam juice
2 cups water
¼ cup rice, washed
2 pounds shrimp
¼ cup finely chopped carrot
¼ cup finely chopped celery
¼ cup finely chopped onion
3 Tbl butter
2 large tomatoes, cored & chopped
1 clove garlic, crushed
2 Tbl cognac
¼ tsp dried thyme
1 bay leaf
2 sprigs of parsley
1½ cups Chicken Broth (page 53 or canned)
½ cup dry white wine
Salt & white pepper
1 Tbl bland cooking oil
1 cup heavy cream
2 Tbl Shrimp Butter (page 168) (optional)

In a saucepan bring the fish broth, or clam juice, and water to a boil. Add the rice and cook it, covered, at simmer for 30 minutes or until the grains are very soft. Drain the rice, reserving the liquid, and force it through a fine sieve. Set the rice and liquid aside for the moment.

Shell and de-vein the shrimp, reserving the shells. In a saucepan over moderate heat brown the carrot, celery, and onion lightly in 2 tablespoons of the butter. Add the tomatoes and garlic, and cook until they are soft. Reserve 6 of the shrimp and add the rest to the vegetables. Heat the cognac, set it ablaze, and pour it over the shrimp and vegetables. Let the flame burn out. Add the thyme, bay leaf, and parsley, and stir in the chicken broth and wine heated together. Season with salt and white pepper to taste. Cover the pan and cook for 5 minutes. Remove the shrimp and set them aside in a bowl. In another saucepan heat the oil and remaining butter. Add the reserved shrimp shells and cook them over low heat, mashing and stirring constantly, until they turn pink. Add ½ the reserved rice liquid and cook, covered, over moderate heat for 10 minutes. Strain the liquid and blend it into the vegetable mixture. Discard the shells. Chop the shrimp and rub them along with the vegetable mixture through a coarse strainer. Force that mixture through a fine sieve (or reduce the chopped shrimp and vegetable mixture to a purée in an electric blender, using as much of the remaining rice liquid as needed to facilitate the blending). Combine the purée and sieved rice in a saucepan and stir in any remaining rice liquid. Blend in the cream and shrimp butter, if used. Let the soup heat through without further boiling and serve it hot. Garnish each of the 6 servings with 1 of the whole shrimp.

Purée of Bean Soup | Purée de Haricots Blancs

2 cups dried white beans
3 Tbl bacon fat
2 stalks celery, thinly sliced
1 large carrot, coarsely chopped
1 medium onion, coarsely chopped
3 quarts cool water
1 clove garlic, finely chopped
Bouquet Garni (see Glossary)
Salt & white pepper
2 Tbl finely chopped parsley

Put the beans to steep for 1 hour in a saucepan with enough boiling-

hot water to cover them. In another saucepan heat the bacon fat and in it lightly brown the celery, carrot, and onion. Drain the beans, add them to the vegetables in the saucepan, and pour in the cool water. Add the garlic, bouquet garni, and salt and white pepper to taste. Cook the beans, covered, at simmer for 2 hours, stirring them occasionally until they are very soft. Strain the liquid through a fine sieve, forcing the beans and vegetables along with it, into another saucepan. Heat the purée and serve it hot, apportioned for 6 servings each with a sprinkling of ½ teaspoon of the parsley.

Cabbage Soup | Soupe aux Choux

2 pounds green cabbage
3 Tbl butter
1 clove garlic, crushed
1 medium onion, thinly sliced
1 quart strained Beef Broth (page 52 or canned), heated
½ cup Fresh-Tomato Purée (page 160)
Salt & pepper
3 Tbl bacon fat
6 moderately thick slices French Bread
Grated Parmesan cheese

Cut the cabbage in half and cut out the core. Blanch the cabbage for 5 minutes in lightly salted boiling water. Drain the cabbage, squeeze it dry, and shred it. In a large saucepan heat the butter and in it lightly brown the garlic. Remove and discard it. Add the onion and cabbage, and sauté them, stirring constantly until they are evenly and well browned. Stir in the broth, tomato purée, and salt and pepper to taste, and cook, partially covered, for 30 minutes. Heat the bacon fat in a skillet and in it lightly brown the slices of bread on both sides. Place a slice of the bread in each of 6 soup plates and ladle the soup over the slices. Serve steaming hot with the cheese passed separately, to be added to individual tastes.

Cream of Chicken Soup | Potage Crème de Volaille

3 Tbl butter
3 Tbl flour
1½ quarts Clarified Chicken Broth (page 54 or canned), heated
3 leeks, white parts only, thinly sliced
2 center stalks celery, thinly sliced
Salt & white pepper
1½ cups heavy cream
2 egg yolks
1½ cups shredded cooked breast of chicken

In a large saucepan melt the butter over low heat. Blend in the flour and cook, without browning, for 2 minutes. Stir constantly. Blend in the hot clarified broth, and add the leeks and celery. Season with salt and white pepper to taste. Cook, partially covered, for 30 minutes or until the vegetables are soft. Strain the broth through a fine sieve into another saucepan and force the vegetables through. Thoroughly combine ¾ cup of the cream and the egg yolks, and blend the mixture gradually into the consommé. Stir in the remaining cream. Add the shredded chicken and heat the soup through without boiling. Serve hot, apportioned for 6 servings.

Curried Cream of Chicken Soup | Crème Sénégalese

Cream of Chicken Soup (above) **1 Tbl curry powder**

Prepare the soup as directed in the recipe, blending the curry powder along with the flour into the melted butter. Proceed as directed. Cool the soup and chill it thoroughly.

Cream of Mushroom Soup | Potage Velouté aux Champignons

¾ pound fresh mushrooms
3 Tbl butter
2 cups Chicken Velouté Sauce (page 145)
3 cups Clarified Chicken Broth (page 54 or canned), heated
1 tsp lemon juice
1 cup heavy cream
1 egg yolk
Salt & white pepper

Lightly wash the mushrooms, dry them well, and slice them thinly. In a large saucepan melt the butter over low heat. Add the mushrooms and cook them slowly, covered, for 3 minutes or until they begin to render some of their juice. Blend in the velouté sauce, and stir in the hot clarified broth and the lemon juice. Cook, uncovered, at simmer for 10 minutes. Remove pan from heat and stir in very gradually the cream and egg yolk combined. Season with salt and white pepper. Return pan to heat for a minute or two to blend the flavors. Do not let the soup boil. Serve hot, apportioned for 6 servings.

Glazed Onion Soup | Soupe à l'Oignon Gratinée

4 Tbl butter
4 medium onions, thinly sliced
¼ tsp sugar
1 Tbl flour
1½ quarts strained Beef Broth (page 52 or canned), heated
Salt & pepper
6 moderately thick slices French Bread
Grated Parmesan cheese

In a saucepan melt 2 tablespoons of the butter over moderate heat. Add the onions, sprinkle them with the sugar, and cook them, stirring frequently, until they are evenly and well browned. Blend in the flour, and cook, stirring, for 2 minutes. Remove pan from heat, whisk in the hot broth, and season to taste with salt and pepper. Return pan to heat and continue cooking, with the pan partially covered, for 30 minutes longer.

In a skillet heat the remaining butter and in it brown the slices of bread well on both sides. Coat them with grated Parmesan cheese

Pungent leeks and robust potatoes combine in a classic and utterly satisfying French soup (page 69).

and place a slice in each of 6 broiler-proof soup dishes. Pour the soup around them and glaze the tops under a hot broiler. Serve at once with additional grated cheese passed separately.

Leek and Potato Soup | Potage Parmentier

3 Tbl butter
3 leeks, white parts only, thinly sliced
1 medium onion, thinly sliced
3 medium potatoes, thinly sliced
3 cups strained Chicken Broth (page 53 or canned)
Salt & white pepper
1½ cups milk
¼ cup heavy cream

In a saucepan heat the butter and in it cook the leeks and onion until the slices wilt. Add the potatoes, stir in the broth, and cook over low heat for 30 minutes or until the vegetables are very soft. Strain the broth and force the vegetables along with it through a fine sieve into a mixing bowl or purée the mixture in an electric blender. Season with salt and white pepper to taste. Return the purée to the saucepan and bring it to a gentle boil over low heat, stirring constantly. Add the milk and cream, and let the soup heat through without further boiling. Apportion the hot soup for 6 servings. *(See photograph, page 67.)*

Vichyssoise | Vichyssoise

Leek and Potato Soup (above)
½ cup heavy cream
¼ cup sour cream
Salt, to taste
Chopped chives

Cool the soup and blend into it the heavy cream and sour cream, combined. Correct the seasoning, adding salt if needed. Chill thoroughly. Apportion the soup in chilled soup cups to provide 6 servings, each with a generous sprinkling of chopped chives.

Cucumber Vichyssoise | Vichyssoise au Concombre

1 medium cucumber
Leek and Potato Soup (above)
½ cup heavy cream
¼ cup sour cream

From the first delicate harvest of the kitchen garden, this Consommé with Spring Vegetables (page 58).

Peel, seed, and finely grate the cucumber, and press out as much of the liquid as possible. Cool the soup and blend the grated cucumber into it. Add the heavy cream and sour cream, combined, and chill thoroughly. Garnish each serving with a thin slice of cucumber, if desired.

Tomato Vichyssoise | Vichyssoise aux Tomates

Leek and Potato Soup (page 69)
1 cup Fresh-Tomato Purée (page 160)

Cool the soup and blend into it the tomato purée. Chill thoroughly.

Purée of Fresh-Pea Soup | Potage Saint-Germain

3 cups shelled fresh peas
½ cup shredded green lettuce leaves
½ cup chopped spinach leaves
2 leeks, green parts only, finely chopped
¼ tsp dried chervil
2 Tbl butter
1 tsp salt
⅛ tsp pepper
2 cups boiling-hot water
1 quart strained Chicken Broth (page 53 or canned)
1 cup heavy cream

In a large saucepan combine the peas, lettuce, spinach, green parts of leeks, chervil, butter, salt, pepper, and hot water. Cook, covered, at simmer for 30 minutes or until the vegetables are very soft. Add more boiling-hot water if needed to complete the cooking. Force the mixture through a fine sieve or purée it in an electric blender, and return it to the saucepan. Blend in the broth and bring it to a boil. Cook, uncovered, for 5 minutes. Correct the seasoning, adding more salt, if needed. Stir in the cream and heat without boiling. Serve hot apportioned for 6 servings.

Cream of Sorrel Soup | Potage Germiny

1 cup fresh sorrel leaves
4 scallions, white parts only
2 Tbl butter
1½ cups Clarified Chicken Broth (page 54 or canned), heated
1 cup heavy cream
2 egg yolks
Salt & white pepper

Finely shred the sorrel leaves. Thinly slice the scallions. In a saucepan melt the butter over low heat and in it cook the scallions until they are soft but not browned. Add the shredded sorrel and when the shreds wilt stir in the hot clarified broth. Cook, uncovered, for 20 minutes. Strain the broth, forcing the sorrel and scallions along with it, through a fine sieve into another saucepan. Reheat the mixture. Blend the cream into the egg yolks and, off the heat, stir the mixture gradually into the sorrel soup. Heat without boiling, stirring until the soup thickens slightly. Season with salt and white pepper to taste. Serve hot or chilled apportioned for 6 servings.

Vegetable Soup Provençale | Soupe de Légumes Provençale

⅓ cup olive oil
2 large onions, thinly sliced
6 center stalks celery, coarsely chopped
2 carrots, peeled & coarsely chopped
4 large tomatoes, peeled, seeded & coarsely chopped
2 quarts boiling-hot water
1 clove garlic, finely chopped
Salt & pepper
⅓ cup rice, washed
2 Tbl finely chopped parsley

Heat the oil in a saucepan and in it cook the onions, celery, and carrots until they are lightly browned. Add the tomatoes and when they have softened pour in the hot water. Add the garlic and the seasonings to taste. Cook, covered, at simmer for 1 hour. Add the rice and continue the cooking for a final 15 minutes or until the grains are tender. Serve the soup hot, apportioned for 6 servings each sprinkled with 1 teaspoon of the parsley.

3 | main courses

The most enduring of all cookery must surely be the French. It is indomitable. It is cooked everywhere in the world, adapted to the dispositions of the people that prepare it, as well as to the ingredients available. It is one thing in Italy, for example, another in Scotland, still another in Chile, and quite another in Japan. Yet despite its being subject, in the alien lands in which it has taken up residence, to an imponderable variety of alterations, substitutions, mutations, and personal culinary whims, it manages stanchly to retain the flavor of France.

Americans are fortunate in having at hand almost all the ingredients of French cuisine, either imported or domestically produced. There are exceptions, however. For those special Mediterranean fish that compose the authentic French bouillabaisse, alas, we must make substitutions of native species. Yet, even as made here, the dish continues to assert the flavor of France. Other instances of culinary translation appear in this chapter: of orange sauce—traditionally the enhancement of chicken livers—with red snapper, of pepper sauce served with domestic duckling rather than the venison it so often accompanies on French tables. All are in the tradition of French cooking, which uses subtlety and contrast in such ways that it is able to beguile the tastes of every nationality.

Custard with Ham and Spinach | Timbales de Jambon et Épinards

4 eggs
4 egg yolks
2⅓ cups Chicken Broth (page 53 or canned)
1 cup heavy cream
⅛ tsp nutmeg
Salt & white pepper
1 pound cooked ham, finely ground
1 pound young spinach, cooked, chopped & drained
2 Tbl butter, cut into small pieces

Preheat oven to 325 degrees. In a mixing bowl beat together the eggs, yolks, broth, cream, and nutmeg. Season with salt and white pepper to taste. Combine ½ the mixture with the ham, and the remainder with the spinach. Butter 6 custard molds each of 1½ cups capacity and apportion the ham mixture equally among them. Fill molds with the spinach mixture. Sprinkle each with 1 teaspoon of the cut butter. Place the molds in a roasting pan. Set pan in preheated oven and pour hot water around the molds to a depth of 1 inch. Bake for 20 minutes, or until a knife inserted in the center of the molds can be withdrawn clean. This recipe provides 6 servings. Homemade Noodles with Sautéed Bread Crumbs (page 200) provide good accompaniment.

Custard with Fresh Salmon | Timbales de Saumon Frais

4 eggs
4 egg yolks
2 cups light cream
1⅓ cups Fish Broth (page 54) or bottled clam juice
1 Tbl lemon juice
Salt & white pepper
1 pound cooked fillet of salmon, flaked
2 Tbl butter, cut into small bits

Preheat oven to 325 degrees. In a mixing bowl beat together the eggs, yolks, cream, broth or clam juice, and lemon juice. Season with salt and white pepper to taste. If clam juice is used, omit the salt. Fold in the flaked fish. Butter 6 custard molds each of 1½ cups capacity and apportion the mixture equally among them. Sprinkle each with 1 teaspoon of the cut butter. Arrange the filled molds in a roasting pan. Set pan in preheated oven and pour hot water around the molds to a depth of 1 inch. Bake for 20 minutes, or until a knife inserted in the center of the custards can be withdrawn clean. Remove the molds and let them stand for 5 minutes before unmolding them onto warm serving plates. Serve the 6 servings with Raw Asparagus Salad (page 204).

Hard-Cooked Eggs | Oeufs Durs

Eggs to be cooked hard should be at room temperature. If they are not, and you are in a rush to get them going, set them first in a pan of warm tap water for 1 minute. Immerse them in boiling-hot (but not boiling) water in a heavy pan and cook them at the gentlest possible simmer for 12 minutes (½ minute or so longer if the eggs are extra large). Drain them immediately and cool them quickly in cold water. The quick cooling is intended to prevent the yolks from discoloring, and it does seem to make the eggs easier to shell. To center the yolks, for a more attractive appearance when the eggs are to be stuffed, move the eggs around in the water frequently, but gently, during the first 5 minutes of cooking.

Cracking during cooking can be reduced if you avoid the hazards. Don't drop very cold eggs into boiling-hot water. Don't cook them in violently bubbling water which will cause them to bounce against each other and the sides of the pan and invariably crack. Cracking may also be caused by cooking the eggs in a thin pan. The heat source is too close to the eggs resting on the bottom and the heat too intense. Pricking the large ends of the eggs very gently with a needle is frequently helpful, but occasionally that becomes more cause than cure, particularly when the shells are thin.

Hard-Cooked Eggs with Artichoke Hearts and Chicken Livers | Oeufs Carême

9 cooked Artichoke Hearts (page 173 or see Note)
¼ pound chicken livers
2 scallions, white parts only, finely chopped
6 Tbl butter
6 ounces button mushrooms
2 Tbl flour
1½ cups Chicken Broth (page 53 or canned)
½ cup dry white wine
¼ cup heavy cream
1 Tbl finely chopped parsley
Salt & white pepper
9 hard-cooked eggs, shelled & halved lengthwise

Cut the artichoke hearts into halves horizontally and set them aside in a bowl. In a skillet over moderate heat cook the chicken livers and scallions in 1 tablespoon of the butter for 3 minutes, or until the livers are cooked through and the scallions are lightly browned. Remove them and, when the livers are cool enough to handle, cut them into large dice. Add them and the scallions to the artichoke hearts. Lightly rinse and thoroughly dry the mushrooms. Trim off the stems flush with the caps and chop them finely. Leave the caps whole. In the skillet in which the livers were cooked heat 3 more tablespoons of the butter. Add the mushrooms, caps and stems, and sauté them quickly until they are lightly browned. Add them, along with any rendered juice, to the ingredients in the bowl. Preheat oven to 350 degrees.

In a saucepan heat the remaining butter and blend the flour into it. Cook gently for 2 minutes, stirring constantly to prevent browning. Combine the broth and wine, and add the mixture gradually to the roux, stirring to produce a smooth sauce. Stir in the cream, and add the parsley. Season with salt and pepper to taste.

Spread the prepared artichoke-chicken-liver-mushroom mixture in a baking dish and arrange the halves of hard-cooked eggs over it. Cover with the prepared sauce. Set the dish in the oven and heat through. This recipe provides 6 servings. A Ring of Rice and Peas (page 198) is suggested as accompaniment. (*See photograph, page 188.*)

NOTE: A 10-ounce package of frozen artichoke hearts may be substituted for the fresh ones. Cook them first according to directions on the package.

How to Season a Skillet

As important as the actual preparation of a French omelette is the pan in which it is cooked. For best results use a 7-inch heavy iron or aluminum skillet about 2 inches deep with sloping sides rounded at the bottom. The pan must be seasoned before it is used to prevent sticking. Scour a new pan with steel wool, wash it with hot soapy water, and rinse and dry it thoroughly. Fill the pan to within ½-inch of the top with bland cooking oil. (Do not use olive oil. The flavor lingers.) Heat the oil very, very slowly almost to the smoking point. If the heat is properly low, this will take about 1 hour. Remove the pan from the heat and let the oil cool completely. Drain off the oil and reserve it (it is still usable for cooking). Wipe the pan with paper toweling, leaving a light film of oil, and store it, wrapped in foil, until it is needed. Reserve the pan exclusively for cooking omelettes and French pancakes, and never wash it again. Clean it by scouring it with salt, and rub it with a little oil before storing it. If the pan should happen to be washed with soapy water, rinse it well, dry it, coat it with oil, and reheat it very slowly. Wipe and store the pan as before.

French Scrambled Omelette | Omelette Brouillée

3 eggs
1 tsp cold water
Salt & white pepper
1 Tbl butter

In a mixing bowl combine the eggs with the cold water and salt and white pepper to taste. Using a table fork beat the eggs just until the whites and yolks are blended and flow from the fork in a thin stream. In an omelette pan (or heavy 7-inch skillet with rounded sides) melt 1 tablespoon butter over high heat, swirling it around to coat the inside completely. Let the butter foam and immediately the foaming subsides pour in the eggs. Begin stirring them at once, vigorously in a circle, with the back of the fork at the bottom of the pan. At the same time push and pull the pan rapidly back and forth over the heat. Continue so for about 20 seconds. Spread the eggs evenly in the pan and sprinkle them, if desired, with chopped parsley (for a Fines Herbes

Omelette) or grated Parmesan cheese. Moist fillings, such as creamed spinach, should be added a second or two later, when the eggs are a little firmer (see Note).

Carefully fold the side of the omelette nearest the handle in to the center. Tilt the pan, with the handle up and the far side held low over a warm serving plate. Slide the omelette out onto the plate, inverting the folded side over the other to form a lightly browned omelette into a handsome oval. Glaze the top by brushing it lightly with a little melted butter. This size omelette is a single serving. The cooking of each omelette should take no longer than 1 minute.

When several omelettes must be served at the same time, they may be made somewhat ahead of time, undercooked, brushed with melted butter, arranged on a lightly buttered heat-proof platter, and covered with foil. At serving time, remove the foil, set the platter under a moderately hot broiler to heat through and complete the cooking. *(See photographs, page 85.)*

NOTE: Filling an omelette in the pan with a moist preparation containing relatively large pieces of solids, such as chicken livers or whole mushrooms, can make it difficult to fold the omelette and roll it out of the pan. Such fillings are best and most attractively added when the omelette has been turned out onto the serving plate. Cut a lengthwise slit into the omelette and fill the opening. Suggestions for such fillings are given in the recipes which follow. Except as noted, all quantities are for single portions.

Omelette with Dried Mushrooms | Omelette à la Forestière

¼ cup dried morel mushrooms
⅔ cup Chicken Broth (page 53 or canned), heated
1 Tbl butter
1 tsp flour
Salt & pepper
French Scrambled Omelette (page 77)

Wash the morels thoroughly to remove any sand which may be imbedded in their grooves. Put the mushrooms in a bowl, pour the hot broth over them, and let them soften for 30 minutes. Drain the mushrooms, reserving the remaining broth. If the broth is in excess of ½ cup, reduce it to that quantity in a saucepan over high heat. In a small saucepan heat the butter and in it cook the mushrooms for 2 minutes. Sprinkle them with the flour, stirring to coat them evenly, and heat for 1 minute. Blend in the broth, stirring until the sauce is smooth. Season with salt and pepper to taste. Prepare and fill the omelette as directed in the recipe.

Tomato-Cheese Omelette | Omelette à la Tomate et au Fromage

1 Tbl butter
2 tsp flour
1 cup milk
¼ cup grated Gruyère cheese
1 small tomato, peeled, seeded & chopped
Dash of Tabasco
Salt & white pepper
2 French Scrambled Omelettes (page 77)

In a saucepan gently heat the butter. Blend in the flour and cook for 2 minutes, stirring to prevent the roux from browning. Gradually blend in the milk, stirring to produce a smooth sauce. Add the cheese and continue stirring until it melts. Remove and reserve ⅓ cup of the sauce. Add the tomato to the remainder and let it heat through. Season with Tabasco and salt and white pepper to taste. Prepare and fill the 2 omelettes in the pan as directed in the recipe. Coat them with the remaining sauce and glaze them under a hot broiler. This recipe provides 2 servings.

Potato Omelette | Omelette Parmentière

1 medium potato, cooked unpeeled
2 Tbl butter
1 tsp finely chopped parsley
Salt & pepper
French Scrambled Omelette (page 77)

Peel the potato, cut it into small dice, and brown it lightly in the butter heated in a skillet. Drain the potato, combine it with the chopped parsley, and season with salt and pepper to taste. Prepare and fill the omelette as directed in the recipe. The omelette may be filled with this preparation in the pan or on the serving plate.

Basque-Style Omelette | Pipérade

4 Tbl bacon fat
6 ounces tenderized ham, cut in julienne
1 medium onion, thinly sliced
1 medium green pepper, cut in fine julienne
3 medium tomatoes, peeled, seeded & finely chopped
1 small clove garlic, peeled
Bouquet Garni (see Glossary)
10 eggs
Salt & pepper

In a skillet heat 2 tablespoons of the bacon fat and in it lightly brown the ham. Add the onion and pepper, and cook them slowly, covered, until they are soft but not brown. Stir in the tomatoes and add the whole clove of garlic and the bouquet garni. Season with salt and pepper to taste. Cover the skillet again and continue cooking over low heat until the vegetables are reduced almost to a paste. Remove and discard the garlic and bouquet garni. Increase the heat slightly and cook, uncovered, for a few minutes until the remaining juice is almost evaporated. Let the mixture cool. Season the eggs with salt and pepper to taste and beat them with a whisk until the whites and yolks are well combined. Stir them into the vegetables. In a heat-proof earthenware casserole gently heat the remaining bacon fat. Reduce the heat to moderate and add the omelette mixture. Stir and cook, but do not fold, as for a traditional French omelette. Let the omelette cook to a creamy consistency, sprinkle it with chopped parsley, if desired, and serve at once from the casserole. The pipérade provides 6 servings.

Poached Eggs | Oeufs Pochés

All dedicated egg poachers agree that to cook an egg in a little pan nested in a ring over water is not to poach it at all. To be properly poached an egg must be cooked *in* a liquid and out of its shell, of course. Poach the egg in a saucepan or skillet, one not so deep that it will be difficult to get the egg into and out of the liquid. And let the liquid not be seasoned unless the egg is destined for a preparation in aspic *(en gelée),* in which case use water, each 2 cups seasoned with 1 teaspoon of white wine vinegar.

Three inches of water is a good depth for poaching eggs, even for extra large eggs. Bring the water to a rolling boil and pour enough of it into a teacup to fill ½ its capacity. Break an egg into the cup, carefully so as not to disturb the yolk, and let it remain for 2 minutes until the white begins to set. If the egg is not completely submerged, gently add a little more water to make it so. With a soft rubber spatula retrieve any straying wisps of egg white and fold them around the yolk until they adhere. When the egg becomes quite opaque roll it out of the cup at an angle into the water. Let it cook so, barely simmering, for 3 minutes longer, or until the white is firm and the yolk seems soft to gentle pressure. Remove the egg with a slotted spoon and let it drain. Serve at once or keep the eggs in lightly salted cool water for later service. They may be reheated, when required, off the heat in hot water for half a minute or so.

Poached Eggs with Bacon and Hollandaise Sauce |
Oeufs Pochés à la Demi-Mondaine

½ tsp cornstarch
Hollandaise Sauce (page 150)
12 slices moderately lean bacon
2 tomatoes, peeled & cored
Flour for dredging
12 thick rounds of toasted white bread, each 3 inches in diameter
12 Poached Eggs (above), cooked soft

Blend the cornstarch into the egg yolks for the Hollandaise sauce and prepare the sauce as directed in the recipe. In a skillet cook the bacon until it is crisp. Drain it, reserving the drippings in the pan, and crumble it finely. Combine the bacon with the Hollandaise sauce. Cut the tomatoes each into 6 thin slices and dredge them lightly with flour. Remove any burned bits of bacon from the fat in the skillet. Reheat the fat and in it brown the slices of tomato well on both sides. Place a slice on each round of toast and set a poached egg on top. Set these arrangements in a serving platter and coat each with some of the combined Hollandaise sauce and bacon. Serve these 6 portions with, if desired, Asparagus (page 174).

Poached Eggs with Puréed Codfish | Oeufs à la Bénédictine

1 pound fillets of salt codfish
1 clove garlic, mashed to a paste
½ cup olive oil
¾ cup milk
12 Poached Eggs (page 81)
Spinach Sauce (page 159)
Paprika

Soak the codfish in water to cover for 12 hours. Drain them and cover again with fresh water in a saucepan. Bring the water just to boil. Remove pan from heat and let the fish steep in the hot water for 5 minutes. Drain them again and remove the skin and any lingering bones. Flake the fish, transfer them to a mortar or a bowl, and blend in the garlic. In separate saucepans warm the olive oil and milk, and keep them warm. Blend these liquids alternately, a little at a time, into the codfish, working them in with a pestle or a wooden spoon. The mixture should be very smooth and of the consistency of heavy cream. Spread equal amounts in 6 gratin dishes and place 2 poached eggs on each. Cover with the spinach sauce and sprinkle with paprika.
NOTE: Brandade de Morue, which is simply the codfish mixture above, may be served with toast as a light entrée or as an hors-d'oeuvre.

Poached Eggs in Red Wine | Oeufs Pochés au Vin Rouge

12 slices French bread, ¾-inch thick
4 Tbl butter
4 cups light red wine, such as Beaujolais
Bouquet Garni (see Glossary)
1 clove garlic, mashed
Salt & pepper
12 eggs
Kneaded Butter (page 164)

Brown the slices of bread on both sides in the butter heated in a skillet. Drain the slices and keep them warm on a side platter. In a saucepan over moderate heat bring the wine to a boil with the bouquet garni and garlic. Remove pan from heat and let the herbs steep for 5 minutes. Strain the wine into the pan in which you will poach the eggs and discard the herbs. Season the wine with salt and pepper to taste. Poach the eggs as directed in the recipe (page 81) in the red wine. Remove them to a platter and keep them warm. Reduce the wine over high heat to 2 cups and thicken it slightly with a little of the kneaded butter. Arrange the slices of browned bread in a warm serving platter with a poached egg on each and pour the wine sauce over them. Serve the 6 portions with, if desired, Braised Endive (page 182).

Shirred Eggs | Oeufs sur le Plat

3 Tbl butter, melted
12 eggs
Salt & white pepper

Preheat oven to 375 degrees. When the oven is hot, set in it 6 individual gratin dishes or shallow heat-proof dishes large enough to accommodate 2 eggs. Let the dishes heat well. Remove them and coat the bottom of each with 1 teaspoon of the melted butter. Break 2 eggs into each dish and float ½ teaspoon of the melted butter over them. Return the dishes to the oven and let them remain until the eggs are set. The whites will be firm but the yolks soft in 3 minutes. Thereafter they harden very quickly. Season them with salt and white pepper to taste, garnish if desired, and serve immediately with a good green salad and French Bread, preferably your own and still warm. Recipes for shirred eggs with different garnishes follow.

Shirred Eggs with Bacon and Cheese | Oeufs sur le Plat Lorraine

2 Tbl butter
1 Tbl flour
2 cups light cream
⅓ cup grated Gruyère cheese
6 strips crisply cooked lean bacon
Salt & pepper
6 servings Shirred Eggs (above)

In a saucepan gently heat the butter. Blend in the flour and cook, stirring constantly to prevent burning. Add the cream, a little at a time, stirring to produce a smooth sauce. Add the cheese and stir until it melts and is incorporated into the sauce. Crumble the bacon and stir it into the sauce. Season with salt and pepper to taste. When the eggs have baked for 2 minutes spread the sauce around them. Continue the baking for 1 to 2 minutes longer.

With a little practice
making beautiful scrambled omelettes becomes
a simple procedure (page 77).

Add salt to eggs and cold water.

2. Add freshly ground pepper.

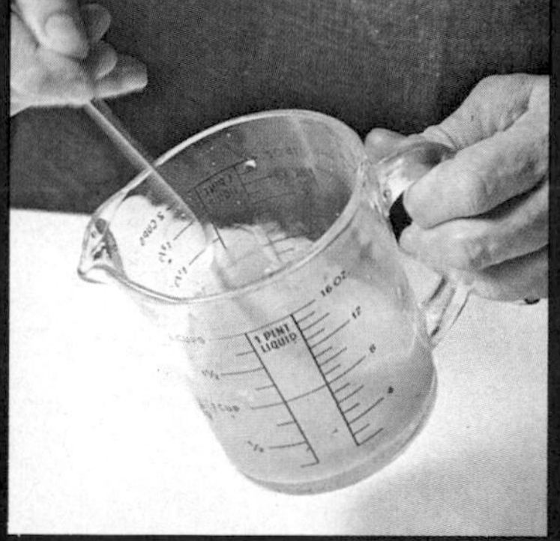
3. Beat eggs until they . . .

4. . . . flow in a thin stream.

Melt butter in omelette pan.

6. Swirl butter to coat sides.

7. Pour eggs into pan.

8. Stirring should begin at once.

Pan is pushed and pulled . . .

10. . . . while stirring continues.

11. Add chopped parsley if desired.

12. Carefully fold side of omelette . . .

. . . nearest handle in to center.

14. Slide omelette out onto plate . . .

15. . . . inverting folded side over other.

16. Result is handsome oval.

CHARTREUSE
CHARTREUSE
LIQUEUR
PAR LES PÈRES
FABRIQUÉE
CHARTREUX
L Garnier
L Garnier

Shirred Eggs with Chicken Livers | Oeufs sur le Plat aux Foies de Volaille Sautés

18 chicken livers
3 Tbl butter
1½ tsp flour
½ cup Chicken Broth (page 53 or canned)
Salt & pepper
6 servings Shirred Eggs (page 84)

Sauté the chicken livers for 3 minutes in the butter heated in a skillet. Remove them to a side dish and keep them warm. Blend the flour into the butter remaining in the skillet and cook, stirring for 2 minutes. Stir in the broth gradually to produce a smooth sauce. Return the livers to the sauce and let them heat through. Season with salt and pepper to taste. When the eggs have baked for 2 minutes, place 3 chicken livers around each serving and continue cooking for 1 to 2 minutes longer.

Chicken and Lobster Soufflé | Soufflé de Volaille et Homard

2 Tbl butter
3 Tbl flour
½ cup Chicken Broth (page 53 or canned)
½ cup light cream
½ cup finely ground cooked chicken
½ cup finely ground cooked lobster
⅛ tsp dried basil
Salt & pepper
4 egg yolks
5 egg whites

Preheat oven to 375 degrees. In a saucepan gently heat the butter. Blend in the flour and cook for 2 minutes, stirring to prevent the roux from taking on any color. Add gradually the chicken broth and the cream, stirring to produce a smooth sauce. Stir in the chicken and the lobster, and let them heat through in the sauce. Add the basil and season with salt and pepper to taste. Remove pan from heat and beat in the egg yolks. Let the mixture cool somewhat. Beat the egg whites until they are stiff but not dry, and stir ¼ of them into the prepared mixture. Fold in the remainder. Butter a 6-cup-capacity soufflé dish and pour the mixture into it. Smooth the top slightly. Bake in the preheated oven

Inspired use of the famous Carthusian liqueur makes this quickly prepared Sautéed Shrimp with Chartreuse (page 100) a memorable dish.

40 minutes, or until the soufflé is well puffed, firm, and nicely browned. The soufflé provides 4 servings. Thinly sliced cucumbers and sweet onions with French Dressing (page 163) are excellent accompaniment.

Ham and Corn Soufflé | Soufflé au Jambon et Maïs

3 Tbl butter
3 Tbl flour
1 cup light cream
½ cup grated fresh corn
½ cup finely ground cooked ham
2 Tbl tomato paste
Salt & pepper
4 egg yolks
5 egg whites

Preheat oven to 375 degrees. In a saucepan heat the butter. Blend in the flour and cook for 2 minutes, stirring to prevent the roux from browning. Gradually add the cream, stirring constantly until the mixture thickens and is smooth. Stir in the corn, ham, and tomato paste, and season with salt and pepper to taste. Let the mixture heat through and remove pan from heat. Beat in the egg yolks and let the mixture cool somewhat. Beat the egg whites until they are stiff but not dry, and stir ¼ of them into the prepared mixture. Fold in the remainder. Butter a 6-cup-capacity soufflé dish and pour the soufflé mixture into it. Smooth the top slightly. Bake in the preheated oven 30 minutes, or until the soufflé is well puffed, firm, and nicely browned. This recipe provides 4 servings which may be served with, if desired, Spiced Sautéed Tomatoes (page 194).

fish and seafood

Casserole of Codfish and Potatoes | Morue et Pommes de Terre en Cocotte

2 pounds fillets of salt codfish
2 cups milk, scalded
6 medium potatoes, unpeeled, thoroughly scrubbed
1 medium onion, thinly sliced
2 Tbl butter
2 tsp flour
White pepper
Salt
2 Tbl grated Parmesan cheese

Soak the codfish in cool water to cover for 12 hours, changing the water 2 or 3 times. Drain the fish, flake it, and remove the skin and any remaining bones. Put the flaked fish in a saucepan, pour the hot milk over it, and cook at bare simmer for 10 minutes. Remove pan from heat and let the fish steep in the hot milk for 5 minutes. Drain it, reserving the milk. Preheat oven to 375 degrees.

Cook the potatoes over moderate heat in water to cover for 15 minutes, or until they are tender but still firm. Remove them to a side platter and let cool. Reheat the water to boiling and in it blanch the onion slices for 2 minutes. Drain them and set aside. When the potatoes are cool enough to handle, peel them and cut into slices about ⅛-inch thick. Set them aside for the moment also.

You will need 1 cup of the milk in which the fish was cooked. If it has reduced during cooking to less than that, add enough light cream to make up the difference. In a saucepan gently heat 1 tablespoon of the butter. Blend in the flour and cook this roux over low heat for 2 minutes, stirring constantly so that it does not brown. Blend in the cup of reserved milk (with the added cream, if needed), a little at a time, to produce a smooth thin sauce. Season with white pepper and, if needed, salt to taste.

Grease a *cocotte* (a heat-proof earthenware casserole) with the remaining butter and in it arrange a layer of ⅓ of the potatoes. Pour over them ¼ cup of the prepared sauce. Cover with ½ each of the codfish and onion, and pour ¼ cup of the sauce over them. Continue with, in order, ½ the remaining potatoes, all of the remaining fish and onion, ¼ cup of the sauce, and the remaining potatoes. Combine the grated cheese with the remaining sauce and spread it over the potatoes. Bake, uncovered, in the preheated oven 15 minutes or until the sauce bubbles and the top is well browned. This recipe provides 6 hearty servings. A green salad with French Dressing (page 163) is suggested as an accompaniment.

Casserole of Mackerel and Leeks |

Maquereaux et Poireaux en Cocotte

2 pounds fillets of mackerel
Salt & pepper
Flour for dredging
5 Tbl butter
6 leeks, white parts only, cut in julienne
1 Tbl finely chopped parsley
½ cup water

Season the fish with salt and pepper to taste and dredge them well with flour. Brown them lightly on both sides in 3 tablespoons of the butter heated in a skillet. Heat the remaining butter in a *cocotte* (a heat-proof earthenware casserole) and lightly brown the leeks in that. Arrange the fish over the bed of leeks, and sprinkle them with the parsley. Blend the water into the juices remaining in the skillet and let it come to a boil. Pour it over the fish. Cover the casserole and cook the fish and leeks over low heat for 30 minutes or until the liquid is completely absorbed. This is a good hearty dish for a winter midday meal, to be made complete with a green salad with French Dressing (page 163) and crusty French Bread, preferably of your own baking.

Pike Dumplings with Creamed Sorrel |

Quenelles de Brochet à l'Oseille à la Crème

2 pounds fillets of pike
4 egg whites
3 cups heavy cream
Salt & white pepper
Fish Broth (page 54) or bottled clam juice
2 pounds fresh sorrel
5 Tbl butter
⅓ cup finely chopped scallions, mostly white parts
⅓ cup additional heavy cream
2 Tbl sour cream

Remove the skin from the fillets of pike and make certain the fish are completely free of bones. Grind them 3 times through the fine blade of a food chopper. Put the ground fish in a mixing bowl and vigorously beat in the eggs whites, 1 at a time. Force the mixture through a fine sieve and work it to a velvety smooth paste in a mortar with a pestle or in a bowl with a wooden spoon (or reduce the ground fish and egg whites directly to a smooth paste in an electric blender). Beat into the paste only enough of the 3 cups of cream to produce a mixture that is just firm enough to hold a shape. Too much cream may cause the dumplings to disintegrate in the poaching liquid. Test frequently by steeping a spoonful in a bowl of boiling-hot water. If it firms, you have added enough cream. Season the remaining paste with salt and white pepper to taste. Using 2 soup spoons shape the paste into ovals and poach them at just below a simmer in equal quantities of fish broth or bottled clam juice and water, or in water alone, lightly salted. Maintain the heat of the poaching liquid for 15 minutes, by which time the quenelles should be properly cooked. Drain them on a cloth or paper toweling and arrange them in a lightly buttered platter. Keep them warm.

Wash the sorrel, dry it between sheets of paper toweling, and cut it into shreds. In a saucepan gently heat 4 tablespoons of the butter and in it cook the scallions until they are soft but not brown. Add the sorrel and cook it, covered, until it wilts and the shreds are tender. Uncover the pan and continue cooking until all rendered liquid evaporates. Remove pan from heat. Combine the ⅓ cup heavy cream and the sour cream, and stir the mixture gradually into the puréed sorrel. Season it with salt and white pepper, add the remaining butter, cut into small bits, and reheat until the mixture thickens slightly. Pour it over the pike dumplings and serve them at once. This recipe serves 6.

Deviled Grilled Salmon | Saumon Grillé à la Diable

6 slices fresh salmon, about 6 ounces each
1½ tsp coarse salt
8 Tbl butter
1 tsp bland cooking oil
½ tsp prepared mustard
⅛ tsp dry mustard
⅛ tsp ground coriander
¼ tsp lemon juice
1 tsp brown sugar
3 Tbl cognac
Lemon wedges

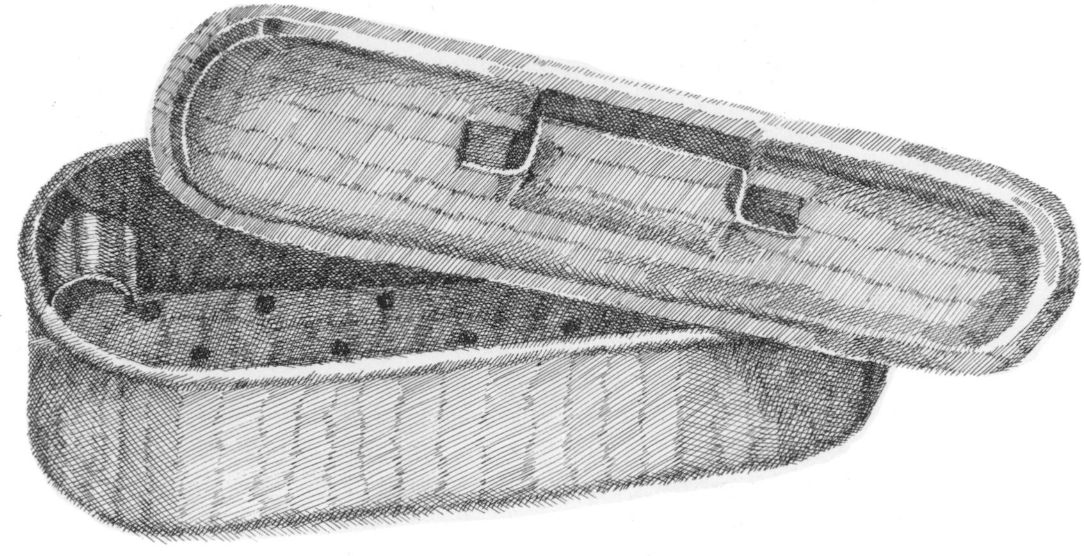

Sprinkle each slice of salmon with ¼ teaspoon coarse salt and let the fish season in the refrigerator for 30 minutes. Prepare a paste in a mixing bowl by combining 6 tablespoons of the butter and all of the remaining ingredients except the cognac and lemon wedges. Remove the fish from the refrigerator and brush the slices to remove excess salt. Coat the slices evenly with the prepared paste. In a skillet melt the remaining butter over moderate heat. When it is properly hot, add the slices of salmon coated sides up in a single layer, and cook them for 3 minutes. Have the cognac ready, gently warmed, set it ablaze, and pour it flaming over the salmon. When the flame expires, transfer the pan to a moderately hot broiler about 3 inches below the heat source and continue the cooking for 3 minutes longer, or until the fish flakes easily when tested with a fork. Place on a serving platter and garnish with lemon wedges. Serve with Cucumbers in Cream (page 40).

Red Snapper with Orange Sauce | Poisson au Four Bigarade

3½- to 4-pound red snapper
1 small hot pepper, split
Juice of 1 orange, strained
Juice of ½ lemon, strained
1 tsp salt
1 large onion, finely chopped
1 Tbl bland cooking oil
3 Tbl butter
2½ cups cool water
1¼ cups medium-dry white wine, such as Graves
2 Tbl white wine vinegar
2 scallions, white & tender green parts, thinly sliced
1 stalk celery, thinly sliced
3-inch length thin orange peel
1 clove garlic, mashed
2 whole cloves
Bouquet Garni (see Glossary)
12 small carrots
6 small potatoes, peeled
6 leeks, white parts only
6 slices unpeeled orange, ⅛-inch thick
1 Tbl tomato paste
Additional salt
1 Tbl arrowroot powder

Have the market clean the fish and bone it whole, leaving the head on. Rub the skin of the fish with the cut sides of the hot pepper, and score the skin lightly on the diagonal in 3 places on each side. Place the fish in a baking pan, pour the fruit juices around it, and stir in the teaspoon of salt. Let the fish marinate so for 1 hour, turning it after 30 minutes to season it evenly.

Preheat oven to 375 degrees. In a large saucepan over low heat cook the onion in the oil and butter until it is soft but not brown. Stir in the water, wine, and vinegar, and bring the liquid quickly to a boil. Add the scallions, celery, orange peel, garlic, cloves, and bouquet garni. Cook, uncovered, over moderate heat for 10 minutes. Add the whole vegetables and cook them, covered, for 10 minutes. Remove and reserve them on a side platter. Strain the liquid and reduce it over high heat to about 3 cups. Pour it over the fish, and blend it with the marinade. Arrange the orange slices, slightly overlapping, on top of the fish. Bake, uncovered, in the preheated oven for 10 minutes. Add the reserved whole vegetables and continue cooking for 10 minutes longer, or until the fish flakes easily when tested with a fork. Transfer it carefully to a warm serving platter and keep it warm. Rearrange the orange slices on top. If the vegetables need further cooking, cover pan and continue cooking until they are tender. Arrange them around the fish.

Strain the cooking liquid into a saucepan, and if it is in excess of 1½ cups reduce it to that quantity. Stir into it the tomato paste, and correct the seasoning, adding salt, if needed. Thicken the sauce with the arrowroot powder dissolved in ⅓ cup of cool water. Pour ¼ cup of the sauce over the fish and pass the rest separately. This recipe provides 6 generous servings of fish and vegetables.

Braised Stuffed Trout | Truites Farcies et Braisées

6 trout, about ¾ pound each
½ pound fillet of flounder
1 egg, separated
2 cups heavy cream
Salt & white pepper
2 Tbl butter
2 leeks, white parts only, thinly sliced
¾ cup dry white wine
¼ cup Fish Broth (page 54) or bottled clam juice
1 Tbl tomato paste
½ tsp paprika
¼ tsp lemon juice

Have the fish market clean and bone the trout without separating the halves, but removing the heads. Keep the fish in the refrigerator until the filling is prepared.

Put the flounder twice through the fine blade of a food chopper. Put it in a bowl and with a wooden spoon vigorously beat in the egg white a little at a time. Force the mixture through a fine sieve and work it to a smooth paste in the bowl with the wooden spoon or in a mortar with a pestle (or reduce the ground fish and egg white immediately to a paste in an electric blender, adding ⅓ cup of the heavy cream to facilitate the blending). Beat 1 cup of the cream by tablespoons into the paste (add only ⅔ cup of the cream to paste made in a blender). Season this mousse with salt and white pepper to taste and chill it thoroughly in the refrigerator. Preheat oven to 375 degrees.

Arrange the boned trout open and flat on the working surface and spread them equally with the prepared mousse. Fold them closed and arrange them in a well-buttered baking dish. Melt the butter in a skillet over low heat and in it cook the leeks until the slices wilt. Spread them over the fish along with butter remaining in the pan. Sprinkle with salt and white pepper to taste. In a saucepan heat together the wine, fish broth or clam juice, and tomato paste, and pour the liquid around the fish. Cover the baking pan securely (with foil if the dish has no cover), set it in the preheated oven, and cook the fish so for 20 minutes or until they are tender. Transfer the fish to a warm serving platter, leaving the leeks and cooking liquid in the pan. Keep the fish warm. Cook the liquid in the baking pan for 2 minutes over moderate heat on top of the stove. Strain it into a saucepan, and if it is in excess of ½ cup reduce it over the heat to that quantity. Stir in the paprika, and gradually blend in the remaining cream combined with the egg yolk. Let the sauce heat through without boiling, stirring until it thickens slightly. Stir in the lemon juice.

Peel off the skin from the exposed sides of the fish. Pour the sauce around the fish and serve at once with Braised Rice (page 197). This recipe provides 6 servings.

Burgundian Fish Stew | Matelote à la Bourguignonne

6 pounds assorted freshwater fish
6 Tbl butter
2 large carrots, finely chopped
1 medium onion, finely chopped
1 stalk celery, finely chopped
2 leeks, white parts only, thinly sliced
2 cloves garlic, crushed
3 cups red Burgundy wine
Salt & pepper
¼ cup marc de Bourgogne (see Note)
Kneaded Butter (page 164)
6 thick slices French Bread
2 Tbl Garlic Butter (page 166)

As Marseille has its bouillabaisse (see page 60), Burgundy has its *matelote;* but while the famous dish of Provence is prepared only with fish from the sea (specifically from the Mediterranean waters of Marseille), the matelote is made only with Burgundy's freshwater fish, such as carp, eel, perch, pickerel, pike, and trout. Traditionally 4 or 5 different fish are used. Serve this preparation as a main course.

Have the fish market clean the fish and remove the heads. Cut the fish across the width into 2- or 3-inch pieces. In a large, moderately deep saucepan melt 4 tablespoons of the butter over low heat. Add the vegetables and garlic, and stir to coat them with the butter. Pour in the wine. Season with salt and pepper to taste, and cook the mixture, covered, for 15 minutes. Arrange the fish over the bed of vegetables. Gently heat the marc, set it ablaze, and pour it over the fish. Shake the pan until the flame expires. Cover pan and continue cooking for 15 minutes or until the fish are tender. Remove them to a warm serving platter and keep them warm. Strain the broth, discarding the residue, and return the liquid to the pan and the heat. Thicken it slightly with kneaded butter and stir in the remaining regular butter. In a skillet brown the slices of bread on both sides in the garlic butter, and arrange a slice in each of 6 soup plates. Surround the slices equally with the fish and pour the sauce over them. Serve at once.

NOTE: Marc de Bourgogne is a brandy distilled from the mash of Burgundy wine.

Provincial Fish Stew | Bourride au Goût de Madame M.

1½ pounds assorted small fish (smelt, trout, perch, carp, etc.)
2 quarts water
2 medium tomatoes, peeled, seeded & chopped
2 medium onions, finely chopped
1 stalk celery, sliced, with leaves
2 cloves garlic
3-inch strip thin orange peel
⅓ cup olive oil
Bouquet Garni (see Glossary)
Salt & pepper
⅛ tsp powdered saffron
1½ pounds fillets of sole
6 slices day-old French Bread
Garlic Mayonnaise (page 157)
2 egg yolks

Have the fish market clean the fish and cut them, without the heads, into serving pieces. In a large saucepan bring the water to a boil with the tomatoes, onions, celery, 1 clove of the garlic, mashed, the orange peel, 2 tablespoons of the olive oil, bouquet garni, and salt and pepper to taste. Simmer, covered, for 20 minutes. Add the saffron, blended with a little of the broth, and cook for 1 minute. Add the fish pieces and cook them, uncovered, over moderate heat for 10 minutes or until they are tender. Remove them to a warm serving platter and keep them warm. Remove the orange peel and bouquet garni from the broth and discard them. Strain the broth through a fine sieve, forcing the vegetables along with it into a large skillet. Heat the mixture and poach the fillets of sole in it, at simmer, for 5 minutes, or just until they flake

easily when tested with a fork. Remove them to the platter of small fish. Reduce the poaching liquid over high heat to 5 or 6 cups and keep this soup warm.

Rub the slices of bread with the remaining clove of garlic, cut, and brown them well in the remaining olive oil heated in a skillet.

In a small bowl blend 2 tablespoons of the garlic mayonnaise into the egg yolks. Beat in enough soup to warm the mixture through and stir it gradually into the remaining soup. Heat gently, stirring constantly, until the soup thickens somewhat. Place the slices of bread in soup plates with the small fish apportioned around them. Pour the soup over the fish. Place a piece of the sole on each slice of bread and top with some of the garlic mayonnaise. Serve hot. The soup may be served with the bread, and the fish separately with the mayonnaise.

Stuffed Scallops | Coquilles Saint-Jacques Farcies

36 large sea scallops
3 cups dry white wine
1 bay leaf, crumbled
½ pound fillet of flounder
½ pound shelled & de-veined shrimp
2 egg whites
Juice of 1 lemon, strained
2 Tbl Fresh-Tomato Purée (page 160)
1 Tbl cognac
⅛ tsp nutmeg
Salt & white pepper
3 Tbl butter, melted
Béarnaise Sauce (page 155)

Rinse the scallops in cool water and drain them. Put them in a glass or china bowl and pour the wine over them. Add the bay leaf. Let the scallops marinate so, under refrigeration, for several hours or overnight. Drain them and dry them thoroughly.

Put the flounder and shrimp together through the fine blade of a food chopper several times (at least 3). Force them through a fine sieve and work them further, in a mortar with a pestle or in a bowl with a wooden spoon, to produce a smooth paste. Beat into it the egg whites, a little at a time, and stir in the lemon juice, tomato purée, cognac, and nutmeg. Season with salt and white pepper to taste. With a sharp, pointed knife cut a pocket in the side of each scallop and, using a pastry bag fitted with a plain tube, pipe in the fish paste, filling the scallops well. Arrange them, not too close together, in a shallow baking pan and brush them with the melted butter. Cook them in a hot broiler for 5 minutes or until they are lightly browned and tender, turning them once. Serve with the Béarnaise sauce. This recipe provides 6 servings.

Clam Hash | Praires Hachés

Steamed Clams (page 14)
4 medium-size boiled potatoes, peeled & finely diced
1 medium onion, finely chopped
2 Tbl finely chopped green pepper
1 tsp finely chopped celery leaves
White pepper
3 Tbl bacon fat

Shell the clams and chop them finely. Combine them in a mixing bowl with the potatoes, onion, pepper, and celery leaves. Season with white pepper to taste. Heat the bacon fat in a skillet and crumble in the clam mixture. Cook, over moderate heat, stirring until the bits begin to brown. With a spatula mold them into a flat cake and continue cooking until it is well browned on the under side. Turn the cake and brown the other side. Serve the 6 portions of the hash with, if desired, sliced tomatoes with French Dressing (page 163).

Crabmeat in French Pancakes | Crêpes au Crabe Mornay

3½ cups cooked crabmeat, flaked
1½ cups Cream Sauce with Cheese (page 144)
18 French Pancakes (page 239)
⅓ cup heavy cream, whipped
¼ cup grated Parmesan cheese

In a saucepan heat the crabmeat in 1 cup of the sauce. Place about ¼ cup of the mixture in the center of each pancake. Roll the pancakes, tucking in the sides to enclose the fillings completely. In a small bowl combine the remaining sauce, cooled, with the whipped cream. Arrange the filled pancakes in a lightly buttered shallow baking pan and coat them equally with the creamed sauce. Sprinkle with the grated cheese. Set the pan under a moderately hot broiler and let it remain for a few minutes until the pancakes are heated and glazed. This recipe provides 3 filled pancakes for each of 6 servings.

Sautéed Shrimp with Chartreuse |
Crevettes Sautées au Chartreuse

2 pounds medium shrimp
4 Tbl butter
2 Tbl orange juice, strained
Salt & white pepper
3 Tbl green Chartreuse
A Ring of Rice and Peas (page 198)

Shell and de-vein the shrimp, rinse them, and dry them well with paper toweling. Heat the butter in a large skillet. Add the shrimp and cook them briskly for 5 minutes, turning them frequently until they are uniformly pink and cooked through. Sprinkle them with the orange juice and season them with salt and white pepper to taste. Reduce the heat to low. In a small saucepan gently heat the Chartreuse, set it ablaze, and pour it flaming over the shrimp. Shake the pan until the flame expires. Unmold the ring of rice and peas onto a warm serving platter and fill the center with the shrimp. Serve at once. A sauce to be served with the shrimp may be quickly prepared by blending into the cooking juices remaining in the skillet 1 cup heavy cream and an

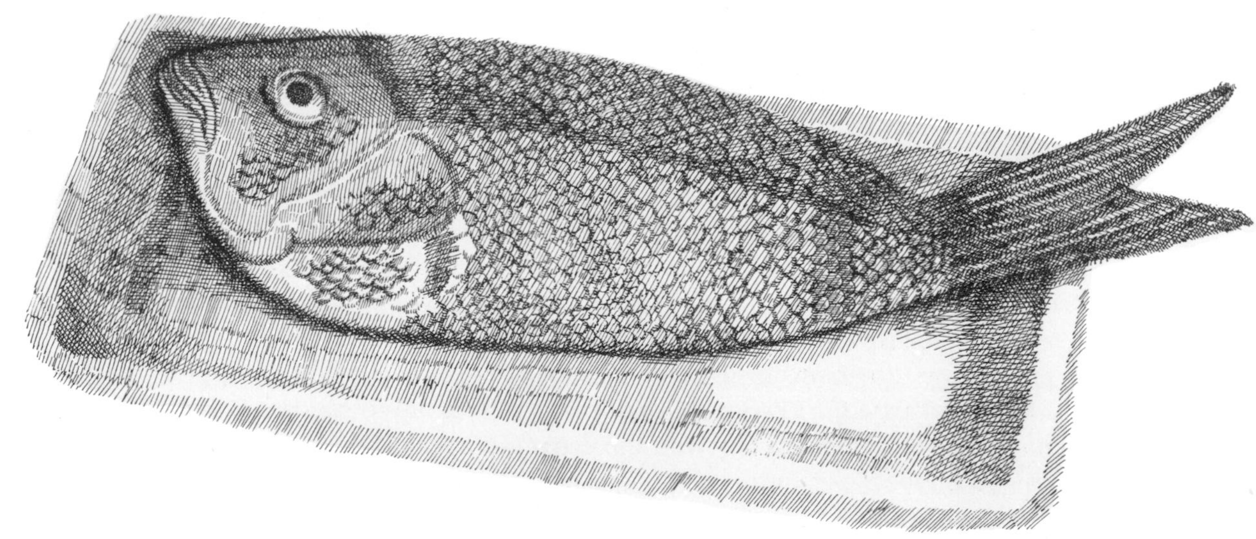

additional tablespoon of Chartreuse. Season to taste with salt and pepper. This recipe provides 6 servings. *(See photograph, page 86.)*

Sautéed Frogs' Legs | Cuisses de Grenouilles Sautées

3 pounds frogs' legs
3 cups milk
Flour for dredging
4 eggs, beaten
2 cups fine dry bread crumbs
8 Tbl Clarified Butter (page 166)
Salt & white pepper
Lemon wedges

Trim the frogs' legs and soak them in the milk for 1 hour. Drain and dry them thoroughly. Dredge the legs lightly with flour, dip them in the beaten eggs, and coat them evenly with the bread crumbs. Sauté ⅓ of the frogs' legs in 3 tablespoons of the butter heated in a skillet, browning the legs well on all sides. Cook the remaining frogs' legs in 2 batches in the same way, adding butter as needed. Each batch of frogs' legs will be properly cooked in about 5 minutes. Drain them and keep them warm at the back of the stove. When all are cooked, arrange them in a warm serving platter to provide 6 servings. Season them with salt and white pepper to taste and garnish the platter with lemon wedges. Serve the frogs' legs with, if desired, fresh Asparagus (page 174) with Creamed Hollandaise Sauce (page 152).

Frogs' Legs Provençale | Cuisses de Grenouilles Provençales

Sautéed Frogs' Legs (above)
1 Tbl butter
1 clove garlic, finely chopped
4 medium tomatoes, peeled, seeded & coarsely chopped
Salt & white pepper
1 Tbl finely chopped parsley

Sauté the frogs' legs as directed in the recipe and keep them warm on a serving platter. Heat the butter in the sauté pan and in it cook the garlic until it is soft but not brown. Stir in the tomatoes and cook them over high heat until they soften somewhat. Season lightly with salt and white pepper. Pour the sauce over the frogs' legs and sprinkle with the chopped parsley.

poultry

Roast Chicken, French Style | Poulet Rôti

1 3-pound young chicken
6 Tbl butter, softened
Salt & pepper

Preheat oven to 400 degrees. Coat the inside of the bird with 3 tablespoons of the butter and sprinkle it with salt and a good grinding of pepper to taste. Truss it, securing the legs and wings close to the body. Coat the outside also with 3 tablespoons of the butter favoring particularly the breasts and legs. Sprinkle the skin also with salt and pepper. Place the bird on its side in a roasting pan and set pan in preheated oven. Roast the chicken so for 15 minutes. Baste with the drippings in the pan and roast 5 minutes longer. Turn the chicken to the other side. Roast another 5 minutes and baste that side. Roast 15 minutes more. Set the chicken upright, on its back, and baste the breast well. Roast 10 minutes, baste, roast 10 minutes longer, and the chicken is done—that is, done medium rare, which is how the French like it. If you prefer chicken a little less pink, reduce oven temperature to 350 degrees and start the whole roasting procedure over, turning and basting at 10-minute intervals, for an additional 30 minutes. Remove the trussings and carve the chicken. The sauce for the chicken is the drippings in the pan. Serve with, if desired, fresh Asparagus (page 174). One 3-pound chicken will provide 3 servings.

Stuffing for Roast Chicken | Farce pour Poulet Rôti

1 medium onion, finely chopped
2 Tbl butter
1 cup Sausage Meat (page 132)
1 cup finely ground veal
3 chicken livers
1 Tbl cognac
⅔ cup day-old white bread crumbs
2 Tbl dry vermouth
2 Tbl light cream
¼ tsp dried thyme
⅛ tsp dried rosemary
⅛ tsp nutmeg
Salt & pepper
3 egg yolks

In a skillet cook the onion in the butter over moderate heat until it is soft but not brown. In a mixing bowl combine the sausage meat, veal, and chicken livers, and add the cooked onion and any butter remaining in the skillet. Put this mixture through the fine blade of a meat chopper. Blend in the cognac. Soften the bread crumbs with the vermouth and cream, and thoroughly combine that mixture, along with the herbs and nutmeg, with the ground meats. Season to taste with salt and pepper. Stir in the egg yolks. This recipe provides sufficient stuffing for a 3-pound chicken.

Roast Chicken with Apple Brandy | Poulet Rôti à la Normande

3 2¼-pound frying chickens
10 Tbl butter
Salt & pepper
1 small onion, finely chopped
1 cup rice
3 cups Chicken Broth (page 53 or canned), heated
1 bay leaf
1 cup heavy cream
2 cups Chicken Velouté Sauce (page 145)
¼ pound mushrooms, cleaned & thinly sliced
¼ cup Calvados (French apple brandy) or applejack
Sprigs of watercress

Trim off the chicken wings and truss the birds, securing the legs firmly to the bodies. The wings are not required for this recipe; reserve them for other uses. Swathe the chickens each in 2 tablespoons of the butter and season them to taste with salt and pepper. Roast them French style (opposite), but reduce oven heat to 350 degrees after the first 40 minutes.

In a casserole heat 2 tablespoons of the butter and in it cook the onion until it is soft but not brown. Add the rice and stir constantly for 3 minutes until the grains are well coated with the butter and have started to turn opaque. Stir in the hot chicken broth and add the bay leaf and salt to taste. Let the broth bubble for a second or two. Cover the casserole securely, transfer pan to oven on a rack above the chickens, and cook the rice for 30 minutes, or until the liquid is completely absorbed and the grains are tender. Remove and discard the bay leaf. Keep the rice warm.

When the chickens are cooked, take them from the oven and remove the trussings. Cut the chickens into halves and carefully remove the breast bones. Set them aside for the moment, but keep them

warm. Drain off most of the fat remaining in the roasting pan. Pour in the cream and blend it into the cooking glaze at the bottom of the pan. Stir in the velouté sauce. Quickly sauté the mushrooms in the remaining butter heated in a skillet. Add them to the roasting pan. Stir in the Calvados or applejack and let the sauce heat through gently.

Spread the prepared rice in a warm serving platter and arrange the 6 portions of chicken over it. Pour the sauce over them. Garnish with sprigs of watercress and serve at once.

Sautéed Breast of Chicken with Cucumbers |
Suprêmes de Volaille Sautés aux Concombres

6 whole chicken breasts, about 1 pound each
1 large cucumber
½ cup Chicken Broth (page 53 or canned)
½ cup dry white wine
4 Tbl butter
¼ cup thinly sliced scallions, white parts only
Salt & white pepper
1 cup heavy cream
¼ tsp finely grated lemon rind

Have the butcher split the chicken breasts and remove the skins and bones. Place the breasts between sheets of waxed paper and, with a meat pounder or flat of a cleaver, flatten the meat to a thickness of about ¼-inch. Set the breasts aside for the moment.

Peel the cucumber, split it lengthwise, and scrape out the seeds. Cut the cucumber into thin slices. Reserve about ⅔ of them. Put the remainder in a saucepan with the broth and wine. Bring the liquid to a boil and immediately remove pan from heat. Let the cucumbers steep so in the liquid for 5 minutes. Remove and discard the slices of cucumber. Keep the liquid warm.

In a large skillet gently heat the butter and in it cook the scallions until they are soft but not brown. Add the chicken breasts, as many at a time as the pan can accommodate, and cook them slowly for 10 minutes or until they are tender, turning once. Season them with salt and white pepper to taste. Remove them to a side platter and keep warm. Remove and discard the scallions. Pour in the prepared broth and wine, and blend it into the cooking glaze at the bottom of the pan. Cook down the liquid until it is reduced to about ¼ cup. Blend in the cream and lemon rind, and season the mixture with salt and white pepper to taste. When the cream has been heated, return the chicken breasts to the skillet and add the reserved cucumber slices. Heat them all in the cream. Transfer the chicken breasts and cucumbers to a warm serving platter and pour the sauce over them. Serve at once with Steamed Rice (page 198). This recipe provides 6 servings.

Sautéed Chicken, Hunter Style | Poulet Sauté Chasseur

2 frying chickens (about 6 pounds)
6 Tbl butter
1 tsp bland cooking oil
Salt & pepper
¼ cup cognac
2 large shallots, finely chopped
1 clove garlic, mashed to a paste
3 large tomatoes, peeled, seeded & chopped
¼ tsp dried basil
½ cup dry white wine
1 cup Brown Sauce (page 148)
¾ pound fresh mushrooms

Cut the chickens into serving pieces. Lightly sponge the pieces with a damp cloth and dry them thoroughly. In a large skillet heat 4 tablespoons of the butter and the oil. Add the chickens, as many pieces at a time as the pan can accommodate without crowding, and, over rather high heat, brown them well on all sides. Season them to taste with salt and pepper. Return all the pieces to the skillet. Gently heat the cognac, set it ablaze, and pour it over the chickens. Shake the pan to prolong the blaze. When the flame expires, reduce heat to moderate, cover the skillet, and cook the chickens so for 20 minutes or until they are tender, basting occasionally. Remove the pieces to a side platter and keep them warm.

To the drippings in the skillet add the shallots and garlic, and cook them until they are soft but not brown. Add the tomatoes and basil, and stir in the white wine. Cook, uncovered, for 5 minutes. Blend in the brown sauce and cook 5 minutes longer.

Lightly wash the mushrooms, dry them well, and trim off the stems. Reserve the stems in the refrigerator for other uses. Thinly slice the caps. In another skillet heat the remaining butter and in it lightly brown the mushrooms. Transfer them and any rendered juices to the sauce in the other skillet. Season with salt and pepper to taste and cook the mixture for 2 to 3 minutes to blend the flavors. Return the cooked chicken to the skillet and baste the pieces with the sauce. Let them heat through and serve them with the sauce. This recipe provides 6 servings.

Sautéed Chicken with Lemon | Poulet Sauté au Citron

8 Tbl butter
2 frying chickens (about 6 pounds), split
1½ quarts Chicken Broth (page 53 or canned), heated to boiling
1 tsp salt
4 peppercorns
¼ cup flour
Juice of 2 lemons, strained
White pepper & additional salt
1 cup heavy cream
2 egg yolks
1 Tbl finely chopped parsley

Melt 5 tablespoons of the butter in a large skillet over low heat and in it cook the chickens, a half at a time, very gently without browning, for 5 minutes each. Transfer the halves to a large saucepan, arranging them as flatly as possible. Pour the boiling hot broth over them and add the teaspoon of salt and the peppercorns. Bring the broth back to boil over low heat, and skim it. Cover the pan partially and cook for 45 minutes or until the chickens are tender. Drain them, reserving the broth, and when they are cool enough to handle, bone them, removing the meat in as large pieces as possible. Strain the broth. In another saucepan melt the remaining butter over low heat and blend in the flour. Cook without browning, stirring constantly, for 2 minutes. Gradually add the reserved broth, stirring constantly to produce a smooth sauce. Blend in the lemon juice and add additional salt, if needed, and white pepper to taste. Combine the cream and egg yolks, and blend the mixture gradually into the sauce. Heat again, without boiling, stirring until the sauce thickens. Add the boned chicken and heat it through. Transfer the chicken and the sauce to a warm serving platter and sprinkle the chopped parsley over them. Serve the 6 portions with Steamed Rice (page 198).

Chicken in Wine Aspic | Poulet au Vin Blanc en Gelée

2 frying chickens (about 6 pounds)
2 quarts Chicken Broth (page 53 or canned)
1½ cups dry white wine
1 veal knucklebone, cracked
6 large carrots
1 large sweet onion
3–4 canned pimientos, drained (4-ounce can)
½ cup olive oil
Salt
9–12 peppercorns
Lettuce leaves

Have the butcher skin and bone the chickens, reserving the bones. Put the bones, necks, wing tips, and giblets (except the livers) in a large saucepan. Pour over them the broth and wine, and add the veal bone. Bring the liquid to a boil and skim it. Partially cover the pan and cook at simmer for 2 hours. Strain the resulting broth and clarify it, if necessary (page 54). Let it cool.

Thinly slice the carrots and the onion, and separate the onion slices into rings. Cut the pimientos into strips. Pour the oil into a large heavy casserole and arrange the chicken breasts in it. Cover them with, in order, a layer each of ⅓ of the carrots, onion, and pimientos. Cover with a layer of chicken. Sprinkle lightly with salt and add 3 or 4 peppercorns. Arrange the remaining ingredients in 2 similar series of layers, seasoning each series (not each layer) with salt and adding peppercorns. Pour over all enough of the prepared broth barely to cover the ingredients. Refrigerate or freeze any remaining broth for other uses.

Bring the broth in the casserole to a boil and skim it. Cover the casserole very securely and cook the chicken and vegetables at simmer for 1½ hours or until the chicken is tender. Remove the cover and let the chicken cool completely. Chill it overnight in the casserole, covered with foil. In the morning drain off the olive oil and reserve it. Return the chicken, still in the casserole and undisturbed, to the refrigerator until serving time. To serve, unmold the chicken and vegetables, now handsomely jellied in the wine and chicken broth, onto a bed of lettuce leaves in a chilled serving platter. Serve with Oven-Browned Matchstick Potatoes (page 191) and a green salad with French Dressing (page 163) made with the reserved drained olive oil. This Chicken in Wine Aspic is sufficient for 8 servings. *(See photograph, page 119.)*

Chicken Livers with Orange | Foies de Volaille à l'Orange

2 pounds chicken livers
6 Tbl butter
Salt & pepper
2 shallots, finely chopped
¾ cup Chicken Broth (page 53 or canned)
½ cup strained orange juice
¼ cup Madeira wine
⅛ tsp dried chervil
1½ cups peeled orange segments, fresh or drained canned
2 tsp sugar

Cut the chicken livers into halves and sauté them for 5 minutes in 4 tablespoons of the butter heated in a large skillet. Stir the livers occasionally so that they brown evenly and cook through. Season them with salt and pepper to taste and transfer them to a warm serving platter. Keep them warm. Add 1 tablespoon butter to that remaining in the pan and in it cook the shallots until they are soft but not brown. Stir in the

broth, orange juice, Madeira, and chervil, and blend the liquids with the juices in the pan. Cook over moderate heat until the liquid is reduced to about ¾ cup and has thickened slightly.

In another skillet melt the remaining butter. Add the orange segments and stir them into it. Sprinkle them with the sugar and caramelize them lightly under a hot broiler. Strain the reduced sauce over the chicken livers and arrange the orange segments around them. Serve these 6 portions of livers with Braised Rice with Saffron (page 197).

Breast of Duckling with Pepper Sauce |

Suprêmes de Caneton, Sauce Poivrade

3 ducklings, about 5 pounds each
3 onions
3 whole cloves
1 cup fresh grapefruit juice
2 cups Chicken Broth (page 53 or canned)
Salt
Pepper Sauce (page 149)

Preheat oven to 350 degrees. Sponge the ducklings with a damp cloth and dry them well. Place an onion with a clove stuck into it into the cavity of each and truss the ducklings to secure the legs. Place the birds on a rack in a roasting pan and roast them, uncovered, in the preheated oven for 2 hours, basting every 15 minutes during the first 1½ hours with the grapefruit juice and broth, heated together. Salt the breasts lightly and complete the roasting, without further basting. Take pan from oven and remove the breasts from the ducklings, leaving the skin intact. Use the remaining meat for a salad or as desired. Arrange the breasts, skin sides up, on a rack in a shallow baking pan. Set the pan under a hot broiler to give the skin a final crisping. Transfer the breasts to a warm serving platter and pour the pepper sauce around them. This recipe provides 6 servings.

Roast Stuffed Goose | Oie Farcie

1 10-pound goose
1 clove garlic, cut
½ lemon
2 Tbl finely chopped onion
3 Tbl goose fat or butter
1 goose liver, coarsely chopped
1½ cups finely ground lean beef
1½ cups finely ground veal
1 cup finely ground raw ham
2 cups coarsely chopped sour apples
½ cup coarsely chopped cooked chestnuts (see Purée of Chestnuts, page 181)
½ cup coarsely chopped mushrooms
1 Tbl finely chopped parsley
½ tsp dried thyme
Salt & pepper to taste
¼ cup cognac
1 egg, beaten

Preheat oven to 425 degrees. Rub the goose with the garlic and lemon. In a skillet lightly brown the onion in the goose fat or butter. In a mixing bowl thoroughly combine the cooked onion, along with any remaining fat, and the remaining ingredients. Stuff the goose with the mixture. Close the opening with skewers or sew it closed, and truss the bird, securing the legs and wings close to the body. Set it on its side on a rack in a roasting pan and cook it in the preheated oven for about 3 hours (18 minutes per pound), turning it from one side to the other every 30 minutes for the first 2 hours and leaving it upright for the last hour. Baste every 15 minutes with the goose fat. Drain off excessive fat as it accumulates. Remove the trussing and open the cavity before carving the goose at table to provide 6 to 8 servings. Serve with a portion of the stuffing.

Molded Roast Turkey with Morels | Émincé de Dindon aux Morilles

2 ounces dried mushrooms, preferably morels
¾ cup Chicken Broth (page 53 or canned), heated to boiling
⅓ cup scallions, white parts only, chopped
6 Tbl butter
2 cups soft white bread crumbs, toasted
6 cups finely chopped cooked turkey meat
1 Tbl finely chopped parsley
1 tsp finely chopped celery leaves
⅛ tsp nutmeg
Salt & pepper
2 eggs, lightly beaten
18–20 slices cooked turkey, each ⅛-inch thick & 2½-inches square
Sprigs of watercress

This is an excellent way to use leftover turkey. Wash and drain the mushrooms. Put them in a bowl, pour the hot broth over them, and let soak for 30 minutes or until they soften. Drain them, reserving the broth, and chop them finely. In a skillet cook the scallions in 3 tablespoons of the butter until they are soft. Blend in the toasted crumbs. Combine the crumbs and onions in a mixing bowl with the chopped turkey, parsley, celery leaves, nutmeg, and salt and pepper to taste. Blend in 2 tablespoons of the remaining butter, melted, and the beaten eggs. Preheat oven to 350 degrees. Coat an 8-cup heat-proof mold with the remaining butter and line it with the sliced turkey, overlapping the slices somewhat. Pack the lined mold with the chopped turkey mixture and cover it with buttered foil. Bake in the preheated oven 45 minutes or until the filling is firm. Unmold onto a serving platter and garnish with sprigs of watercress. Serve cut in slices. This recipe provides 6 to 8 servings. It may be doubled or tripled for buffet service.

meat

Boiled Beef | Boeuf Bouilli

5 pounds cross rib of beef
2 sprigs parsley
12 large carrots
1 small parsley root, peeled
1 small celery root, peeled & sliced
1 small turnip, quartered
2 medium tomatoes, cored & quartered
2 large leeks, white parts only
1 cup sliced mushrooms
2 quarts Beef Broth (page 52 or canned)
6 peppercorns
Salt
Chive Sauce (page 158)

Trim the piece of cross rib of most of the fat and put the meat in a large saucepan along with the parsley sprigs, vegetables, and mushrooms. Pour in the beef broth augmented by enough cool water to barely cover the meat. Add the peppercorns and 1 teaspoon salt for each quart of liquid. Bring the liquid to boil and skim it. Cook, covered, at simmer for 2½ hours or until the meat is tender. Take out the carrots after the first hour and reserve them to serve with the meat. Cut the meat into generous slices, arrange on a serving platter, and pour a little of the cooking liquid over them. Serve the remaining broth separately or reserve it for other uses. Garnish the platter with the cooked carrots, reheated. Serve with boiled potatoes, and pass the chive sauce. This recipe provides 6 to 8 servings. *(See photograph, page 120.)*

Short Ribs of Beef Braised with Red Burgundy Wine | Plat de Côtes Braisées au Vin Rouge de Bourgogne

6 pounds short ribs of beef, cut into serving pieces
Flour for dredging
⅓ cup bacon fat
Salt & pepper
1 medium onion, finely chopped
1 carrot, finely chopped
1 stalk celery, finely chopped
¼ tsp dried savory
½ cup Beef Broth (page 52 or canned)
1¼ cups red Burgundy

Preheat oven to 300 degrees. Dredge the short ribs in the flour, coating them completely but lightly, and brown them on all sides in the bacon fat heated in a skillet. Season with salt and pepper to taste. Over the bottom of a heavy casserole of sufficient size to accommodate the short ribs in 1 layer, spread the vegetables and sprinkle the savory over them. Arrange the short ribs on top. Heat the broth and wine together in a saucepan and pour the mixture over the meat. Cover the casserole and set it in the preheated oven. Cook the short ribs for 3 hours or until they are tender. This recipe provides 6 generous portions. They may be served with Homemade Noodles with Sautéed Bread Crumbs (page 200).

Fillet of Beef in Pastry | Filet de Boeuf en Croûte

½ pound chicken livers
2 scallions, white parts only, finely chopped
8 Tbl butter
2 Tbl dry vermouth
2 Tbl Mushroom Flavoring (page 162)
2 Tbl soft white bread crumbs
Salt & pepper
2 pounds fillet of beef, trimmed
½ cup coarsely chopped celery
1 small onion, sliced
1 small bay leaf
¼ tsp dried rosemary
Flaky Pastry (page 235)
1 egg, beaten
¼ cup cognac
1½ cups Brown Sauce (page 148)
¼ cup Fresh-Tomato Purée (page 160)
2 Tbl Madeira wine

Preheat oven to 425 degrees. In a skillet over moderate heat, brown the chicken livers and scallions in 2 tablespoons of the butter. Add the vermouth, cover pan, and let the livers simmer for 3 minutes or until they are cooked through. Force the livers, scallions, mushroom flavoring, and any remaining cooking liquid through a fine sieve into a mixing bowl. Blend in the bread crumbs, and season with salt and pepper to taste. Set the mixture aside for the moment.

Season the beef with salt and pepper to taste and coat it completely with 5 tablespoons of the remaining butter. Place the meat in a roasting pan with the celery, onion, and herbs, and roast it in the preheated oven for 20 minutes. Remove pan and let the meat cool completely in it. Turn off oven heat. Take the cooled fillet from the roasting pan. Do not disturb the remaining vegetables and juices; they will be used in preparing a sauce. Cut the fillet into 6 slices of equal size. Save any juice and add it to the roasting pan. Pat the slices dry and coat each with a ⅛-inch-thick layer of the liver paste. Reheat oven to 425 degrees.

Divide the pastry into 6 parts and roll each ⅛-inch thick and of a size to encase a slice of the fillet. Wrap the prepared slices neatly in the pastry, enclosing them completely. Brush the edges with beaten egg and press together to secure them. Cut decorative shapes from the pastry trimmings and secure them with beaten egg to the pastry-enclosed slices. Arrange the slices bottom seams down on a lightly buttered baking sheet. Brush them with beaten egg and bake them in the reheated oven for 20 minutes or until the pastry is golden brown.

Gently reheat the vegetables and drippings remaining in the roasting pan and de-glaze the pan by stirring in the cognac. Blend in the brown sauce and tomato purée. Let the sauce bubble over the heat and stir in the wine and remaining butter. Strain the sauce and serve it at once with the 6 portions of fillet of beef in pastry. Artichoke Hearts with Purée of Fresh Peas (page 173) provide suitable accompaniment to this elegant main course.

Steak, French Style | Le Steak à la Française

6 rib beef steaks, boned, about 6 ounces each
4 Tbl butter
Salt & pepper
3 Tbl cognac
1 cup dry white wine
⅓ cup heavy cream
⅓ cup thinly sliced beef marrow

Sauté the steaks for 1 minute on each side in the butter heated until very hot in a skillet. They will be rare. Transfer them to a warm serving platter and keep them warm. Season with salt and pepper to taste. In a small saucepan gently heat the cognac, set it ablaze, and pour it flaming over the steaks. When the flame expires, drain the liquid into the sauté pan with the remaining drippings. Return pan to moderate heat and stir in the wine, blending it with the cooking glaze at the bottom of the pan. Stir in the cream, and heat without boiling. Poach

the marrow for 2 minutes in a pan of lightly salted simmering water. Drain the slices and add them to the sauce in the skillet. Let them heat through and pour the sauce over the steaks. Serve at once with Oven-Browned Matchstick Potatoes (page 191).

Fillet Steak, Monaco Style | Tournedos Monégasque

1 small eggplant
½ tsp salt
Bland cooking oil
2 Tbl butter
6 slices fillet of beef, each 1 inch thick
Additional salt & pepper
1½ cups Fresh-Tomato Purée (page 160)
1 cup Bordelaise Sauce (page 149)
½ cup pitted black olives, sliced
2 Tbl finely chopped parsley

Cut the eggplant, unpeeled, into 6 slices each ½-inch thick, and sprinkle them with the ½ teaspoon salt. Set the slices on a rack in a baking pan and let them drain for 30 minutes. Dry them well. Pour cooking oil to a depth of ½-inch into a deep skillet and heat it. Add the slices of eggplant and brown them well, 2 or 3 at a time. Drain them on paper toweling and keep them warm. In another skillet heat the butter and in it sauté the slices of beef, cooking them for 1½ minutes on each side for rare meat, 2 to 3 minutes for medium, and 4 minutes or longer for well done. Season the meat with salt and pepper to taste. Arrange the slices on a warm serving platter and place a slice of the eggplant on each. Quickly heat together the tomato purée and Bordelaise sauce in the skillet in which the meat was cooked, and cover the tournedos equally with the mixture. Sprinkle them with the sliced olives and chopped parsley. Serve the 6 portions at once with, if desired, Oven-Browned Potato Balls (page 190).

Beef Tongue Braised with Vegetables |

Langue de Boeuf Braisée aux Légumes

1 4-pound beef tongue
2 sprigs parsley
1 clove garlic
1 onion
1 clove
3 Tbl bacon fat
1 medium onion, finely chopped
1 large carrot, finely chopped
1 stalk celery, finely chopped
2 Tbl flour
4 cups Beef Broth (page 52 or canned)
1 cup white wine
Salt & pepper
¼ tsp dried thyme
1 small bay leaf
18 tiny carrots
18 tiny white onions
12 small turnips
12 small potatoes

Wash the tongue, put it in a large saucepan, and cover it with boiling-hot water. Add the parsley, garlic, and the onion stuck with the clove. Bring the water back to boil over low heat and skim it. Cover pan and cook the tongue at simmer for 3 hours or until it is tender. Drain the tongue and, when it is cool enough to handle, remove the bones, trim out the roots, and peel off the skin.

In a skillet heat the bacon fat and in it lightly brown the chopped onion, carrot, and celery. Blend in the flour and cook, stirring for 2 minutes until the flour is well combined. Add the broth gradually, stirring until the mixture thickens somewhat. It will not be very thick. Strain it into another saucepan, reserving the vegetables. Over the bottom of a heavy casserole large enough to accommodate the tongue, spread the reserved vegetables and place the prepared tongue on them. Stir the white wine into the strained sauce in the saucepan, season with salt and pepper to taste, and add the thyme and bay leaf. Heat the mixture and pour it over the tongue in the casserole. Cover and cook at simmer for 2 hours.

Cook the carrots, onions, turnips, and potatoes together in a saucepan of lightly salted boiling water for 5 minutes. Drain them and add to the casserole during the last 10 to 15 minutes of cooking so that they will be tender when the tongue is done. Transfer the tongue to a cutting board and slice it. Arrange the slices on a warm serving platter, strain the sauce over them, and place the whole vegetables around them. This recipe provides 6 generous servings.

Meatballs in Sour Cream | Boulettes à la Crème

2½ pounds finely ground lean beef
1 small onion, finely chopped
1 Tbl finely chopped fresh dill (or ½ tsp dried dill weed)
Salt & pepper
6 Tbl butter
1 cup Beef Broth (page 52 or canned), heated
½ cup Fresh-Tomato Purée (page 160)
½ cup sour cream

In a mixing bowl combine the beef with the onion and dill, and season it with salt and pepper to taste. Shape the meat into balls about 1½ inches in diameter, and brown them well in the butter heated in a skillet. Blend in the broth and tomato purée, and cook at simmer for 5 minutes. Remove the meat to a serving platter. Reduce the remaining liquid to ¾ cup and blend the sour cream into it, being careful not to let it boil. Correct the seasoning, adding salt and pepper if needed, and pour the sauce over the meatballs. Serve these 6 portions with, if desired, Steamed Potatoes (page 186).

Sautéed Veal in Anchovy Cream |

Sauté de Veau à la Crème d'Anchois

2 pounds boneless leg of veal, thinly sliced
Flour for dredging
3–5 Tbl butter
Anchovy paste
2 Tbl finely chopped carrot
2 Tbl finely chopped celery
2 Tbl finely chopped parsley
2 Tbl finely chopped shallots
¼ tsp ground coriander
White pepper
¼ cup cognac
¼ cup Madeira wine
½ cup Chicken Broth (page 53 or canned)
¾ cup heavy cream
1 tsp paprika
Sprigs of parsley

If the slices of veal are thicker than ⅛-inch, pound them to that thickness between sheets of waxed paper, and cut them into little cutlets about 3 inches in diameter. Dry them thoroughly between sheets of paper toweling and dredge lightly with flour. Brown them lightly in 3 tablespoons of the butter, or more as needed, heated in a skillet. Drain the cutlets and coat each, on 1 side only, with a thin film of anchovy paste. Arrange them, slightly overlapping, in layers in an oven-proof casserole, sprinkling each layer with a little of the carrot, celery, parsley, shallots, and coriander, combined, and with white pepper to taste. Preheat oven to 325 degrees.

Gently heat the cognac, set it ablaze, and pour it over the meat in the casserole. Let the flame burn out. Gently reheat the skillet in which the cutlets were browned and de-glaze it by blending the Madeira and chicken broth into the brown bits at the bottom of the pan. Stir in the cream and heat the mixture without boiling. Pour it over the layered cutlets in the casserole. Cover the casserole, set it in the preheated oven, and let the meat cook for 1 hour or until it is very tender, basting it from time to time with the cooking liquid. The meat is properly cooked when the stack can be pierced easily with the tines of a cooking fork. Carefully strain the cooking liquid into a saucepan, using a plate to hold the veal in place. Transfer the stack intact to a warm serving platter and keep it warm. Reheat the sauce, reducing it, if necessary to thicken it slightly. Stir in the paprika. Pour the sauce over the veal and decorate the platter with sprigs of pars-

A summer luncheon table beckons with cool and tempting Chicken in Wine Aspic (page 107), Oven-Browned Matchstick Potatoes (page 191), and a salad of crisp lettuce.

ley. Cut the meat into slices, straight through the stack, for 6 servings.

Veal Scallops with Fresh Figs | Escalopes de Veau Glacées aux Figues Fraîches

2 pounds leg of veal, thinly sliced
Flour for dredging
5 Tbl butter
¼ cup Chicken Broth (page 53 or canned)
8 fresh figs (see Note)
2 Tbl strained lemon juice

Pound the slices of veal paper thin between sheets of waxed paper, and cut the slices into small scallops. Dredge them lightly and cook them slowly, in 4 tablespoons of the butter heated in a skillet, until they are golden brown and tender. Transfer them to a side platter and keep them warm. Stir the chicken broth into the skillet and blend it into the cooking glaze at the bottom of the pan. Add the figs and let them heat through. Force them, along with the cooking liquid, through a fine sieve, or purée them in an electric blender and strain out the seeds. Add the lemon juice and reheat the purée in the skillet. Add the remaining butter and stir until it is incorporated. Brush the scallops with the purée and glaze them under a hot broiler. This recipe provides 6 servings.

NOTE: Out of season, substitute drained canned figs for the fresh figs.

Stuffed Veal Rolls | Paupiettes de Veau Farcies

2 pounds boned leg of veal, cut into 12 thin slices
1 pound young spinach leaves, washed & drained
2 shallots, chopped
5 Tbl butter
1 Tbl heavy sweet cream
1 Tbl sour cream
¼ cup finely chopped Bayonne-type ham or prosciutto
⅓ cup grated Gruyère cheese
¼ cup fine dry bread crumbs
Salt & pepper
1 cup Chicken Broth (page 53 or canned)
¼ cup Fresh-Tomato Purée (page 160)
1 Tbl Demi-Glaze (page 56 or see Note)

Simple flavors of boiled beef, tender carrots, and young potatoes are refined with the addition of a chive-flavored sauce (page 112).

With a meat pounder or the flat of a cleaver flatten the slices of veal between 2 sheets of waxed paper to a thickness of about 1⁄16-inch, taking care not to break them. Cook the spinach in a saucepan for 3 minutes in just the water that clings to the leaves. Drain the spinach and chop it. In a small skillet cook the shallots in 1 tablespoon of the butter until they are soft. In a mixing bowl thoroughly combine the spinach, shallots, sweet and sour creams, ham or prosciutto, and grated cheese. Sprinkle each of the slices of veal with a teaspoon of the bread crumbs, and spread them equally with the spinach mixture. Roll the slices, tucking in the sides, to enclose the fillings completely. Tie the rolls with thread to secure them.

In a skillet heat the remaining butter and in it brown the veal rolls, as many at a time as the pan can accommodate, well on all sides. Season them with salt and pepper, and transfer them to a casserole. Preheat oven to 350 degrees.

Blend the chicken broth into the drippings remaining in the skillet, and pour the blended liquid over the veal rolls. Cover the casserole and set it in the preheated oven. Cook for 45 minutes or until the rolls are tender. Remove them, cut off the bindings, and arrange the rolls on a warm serving platter. Keep them warm.

Blend the tomato purée into the liquid remaining in the casserole and heat it. Add the demi-glaze and stir until it is incorporated and the sauce thickens. Pour it over the veal rolls and serve them at once with Sautéed Shredded Potatoes (page 191). This recipe provides 6 servings.

NOTE: Commercial preserved *demi-glace de viande* may be substituted for the demi-glaze.

Casserole of Veal and Lemon |

Côtelettes de Veau au Citron en Cocotte

4 Tbl olive oil
2 pounds leg of veal, thinly sliced
3 Tbl strained lemon juice
Salt & pepper

Preheat oven to 300 degrees. Brush a heat-proof earthenware casserole with 1 tablespoon of the olive oil and arrange over it a layer of

⅓ of the sliced veal, cut scallop size. Dribble over that 1 tablespoon each of the oil and lemon juice and season lightly with salt and pepper. Arrange over that series of ingredients 2 more in the same order. Cover the casserole very tightly, set it in the preheated oven, and let the veal cook for 3 hours or until it is very tender. This recipe provides 6 servings to be accompanied, if desired, with Vegetable Stew Provençale (page 196) and Oven-Browned Potato Balls (page 190).

Stuffed Shoulder of Veal in Aspic |

Épaule de Veau Farci en Gelée

1 2½-pound piece shoulder of veal
½ pound calf's liver
½ pound ham
1 cup dry bread crumbs
1 scallion, including green, finely chopped
2 Tbl finely chopped parsley
¼ tsp dried thyme
¼ tsp dried basil
⅓ cup shelled salted pistachio nuts
1 small clove garlic, mashed to a paste
1 small onion, finely chopped
6 Tbl butter
1 egg
1 egg yolk
Salt & pepper
1 quart Chicken Broth (page 53 or canned)
1 cup dry white wine
1 pound veal knucklebone, cut into small pieces
Sprigs of watercress

Cut a deep pocket in the veal shoulder and fill it with a mixture prepared as follows: Put the liver and ham together through the fine blade of a food chopper. Combine the ground meats in a mixing bowl with all of the ingredients through the garlic. In a small skillet lightly brown the onion in 1 tablespoon of the butter, and blend it along with the whole egg and egg yolk into the meat mixture. Season with salt and pepper to taste. Fill the veal with the mixture, and sew up the opening with kitchen twine. Brown the stuffed shoulder in the remaining butter heated in a skillet. Transfer the shoulder to a roasting pan, cover it with the broth and wine, and add the veal knucklebone. Cover pan and cook the veal at simmer for 2 hours, turning it after the first hour.

Transfer the meat to a platter and let it cool. Strain the broth into a bowl and let it cool also. Chill the cooled veal and broth overnight.

Remove the twine with which the veal was sewed and place the meat on a serving platter. Remove the hardened fat from the broth, and spread the broth, now jellied, over the meat. Rechill until the jelly is firm. Decorate the platter with the watercress and serve the stuffed shoulder in slices as needed to provide 8 servings. Oven-Browned Matchstick Potatoes (page 191) may be served with this.

Sweetbreads in Cream | Ris de Veau à la Crème

6 sweetbreads,
about ¾-pound each
Salt
Lemon juice
Additional salt & pepper
6 Tbl butter
⅓ cup finely chopped carrot
⅓ cup finely chopped onion
⅓ cup finely chopped celery
⅓ cup finely chopped ham
4 sprigs parsley
½ bay leaf
¼ tsp thyme
½ cup Chicken Broth
(page 53 or canned)
½ cup dry white wine
½ cup white port wine
2 Tbl flour
1 cup light cream, scalded
½ cup heavy cream
¼ tsp lemon juice
2 Tbl cognac

Soak the sweetbreads for 1 hour in ice-cold water. Drain them, put them in a saucepan with boiling water to cover, and add 1 teaspoon salt and 1 tablespoon lemon juice for each 4 cups of water used. Cook the sweetbreads at simmer for 10 minutes. Drain and dry them, and remove the tubes and membrane. Sprinkle the sweetbreads with salt and pepper to taste. Preheat oven to 325 degrees.

Heat 4 tablespoons of the butter in a casserole and in it brown the vegetables and ham. Add the parsley, bay leaf, and thyme. Add the sweetbreads, cover the casserole, and cook them over moderate heat for 10 minutes, turning them occasionally to brown them evenly. In a saucepan heat together the broth and wines, and pour the mixture over the sweetbreads. Cover the casserole again and transfer it to the preheated oven. Cook the sweetbreads for 20 minutes or until they are tender. Remove them and cut into halves. Arrange them on a warm platter and keep them warm.

In a saucepan heat the remaining butter and blend the flour into it. Cook for 2 minutes, stirring to prevent the roux from browning. Add the hot light cream, and stir vigorously with a whisk to produce a smooth sauce. Reduce the cooking liquid remaining in the casserole over high heat to ½ its volume. Reduce heat to low and stir in the prepared white sauce. Add the heavy cream and let the mixture heat through without boiling. Add the lemon juice.

In a small saucepan gently heat the cognac, set it ablaze, and pour it flaming over the sweetbreads in the platter. Let the flame expire, and strain the cream sauce over the sweetbreads. Serve them at once with Steamed Rice (page 198). This recipe provides 6 servings.

Cream-Puff Veal Sausages | Godiveau

2 cups water
1 tsp salt
3 Tbl butter
¾ cup flour
2 eggs
1 pound lean shin of veal
¾ pound beef kidney suet
⅛ tsp nutmeg
White pepper
Tomato-Mushroom Purée (page 161)

In a saucepan bring the water to a boil with the salt and butter. When the butter melts add the flour all at once, stirring vigorously until the mixture frees the sides of the pan and is formed into a ball. Off the heat thoroughly beat in the eggs, 1 at a time. Preheat oven to 350 degrees.

Put the veal and suet through the fine blade of a food chopper and combine it with the prepared batter. Blend in the nutmeg and the white pepper to taste. Spread the mixture on a platter and chill it in the refrigerator for 3 hours or until it is firm. Shape the chilled mixture into little sausages about 3 inches long and ¾-inch wide, and arrange them, separated somewhat, on a lightly greased baking sheet. Set the sheet in the preheated oven and bake the sausages for 20 minutes or until they are well puffed and nicely browned. Serve them hot, with the tomato-mushroom purée, for 6 portions.

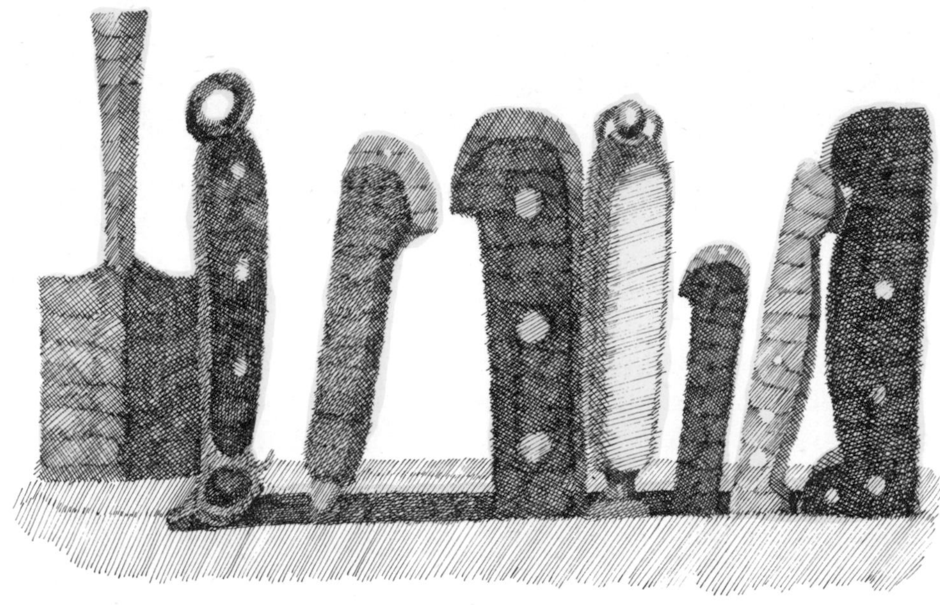

Stuffed Pork Chops Braised Normandy Style | Côtes de Porc Braisées à la Normande

4 Tbl butter
¼ pound lean pork, finely ground
1 stalk celery, finely chopped
1 medium onion, finely chopped
1 cup coarse white bread crumbs, toasted
¼ tsp dried thyme
Salt & pepper
6 loin pork chops, each 1-inch thick
¼ cup Calvados or applejack
1½ cups apple cider, heated
1 Tbl finely chopped parsley

Preheat oven to 325 degrees. In a skillet heat 1 tablespoon of the butter and in it brown the ground pork well. Transfer the meat to a mixing bowl. Heat 1 tablespoon more of the butter with that remaining in the skillet. Add the celery and onion, and cook them over low heat until they are soft. Stir in the bread crumbs, coating them with the fat and blending them with the vegetables. Combine the mixture and the thyme with the ground pork. Season with salt and pepper to taste.

Cut a deep pocket into each of the chops and fill them equally with the prepared mixture. Do not stuff them too firmly. Sew the openings closed or secure them with toothpicks. Sprinkle the chops lightly with salt and pepper. Wipe out the skillet and in it heat the remaining butter. Add the chops, as many at a time as the pan can accommodate, and brown them well on both sides. Transfer them to a large heat-proof casserole, overlapping them to fit in a single layer. In a small saucepan gently heat the Calvados or applejack, set it ablaze, and pour it over the chops. Let the flame burn out. Add the hot apple cider, and bring the liquid back to boil. Cover the casserole and set it in the preheated oven for 1 hour or until the chops are tender. Remove them to a warm serving platter and keep them warm. Skim the fat from the remaining cooking liquid and reduce the liquid, if necessary, until it thickens. Pour it over the chops. Sprinkle them with the chopped parsley and serve at once. This recipe provides 6 servings. Purée of Green Beans (page 175) provides fine accompaniment.

Pork Cutlets in Juniper Aspic |

Escalopes de Porc en Gelée de Genièvre

4 pounds loin of pork
1 pound veal knucklebone, cracked
3 cups Clarified Chicken Broth (page 54 or canned)
3 cups dry white wine
1 small clove garlic, sliced
8 juniper berries, crushed
3 white peppercorns
Salt
Sprigs of parsley

Have the butcher bone the meat in 1 piece, but cut the bones apart.

Preheat oven to 400 degrees. Trim the meat of all but ¼-inch layer of the fat. Discard the trimmings or render the fat and store it in the refrigerator for other uses. Soak the veal knucklebone in boiling-hot water for 5 minutes and drain it. Spread the pork bones in a baking pan and brown them in the preheated oven, turning them from time to time to prevent their burning. Remove pan from oven and drain off all the fat. Reduce oven temperature to 325 degrees.

Place the loin in a deep casserole and arrange all of the bones around it. Add the remaining ingredients, except the salt and parsley, covering about ⅔ of the meat. Bring the liquid in the casserole to a boil on top of the stove and skim it. Cover the casserole, transfer it to the oven, and cook at the reduced heat for 1 hour. Add salt to taste and continue cooking for 1½ hours or until the meat is tender. Let it cool in the broth. Remove and chill it. Skim the broth of as much fat as possible. Strain the broth into a bowl and chill it also for several hours until any remaining fat solidifies. Remove that fat, leaving the clear amber jelly beneath it.

Cut the meat into slices slightly less than ¼-inch and arrange them, slightly overlapping, in a serving platter. Heat the jelly in a saucepan over very low heat until it melts and pour it over the meat. Chill the meat again until the jelly sets. Garnish the jellied pork with sprigs of parsley and serve it with Oven-Browned Matchstick Potatoes (page 191). This quantity of jellied pork is sufficient for 6 servings.

The meat may be glazed in 1 piece, if desired. Baste it with a little of the melted jelly and chill it until it sets. Continue so, with several layers, until the meat is completely coated. Surround the meat in the platter with little molds of the remaining jelly.

Roast Loin of Pork with Onions | Carré de Porc Rôti aux Oignons

3 pounds boned loin of pork
Fat trimmings from loin
1 Tbl Dijon-type mustard
6 medium onions, peeled & halved
Salt & pepper

Preheat oven to 325 degrees. The meat should be boned in 1 piece and trimmed of all but a thin layer of the fat. Place the trimmings in a skillet and heat them slowly until they have rendered about 3 tablespoons of liquid fat. Remove and discard the remaining solids. Increase the heat to moderate, add the meat, and brown it well on all sides. Brush the meat with the mustard and transfer it to an oven-proof casserole with the onions around it. Dribble about a tablespoon of the cooking fat over the onions, and season them and the meat with salt and pepper to taste. Cook in the preheated oven, partially covered (see Note) for 1½ hours and uncovered for 1 hour longer, or until a

BOUCHERIE CHARCUTERIE

meat thermometer inserted in the roast registers 185 degrees.

Serve these 6 portions of the pork in moderately thick slices with the onions and, if desired, Turnip Soufflé (page 195).

NOTE: If the casserole cover will not stay in a position partially covering the meat, use foil instead. Shape it over, but not touching, the meat and secure it to the rim of the casserole. Poke 5 or 6 holes in the foil.

Piquant Meat Cakes | Fricadelles Piquantes

2 shallots, finely chopped
4 Tbl butter
2 cups soft bread crumbs
¾ cup dry white wine
¼ cup milk
3 pounds lean pork, finely ground
2 eggs, lightly beaten
⅓ cup finely grated raw potato
Salt & white pepper
⅛ tsp nutmeg
Flour for dredging
1½ cups Beef Broth (page 52 or canned)
¼ cup Fresh-Tomato Purée (page 160)
½ cup tiny pickled onions, drained
¼ tsp sugar
⅛ tsp dried oregano
⅛ tsp paprika
Additional salt & pepper

In a skillet over moderate heat, cook the shallots in 1 tablespoon of the butter until they are soft but not brown. In a mixing bowl moisten the bread crumbs with ¼ cup of the wine and the milk. Add the shallots, pork, eggs, grated potato, and salt and white pepper. Blend in the nutmeg. Beat the mixture well with a wooden spoon. Form the mixture into medium-size balls and dredge them with the flour. Brown them well in the remaining butter heated in a skillet. Transfer them to a heavy heat-proof casserole and keep them warm over low heat. Pour off any fat remaining in the skillet and de-glaze the pan by stirring into it the beef broth, tomato purée, and remaining wine. Add the pickled onions, sugar, oregano, paprika, and salt and pepper to taste. Pour the mixture over the fricadelles in the casserole. Cook, covered, at simmer for 30 minutes. Serve the fricadelles in their sauce with, if desired, Whipped Potatoes (page 186). This recipe provides 6 generous servings.

Baked Fresh Ham in Chartreuse | Jambon Frais Rôti au Chartreuse

1 4–6-pound fresh ham (leg of pork), whole or half
½ tsp dried chervil
Salt & pepper
12–18 small potatoes, peeled
4 Tbl green Chartreuse

Preheat oven to 350 degrees. Remove the skin of the fresh ham. If you like, roast it separately until it is crisp to provide cocktail snacks. Trim the ham of excess fat, leaving a layer about ¼-inch thick. Score the top in a diamond pattern, rub it with the chervil, and sprinkle it with salt and pepper to taste. Cook the ham, uncovered, in a baking pan in the preheated oven 30 minutes per pound for a whole ham, 40 minutes per pound for a half ham, or until a meat thermometer inserted in the thickest part of the meat registers 185 degrees. Add the potatoes during the last 45 minutes of cooking. When they are tender and nicely browned, remove them to a saucepan on top of the stove along with some of the drippings from the roasting pan. Keep the potatoes warm over low heat. Sprinkle the ham with 2 tablespoons of the Chartreuse and continue cooking for 5 minutes. Sprinkle with the remaining liqueur and cook for a final 5 minutes. Remove the ham to a warm serving platter and let it rest for 10 minutes before carving it as needed to provide 6 to 8 servings. Drain the potatoes and serve them with the ham along with Braised Lettuce (page 184).

Glazed Ham in Cream | Jambon Gratiné à la Crème

1 10-pound tenderized smoked ham
3 carrots, thinly sliced
2 medium onions, thinly sliced
2 stalks celery, thinly sliced
3 large tomatoes, peeled, seeded & chopped
Bouquet Garni (see Glossary)
6 peppercorns
1 cup Chicken Broth (page 53 or canned)
2 cups dry white wine
1¼ cups port wine
1 cup heavy cream
¼ cup sour cream
2 Tbl butter
¼ cup grated Parmesan cheese

Soak the ham in cool water for 1 hour. Drain it, put it in a kettle large enough to accommodate it, and cover it with fresh water. Bring the water to a boil and cook the ham, covered, for 45 minutes. Drain it again and dry it. Preheat oven to 325 degrees.

Trim the ham of all but ¼-inch layer of fat. In a roasting pan heat enough of the trimmings to provide about 3 tablespoons of rendered fat, and in it lightly brown the carrots, onions, and celery. Add the tomatoes, bouquet garni, peppercorns, and broth, and cook the mixture at simmer for 10 minutes. Place the ham on top of the vegetables, and pour the white wine and 1 cup of the port over it. Set pan in the preheated oven and cook it for 2 hours or until it is tender, basting every 15 minutes. Remove the ham to a warm platter and keep it warm. Strain the cooking liquid into a saucepan through several thicknesses of cheesecloth (to remove all the fat) and reduce the liquid over high heat to 1¼ cups. Whip the heavy cream just until it thickens, and blend the sour cream into it. Blend the cream mixture into the liquid in the saucepan along with the butter and remaining port. Cook the sauce, without boiling, stirring until it thickens.

Cut the ham into fairly thick slices. Arrange the slices on a broiler-proof platter and pour the sauce over them. Sprinkle with the grated cheese and brown lightly under a hot broiler. This recipe provides 12 to 14 servings.

Sausage Meat | Chair à Saucisses

2 pounds lean pork
½ pound fresh pork fat
1 large onion, very finely chopped
2 cloves garlic, mashed to a paste
¼ cup cognac
1 Tbl white wine vinegar
¼ tsp powdered sage
2 tsp salt
⅛ tsp white pepper

Coarsely grind the pork and pork fat into a mixing bowl and blend in the remaining ingredients. Cover the bowl and let the mixture season in the refrigerator for several hours or overnight before using it to prepare link sausages or, as is, shaped into small patties and sautéed. This is rather mild sausage meat. If a spicier mixture is preferred, add ⅛ teaspoon white pepper, or more, and a dash or two of Tabasco.

Link Sausages | Saucissons

2 lengths sausage casings, each about 48 inches (see Note)
Sausage Meat (above)

Sausage casings are usually preserved in salt and must be soaked in warm water for 3 to 4 hours and thoroughly rinsed in cool water. To rinse the insides fit 1 end of a casing over a cold-water faucet and let the water run gently through. If the casings are not to be filled immediately, put them in a bowl and cover them with cool water.

To fill for link sausages, drain the rinsed casings and dry them lightly but well between sheets of paper toweling. Tie 1 end of each casing with kitchen twine and force out all the air through the open end. If you have a stuffing attachment for your electric mixer, follow the directions for its use. Lacking such equipment, fill the casings by piping the sausage meat into them with a pastry bag fitted with a very large plain tube or by forcing the meat into the casings through a funnel. Do not pack the meat in too tightly; space must be allowed for separations. Tie the filled casings securely, or twist them tightly, every 3 or 4 inches to provide about 24 sausages. Let the sausages season under refrigeration for 24 hours before using them. They will keep in the refrigerator for 2 to 3 weeks. They may be frozen for considerably longer storage.

NOTE: Sausage casings are available generally in shops specializing in French, Italian, or Spanish-style meat products.

Pork Sausage with Sauerkraut and Apricots | Saucisses aux Choucroute et Abricots

½ pound large dried apricots
2 cups (approximate) medium-dry white wine
1 Tbl butter
1 small onion, finely chopped
1 pound sauerkraut
⅛ tsp white pepper
1 medium potato, peeled & finely grated
Sausage Meat (page 132)

Wash the apricots, put them in an enamel-coated or stainless steel saucepan, and cover them with boiling-hot water. Let them soak for

2 hours. Drain the apricots and pour the wine over them. Cook, covered, over moderate heat for 15 minutes or until they are tender but still firm. Drain the apricots, reserving the wine, and set them aside for the moment.

Heat the butter in a small skillet, and in it cook the onion until it is soft but not brown. Combine the onion, any remaining butter, and the sauerkraut in a heat-proof casserole, and pour in the drained wine. Season with the white pepper. Cover the casserole and cook the sauerkraut at simmer for 1 hour or until the shreds are very tender. Add more wine, if needed, to complete the cooking. When completely cooked, the sauerkraut should still be quite moist. Stir into it the grated raw potato and continue cooking, stirring until it has been completely incorporated and the sauerkraut has thickened. Combine the apricots with the sauerkraut, and remove pan from heat. Preheat oven to 350 degrees.

Shape the sausage meat into patties about ½-inch thick and 2½ inches in diameter. Cook them in a skillet over moderate heat for 10 minutes, turning them once midway during the cooking. No fat will be needed. The sausage meat will provide its own. Drain it off as it is rendered. Drain the cooked patties on paper toweling and arrange them, slightly overlapping, if necessary, over the sauerkraut and apricots. Cover the casserole, transfer it to the preheated oven, and cook 20 minutes. Remove the cover and continue cooking 15 minutes longer. Serve the 6 generous portions which this recipe provides with, if desired, Steamed Potatoes (page 186).

Roast Leg of Baby Lamb | Gigot d'Agneau Rôti

3 2-pound legs of baby lamb **Salt & pepper**

Preheat oven to 400 degrees. Sponge the legs with a damp cloth and dry them thoroughly. Season them with salt and pepper to taste. Put them in a roasting pan, but do not crowd them. Use 2 pans if necessary. Brown the legs for about 3 minutes under a very hot broiler and transfer them immediately to the preheated oven. Let them roast uncovered for 20 minutes for rare meat, 30 to 35 minutes for medium done (pink), and 40 minutes for well done. Serve the lamb with Buttered Flageolet Beans (page 175), the traditional accompaniment for lamb.

Roast Parsleyed Rack of Lamb | Carré d'Agneau Persillé

2 racks of spring lamb, about 3 pounds each
Salt & pepper
½ cup melted butter
2 Tbl finely chopped parsley
2 cloves garlic, very finely chopped
2 cups day-old white bread crumbs

Preheat oven to 325 degrees. Season the lamb with salt and pepper to taste and sear the racks, fat sides up, under a hot broiler for 5 minutes. Transfer the racks to a roasting pan and cook them in the preheated oven for 35 minutes.

In a mixing bowl with a wooden spoon work to a paste the butter, parsley, garlic, and bread crumbs. Season to taste with salt and pepper. Take the racks of lamb from the oven at the end of the indicated time and coat them thickly with the crumb mixture. Return them to the oven and continue cooking for 15 minutes longer or until the crumb coating is browned. Let them rest for 10 minutes before carving in portions 2 chops thick for each of the 6 servings. Suggested accompaniment: Carrots Vichy (page 178).

Roast Rack of Lamb, Provençale | Carré d'Agneau Provençale

A rack of lamb, about 3 pounds
2 small cloves garlic
1 2-ounce can anchovy fillets, drained
Pepper
½ tsp dried rosemary
Hollandaise Sauce (page 150)
1 Tbl Dijon-type mustard

Preheat oven to 325 degrees. Using a very narrow, sharply pointed knife or a metal skewer, pierce the rack in 3 or 4 places between each bone, puncturing the meat through the skin and making the slits deep and equidistant. Cut 1 clove of the garlic into thin slivers. Reserve 6 of the anchovy fillets and cut the rest into ¾-inch lengths. Into each slit in the meat insert a sliver of garlic and a length of anchovy. Season the rack with pepper to taste (the anchovies will provide enough salt), and rub it well with the rosemary. Place the lamb on a rack in a pan and roast it in the preheated oven 40 minutes for rare meat, 50 minutes for medium (pink), and 60 minutes for well done, with meat thermometer readings respectively of 145, 160, and 175 degrees.

Prepare the Hollandaise sauce as directed in the recipe. In a mortar with a pestle or in a bowl with a wooden spoon, work the reserved anchovies and the remaining clove of garlic to a smooth paste. Blend the paste into the sauce along with the mustard. Cut the rack of lamb to provide 6 servings. Pass the sauce separately.

Spring Lamb Stew | Navarin

3 pounds boned shoulder of spring lamb
6 Tbl butter
2 Tbl flour
Salt & pepper
2 cups Chicken Broth (page 53) or water, heated to boiling
4 large tomatoes, peeled, seeded & chopped
1 medium onion
1 whole clove
1 clove garlic, crushed
Bouquet Garni (see Glossary)
18 new potatoes, peeled
18 small white onions
18 tiny carrots
6 small turnips, quartered
½ pound green beans, trimmed
1 pound new peas, shelled

Cut the meat into large cubes and brown them well in 3 tablespoons of the butter heated in a skillet. Transfer the meat as it browns to a heavy heat-proof casserole, and sprinkle it with the flour and salt and pepper to taste. Cook over moderate heat, stirring until the flour is well browned. Drain off the fat remaining in the skillet, and stir the hot broth or water into the glaze at the bottom of the pan. Pour the liquid over the meat in the casserole, and add the tomatoes, the onion stuck with the clove, garlic, and bouquet garni. Cover the casserole and cook the meat at simmer for 1½ hours. Remove the cubes of meat to a side platter and keep them warm. Strain the cooking liquid, discarding the residue. Return the meat to the casserole and the heat, and pour the strained sauce over it. Add all of the vegetables except the beans and peas, and continue cooking for 20 minutes. Add the beans and peas, after blanching them for 2 minutes in lightly salted boiling water. Cook the stew for 10 minutes longer or until the last additions are tender. Serve the navarin steaming hot with crusty French Bread. This recipe provides 6 servings.

Skewered Lamb Kidneys | Rognons de Mouton en Brochette

42 small white onions
½ cup olive oil
¼ cup red wine vinegar
12 lamb kidneys
Salt & pepper

Cook the onions in a saucepan in lightly salted simmering water for 5 minutes. Drain the onions, put them in a bowl, and cover them with the oil and vinegar combined. Let the onions marinate under refrigeration overnight. Drain them well, but do not dry them. Remove the membranes from the kidneys and trim off the hard fat. Cut the kidneys each into quarters and thread them 8 quarters to a skewer with an onion between each. Arrange the 6 skewers on a rack in a broiler pan and set them under a very hot broiler. Cook them so for 10 minutes, turning them frequently. Do not overcook the kidneys or they will toughen. Serve them immediately, 1 skewer to a portion. Serve with Braised Rice (page 197).

game

Jugged Hare | Civet de Lièvre

2 3-pound dressed hares
¼ cup red wine vinegar
Marinade for Game (page 169)
6–8 Tbl bland cooking oil
Salt & pepper
⅓ cup Madeira wine
1 cup heavy cream
1 Tbl finely chopped parsley

Cut the hares into serving pieces and put them in a large mixing bowl. Stir the vinegar into the marinade and pour the mixture over the pieces of hare. Cover the bowl and let the hares season so under refrigeration for 24 hours. In a skillet heat some of the cooking oil and in it, over moderately high heat, cook the pieces of hare, as many at a time as the pan can accommodate, until they are well browned on all sides. Add oil as needed to complete the cooking. Transfer the pieces to a warm serving platter as they are cooked and keep them warm. Season them with salt and pepper to taste. Drain off any oil remaining in the skillet and pour in the wine. Blend it with the cooking glaze at the bottom of the pan and reduce the liquid over high heat to about 2 tablespoons. Reduce the heat and stir in the cream and parsley. Let the sauce heat through.

This recipe provides 6 portions of jugged hare. Serve them with, if desired, Purée of Chestnuts (page 181) combined with ⅓ cup Fresh-Tomato Purée (page 160). Pass the sauce separately.

Partridge with Artichokes | Perdrix aux Artichauts

½ pound button mushrooms
6 small partridges
Salt & pepper
6 Tbl butter
¼ tsp dried rosemary
¼ tsp dried basil
1 cup dry sherry
½ cup Chicken Broth (page 53 or canned)
25 small cooked Artichoke Hearts (page 173 or see Note)
2 tsp cornstarch

Trim the mushrooms flush with the caps and chop the stems. Lightly

season the partridges inside and out with salt and pepper. Heat 4 tablespoons of the butter in a skillet and in it cook the partridges over moderate heat for 8 to 10 minutes, turning the birds to brown them well on all sides. Transfer them to a warm heat-proof casserole and keep them warm. Add the remaining butter to the skillet, heat it, and in it lightly brown the mushrooms. Transfer them to the casserole. To the drippings in the skillet add the herbs and pour in the sherry and

broth. Heat through, stirring to blend in the glaze at the bottom of the pan, and pour the heated mixture over the partridges and mushrooms in the casserole. Cover the casserole and cook at simmer for 15 minutes. Add the artichokes and continue cooking for 20 minutes longer or until the birds are tender. Remove the partridges to a warm serving platter and keep them warm. Drain the mushrooms and artichokes, reserving the cooking liquid, and arrange them around the partridges. Reheat the liquid in the casserole and thicken it slightly with the cornstarch dissolved in a little cool water. Pour the sauce over the partridges and serve at once, each bird to provide a serving.
NOTE: Frozen artichoke hearts cooked according to package directions may be substituted.

Pheasant Molded with Vegetables | Faisan en Chartreuse

3 young pheasants
6 Tbl butter
1 head green cabbage
1 large onion, thinly sliced
3 carrots, cut in thick julienne
1 pound moderately lean bacon, in slices about 1/8-inch thick
2 large tomatoes, peeled & thickly sliced
1 Tbl finely chopped parsley
Salt & pepper
4 cups Chicken Broth (page 53 or canned)
1/2 cup cooked peas

The Chartreuse which designates this preparation refers to a method of cooking said to have been created at the Carthusian monastery in the Chartreuse Massif region of France. Since the fathers there ate no meat, the method was for the preparation of vegetables only. The pheasants and bacon were presumably added by the local laity.

Preheat over to 375 degrees. Coat the pheasants each with 1 tablespoon of the butter and truss them. Roast them on a rack in a pan in the preheated oven for 15 minutes on each side and 15 minutes upright. Remove the birds and cut them into serving pieces. Reserve the juices from the cutting and those in the roasting pan. Reduce oven heat to 325 degrees.

Core the cabbage and blanch it in boiling-hot water for 10 minutes. Drain, separate the leaves, and freshen them in cold water. In a casserole lightly brown the onion and carrots in 2 tablespoons of the remaining butter. Cover them with layers of, in order, ½ the cabbage leaves, the bacon, the remaining cabbage leaves, and the sliced tomatoes. Sprinkle with the parsley and season to taste with salt and pepper. Pour over all the chicken broth and the reserved pheasant juice. Cover the casserole, set it in the oven (now at 325 degrees), and cook for 2 hours. Drain the juice from the casserole and reserve it, cooled and under refrigeration, for other uses.

Grease a rounded mold with the remaining butter and arrange the carrots and peas decoratively over the bottom. Press the slices of bacon over them. Press over them, in order, layers of ½ the cabbage, the pieces of pheasant, the tomatoes and onions, and the remaining cabbage. Fit a plate just inside the casserole over the filling and press out as much of the juice as possible. Set the mold in the still heated oven and leave it for 15 minutes. Unmold carefully onto a warm serving platter and serve at once. This recipe provides 6 generous servings.

NOTE: This chartreuse may also be prepared with partridges.

Sautéed Sliced Loin of Venison | Grenadin de Chevreuil Sauté

2 pounds loin of venison, free of bone
Marinade for Game (page 169)
⅓ cup bland cooking oil
Salt & pepper
Pepper Sauce (page 149)

Cut the venison into slices about 1 inch thick and arrange them in a shallow baking dish in a single layer. Pour the marinade for game over them. Cover the dish and let the meat marinate so in the refrigerator for 2 days, turning the slices several times so that they become uniformly seasoned. Drain the slices and dry them well.

In a skillet heat the bland cooking oil and in it cook the slices of venison over moderately high heat for 5 minutes, turning them once at the midway point. Season these 6 portions with salt and pepper to taste and serve them with Turnip Soufflé (page 195). Heat the pepper sauce and pass it separately.

4 | sauces and butters

Down through the years, plain old American gravy has been good enough for generations of Americans. Of course, there was never anything wrong with it, nor is there now. But two hundred or more French sauces can't be wrong either, and their influence has finally made itself felt in American kitchens. Perhaps the first one to breach our complacence was that wonder of all wondrous French sauces—Hollandaise.

Hollandaise is considered to be one of the trickiest preparations in the entire French sauce repertoire. It is regarded with awe by tyro cooks and is sometimes approached with apprehension even by experienced chefs. I can understand that. I've had several failures with Hollandaise myself. This book offers two methods—the classic one, made over hot water, and a modern, blender-made version—from which to choose; your opportunities to use the elegant Hollandaise should thereby be increased.

It remains to mention the key ingredient to all these sauces: patience. A sauce develops as it cooks; to try to hurry the process is futile and only risks the waste of good ingredients.

sauces

sauces 144 White Sauce | Sauce Béchamel

2 Tbl butter
2 Tbl flour
1½ cups milk, scalded
Salt

In a saucepan gently heat the butter. Blend in the flour and cook over low heat for 2 minutes, stirring constantly to prevent browning. Add the hot milk, stirring it in gradually to produce a smooth sauce. Season with salt to taste. This recipe provides about 1½ cups of sauce to be used as a basis for other sauces, for creamed preparations, or as required.

Cream Sauce | Sauce Crème

2 Tbl butter
2 Tbl flour
1 cup milk, scalded
⅓ cup heavy cream
1 egg yolk (optional)
Salt

In a saucepan gently heat the butter. Blend in the flour and cook over low heat for 2 minutes, stirring constantly to prevent browning. Add the hot milk, stirring it in gradually to produce a smooth sauce. Blend in the cream or, if desired, combine the cream and egg yolk, add enough of the prepared sauce to warm the mixture through, and stir it into the remaining sauce. Season with salt to taste, and heat through without boiling. This recipe provides about 1⅓ cups of sauce to be used for creamed preparations or as required.

Cream Sauce with Cheese | Sauce Mornay

2 Tbl butter
2 Tbl flour
1 cup milk, scalded
⅓ cup heavy cream
2 Tbl grated Gruyère cheese
2 Tbl grated Parmesan cheese
Salt & white pepper

In a saucepan gently heat the butter. Blend in the flour and cook over low heat for 2 minutes, stirring constantly to prevent browning. Add the hot milk, stirring it in gradually to produce a smooth sauce. Blend in the cream and the cheeses and heat without boiling until the cheeses are incorporated. Season to taste with salt and white pepper. Use the 1½ cups of sauce provided by this recipe to coat fish, eggs, or vegetables to be glazed under a broiler, or for other preparations as required.

Tomato Cream Sauce | Sauce Aurore

2 medium tomatoes, peeled, seeded & finely chopped
2 Tbl butter
2 Tbl flour
1½ cups milk, scalded
2 Tbl heavy cream
¼ tsp paprika
Salt & white pepper

Cook the tomatoes in a saucepan, covered, over low heat until they are reduced to a thick paste. Force the paste through a fine sieve and set the purée aside for the moment.

In another saucepan gently heat the butter. Blend in the flour and cook over low heat for 2 minutes, stirring constantly to prevent browning. Add the hot milk, stirring it in gradually to produce a smooth sauce. Blend in the cream and the prepared purée. Add the paprika and salt and white pepper to taste. Heat the sauce through without boiling. This recipe provides about 2 cups of sauce, sufficient for 8 to 10 servings with poached eggs, fish, or chicken, or as a coating for sweetbreads to be glazed under a broiler.

Chicken or Fish Velouté Sauce | Sauce Velouté

2 Tbl butter
2 Tbl flour
3 cups Chicken Broth (page 53 or canned), or Fish Broth (page 54), or bottled clam juice
Salt & white pepper

This sauce is prepared with chicken broth or fish broth, depending upon its use. Recipes requiring velouté sauce in this cookbook specify which is to be used.

Gently heat the butter in the top pan of a double-boiler. Blend in the flour and cook over low heat, stirring to prevent the roux from taking on too much color. It should remain quite pale. Add the required broth or clam juice gradually, stirring to dissolve the roux completely. Bring the liquid slowly to a boil, stirring constantly until the sauce thickens and is velvety smooth. Season it with salt and white pepper to taste. Set pan over bottom part of the double-boiler containing barely simmering water, and cook the sauce, covered, for 45 minutes, stirring it occasionally until it is reduced to 2 cups. Serve the sauce with poached chicken, fish, eggs, or vegetables, or as required.

Velouté Cream Sauce | Sauce Suprême

1 cup Velouté Sauce (above)
⅓ cup heavy cream
½ tsp lemon juice

Following directions in the recipe, prepare the 1 cup of velouté sauce, chicken or fish, as required. Stir into it the cream, a little at a time, and the lemon juice. Reheat the sauce briefly in the top pan of a double-boiler over simmering water. Use the sauce as Cream Sauce (page 144) is used, with chicken, fish, eggs, vegetables, or as required. This recipe provides 1⅓ cups.

White Wine Sauce | Sauce au Vin Blanc

1½ cups dry white wine
2 medium mushrooms, finely chopped
1 cup Chicken or Fish Velouté Sauce (page 145)
½ cup heavy cream
¼ tsp lemon juice
Salt & white pepper

In a saucepan cook the wine and mushrooms, covered, at simmer until the liquid is reduced to ½ cup. Strain the wine, discarding the mushrooms, and return it to the saucepan. Blend into it the velouté sauce and cook the mixture at simmer for 2 minutes to blend the flavors. Add the cream and lemon juice, and season with salt and white pepper to taste. Reheat the sauce, without boiling, and serve it

with poached or sautéed fish or chicken. This recipe provides 2 cups of white wine sauce.

Wine Sauce for Fish | Sauce Bercy

1 cup Fish Broth (page 54) or bottled clam juice
1 cup dry white wine
3 Tbl butter
1 small shallot, finely chopped
2 Tbl flour
⅓ cup heavy cream
½ tsp lemon juice
Salt & white pepper
1 tsp finely chopped parsley

In a saucepan combine the fish broth or clam juice and the wine, and reduce the mixture over high heat to 1 cup. In another saucepan gently heat 2 tablespoons of the butter and in it cook the shallot until it is soft but not brown. Blend in the flour and cook for 2 minutes, stirring to prevent the flour and shallot from taking on color. Add the broth-wine reduction, stirring it in gradually to produce a smooth sauce. Stir in the cream and lemon juice, and season with salt and white pepper to taste. Let the sauce heat without further boiling. Blend in the remaining butter and the parsley. This recipe provides 1⅓ cups of wine sauce for fish or for use as required in specific recipes.

Brown Sauce | Sauce Brune

¼ pound lean ham, coarsely ground
1 large carrot, coarsely chopped
1 stalk celery, coarsely chopped
1 medium onion, coarsely chopped
3 Tbl butter
2 Tbl flour
5 cups Beef Broth (page 52 or canned)
¼ cup tomato juice
Bouquet Garni (see Glossary)
4 peppercorns
½ cup red wine
1 Tbl red wine vinegar

Lightly brown the ham and vegetables in the butter heated in a saucepan. Blend in the flour and let it, along with the meat and vegetables, brown well. Combine the broth and tomato juice, and add the liquid gradually, stirring constantly to dissolve the flour. Add the bouquet garni and the peppercorns. Cook, partially covered, at simmer for 1 hour. Add the wine and vinegar, and continue cooking for 1 hour longer. Strain the sauce and use it as required. Cooled and refrigerated the sauce may be kept for about 1 week. Reheated to boil, it will keep for 1 week longer. For longer storage, the sauce should be frozen. This recipe provides about 2 cups of the sauce.

Madeira Sauce | Sauce Madère

2 cups Brown Sauce (above)
⅓ cup Madeira wine

In a saucepan reduce the brown sauce over moderate heat to 1½ cups. Stir in the wine and cook just long enough to reheat the sauce. Serve with roasts of beef, veal, pork (particularly ham), and poultry. This recipe provides about 2 cups of the sauce.

Marrow Sauce | Sauce Bordelaise

1½ cups red wine
1½ cups Brown Sauce (page 148)
1 4-inch length beef marrowbone (with marrow)
1 tsp finely chopped parsley
Salt & pepper
1 Tbl butter

In a saucepan over high heat reduce the wine to ½ cup. In another saucepan over moderate heat reduce the brown sauce to 1 cup. Stir the reduced wine into the reduced sauce and keep the mixture warm. With a sharp slender knife remove the marrow from the bone and cut it into small dice. Put the dice in a saucepan, cover with boiling water, and poach at simmer for 3 minutes. Drain the marrow and stir it into the combined wine and sauce. Add the parsley and season with salt and pepper to taste. Reheat the sauce briefly and stir in the butter. This recipe provides about 1¾ cups of marrow sauce to serve with grilled or sautéed steak or kidneys or use as required in specific recipes.

Pepper Sauce | Sauce Poivrade

3 Tbl butter
1 large carrot, finely chopped
1 medium onion, finely chopped
¼ cup finely chopped boiled ham
2 Tbl flour
4 cups Beef Broth (page 52 or canned)
1 medium tomato, peeled, seeded & finely chopped
2 sprigs parsley
1 small bay leaf
¼ tsp dried thyme
½ cup red wine
½ cup red wine vinegar
¼ cup Marinade for Game, if any (see Note)
Salt
6 peppercorns, crushed
Ground pepper

In a large saucepan gently heat 2 tablespoons of the butter and in it lightly brown the carrot, onion, and ham. Blend in the flour and let it brown well with the vegetables and ham. Add the broth, stirring it in gradually to dissolve the flour completely. Continue stirring until the broth thickens. Add the tomato, parsley, bay leaf, and thyme, and cook, covered, at simmer for 30 minutes. In another saucepan combine the wine, vinegar, and marinade, if used, and reduce the mixture over high heat to ⅓ cup. Stir the reduction into the simmering liquid. Season with salt to taste and continue cooking, with the pan again covered, for 1 hour. Remove pan from the heat, add the peppercorns, and let them steep for 10 minutes. Strain the sauce (there will be about 2 cups) and stir in the remaining butter. Add enough freshly ground pepper, if needed, to produce a lustily spicy dressing for game or dark meat poultry.

NOTE: Use the marinade only if the meat with which the pepper sauce is to be served has been steeped in it.

Red Wine Sauce | Sauce au Vin Rouge

1 small onion, finely chopped
2 medium mushrooms, finely chopped
2 Tbl butter
1½ cups Beef Broth (page 52 or canned)
1½ cups red wine
2 Tbl red wine vinegar
1½ cups Brown Sauce (page 148)

Lightly brown the onion and mushrooms in the butter heated in a saucepan. Add the broth, wine, and vinegar, and cook, covered, at simmer until the liquid is reduced to 1½ cups. Stir in the brown sauce, and continue cooking, with the pan again covered, until the mixture is reduced to 2 cups. Strain the sauce, discarding the onion and mushrooms, and serve it with roast or grilled beef, poultry, or game, or use as required.

Hollandaise Sauce | Sauce Hollandaise

1 cup unsalted butter (2 sticks)
3 egg yolks
1 Tbl lemon juice
¼ tsp salt

Divide the butter into 8 equal parts and let them soften somewhat at room temperature. In the top pan of a double-boiler thoroughly combine the egg yolks, lemon juice, and salt. Add 1 part of the butter, set pan over the bottom part of the double-boiler containing barely simmering water, and stir constantly until the butter is almost completely incorporated with the yolks. Add a second part of the butter and stir until it, too, is almost all incorporated. Continue so with each of the remaining parts of butter until the sauce has the consistency of very thick cream. Remove pan from over the hot water and keep the sauce warm at back of stove until serving time.

If the sauce is cooked over too hot water or the butter is added too quickly, the mixture may separate. If it does, immediately remove the pan from over the water and pour ½ of the sauce into another container. Beat into the sauce remaining in the pan 1 tablespoon boiling-hot water and 1 egg yolk. Return the pan to the hot water and beat in the other ½ of the sauce, a little at a time, until the emulsion is restored. The possibility of separation may be reduced by dissolving ½ teaspoon cornstarch in the lemon juice and combining it with the

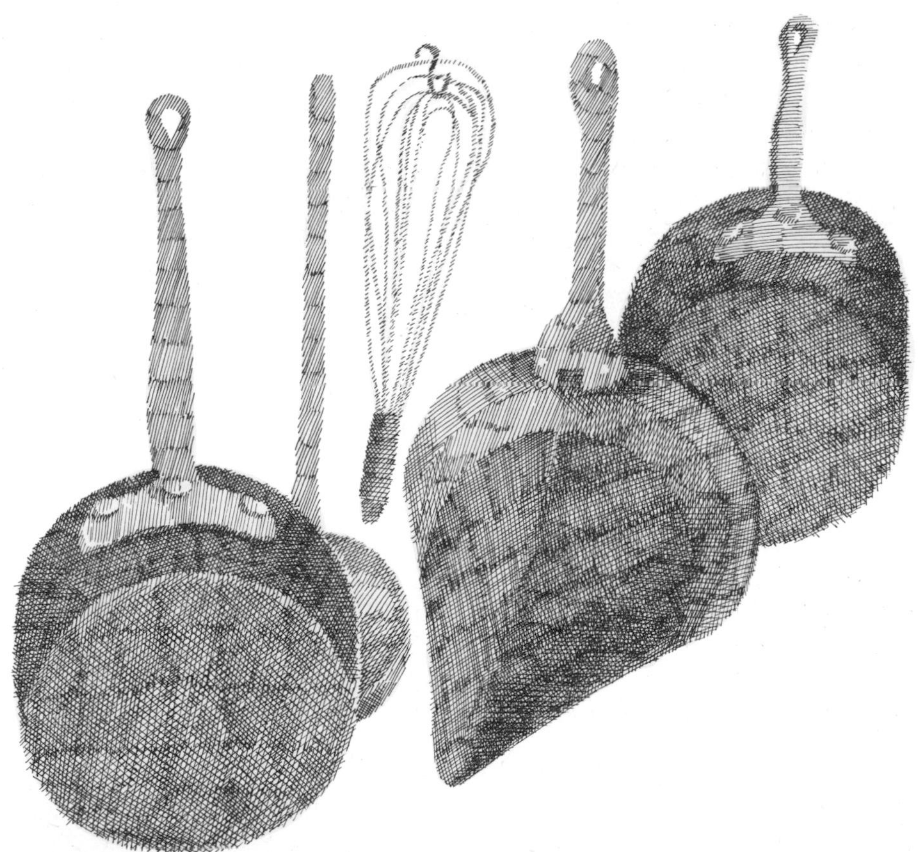

egg yolks before cooking.

This recipe provides about 1½ cups of sauce, sufficient for 6 servings with eggs, fish, or vegetables, or as required.

Hollandaise Sauce Made in an Electric Blender

3 egg yolks
1 Tbl lemon juice
¼ tsp salt
½ cup unsalted butter, heated to foaming

Warm a blender container by pouring warm water into it. Drain the container and dry it well. Put into it the egg yolks, lemon juice, and salt, and blend them at high speed for 2 seconds or only as long as it takes to turn the switch on and off. Turn it on again and start immediately pouring the foaming hot butter into the yolks. Pour steadily in a thin stream. Immediately the last of the butter has been added, stop the blending. Keep the sauce warm until serving time in the blender container set in a pan of warm (not hot) water. This recipes provides about ¾ cup of sauce.

Do not prepare greater quantities of Hollandaise sauce in the blender. Increasing the ingredients will result in a sauce too thick to blend. To double the quantity of this recipe, transfer the prepared sauce from the blender container to a warm mixing bowl and beat into it, a little at a time, an additional ½ cup unsalted butter, melted and warm.

Creamed Hollandaise Sauce | Sauce Mousseline

1½ cups Hollandaise Sauce (page 150)
½ cup heavy cream, whipped

Prepare the Hollandaise sauce as directed in the recipe. Let the sauce cool slightly and fold in the whipped cream. Serve the 2½ cups of sauce immediately to provide 10 portions of dressing for fish, shellfish, vegetables, or poached or hard-cooked eggs.

Proper equipment is needed to produce the fine sauces essential to French cuisine.

Béarnaise Sauce | Sauce Béarnaise

¼ cup dry white wine
¼ cup white wine vinegar
1 Tbl finely chopped shallots
1 tsp dried tarragon
⅛ tsp pepper
1 cup unsalted butter (2 sticks)
3 egg yolks
1 tsp lemon juice
⅛ tsp salt

In a skillet combine the wine, vinegar, shallots, tarragon, and pepper, and cook them over low heat until the liquid is reduced to ¼ cup. Strain it, discarding the solids, and reduce it further to 2 tablespoons.

Divide the butter into 8 equal parts and let them soften at room temperature. Put the egg yolks, lemon juice, and salt in the top pan of a double-boiler and combine the prepared wine-vinegar essence with them. Cook as for Hollandaise Sauce (page 150), adding the butter as directed. This recipe provides about 1½ cups of sauce, sufficient for 6 servings with grilled meats and fish.

Béarnaise Sauce with Tomato | Sauce Choron

¼ cup dry white wine
¼ cup white wine vinegar
1 Tbl finely chopped shallots
1 tsp dried tarragon
⅛ tsp pepper
2 medium tomatoes, peeled, seeded & finely chopped
1 cup unsalted butter (2 sticks)
3 egg yolks
1 tsp lemon juice
⅛ tsp salt

In a skillet combine the wine, vinegar, shallots, tarragon, and pepper, and cook them over low heat until the liquid is reduced to ½ cup. Strain it, discarding the solids, and reduce it further to 2 tablespoons. Cook the tomatoes in a saucepan, covered, over low heat until they are reduced to a thick paste. Force the paste through a fine sieve.

Divide the butter into 8 equal parts and let them soften at room temperature. Put the egg yolks, lemon juice, and salt in the top pan of a double-boiler and combine the prepared wine-vinegar essence and tomato paste with them. Cook as for Hollandaise Sauce (page 150), adding the butter as directed. This recipe provides about 2 cups

A cream-based sauce
is smooth and subtle and not to
be hurried in the making.

of sauce, sufficient for 8 servings with grilled meats and fish, or as required.

Mayonnaise | Sauce Mayonnaise

2 egg yolks
½ tsp prepared mustard
1 tsp salt
⅛ tsp white pepper
2 Tbl white vinegar
1 cup bland cooking oil (such as peanut oil)
½ cup olive oil

In a mixing bowl beat the egg yolks until they are thick. Blend in the mustard, salt, pepper, and vinegar. Combine the oils and add the mixture, a few drops at a time, beating constantly until about ⅓ of the oil has been incorporated and the mixture has thickened to the consistency of thick cream. Increase the additions of oil to about 1 tablespoon at a time, beating each in thoroughly. When all of the oil has been incorporated and the sauce drops rather than flows from the whisk, beat no longer. Overbeating may cause the mayonnaise to separate. If it does, beat in a drop or two of hot water until the emulsion is restored. If it is not, beat the separated sauce, a little at a time, into 1 egg yolk in a mixing bowl. That will do it. This recipe provides slightly less than 2 cups of mayonnaise.

Mayonnaise Made in an Electric Blender

Mayonnaise may also be prepared in an electric blender, using the same ingredients (recipe above). In the blender combine all of the ingredients except 1 cup of the combined oils. Blend them at high speed for 2 seconds or only as long as it takes to turn the switch on and off. Turn the blender on again and begin immediately to pour in the remaining oil. Pour it steadily in a thin stream. When the last of the oil has been added, the mayonnaise should be of the proper consistency. If it is not, continue the blending for a few seconds longer until the mixture "gurgles." The sound is unmistakable. Stop the blending immediately. Further blending will cause the mixture to separate. The

emulsion can be restored by adding 1 egg yolk to the mixture and blending for just a few seconds.

Store handmade and blender-made mayonnaise in a covered container in the least cold area of the refrigerator, where it will keep for about 2 weeks. Mayonnaise cannot be frozen.

Garlic Mayonnaise | Sauce Aïoli

2 cloves garlic, mashed to a paste
1 Tbl soft white bread crumbs
2 egg yolks
¼ tsp salt
1½ cups olive oil, at room temperature
½ tsp lemon juice

Set a mixing bowl on a dampened towel to secure it in place on the working surface. Put the garlic and bread crumbs into the bowl and, with a wooden spoon, work them to a smooth paste. Thoroughly blend in the egg yolks and salt. Hold the container with the olive oil in your left hand and the spoon in your right (or the reverse if you are left-handed). Pour in the olive oil, drop by drop, continuously, forcing it into the garlic paste constantly with the spoon. When about ½ the oil has been incorporated and the mixture is creamy, beat in the remaining oil with a whisk, adding a little more of it at a time, but beating it in just as constantly. When all of the oil has been added, the sauce should be very thick and sturdy enough to hold a small spoon upright for a few seconds. Stir in the lemon juice and correct the seasoning, adding more salt, if needed. This recipe provides 1½ cups of the sauce, enough for 8 to 10 servings of provincial-style hot fish preparations, such as Fish Stew (page 96), or cold poached fish.

The sauce may be made rather more effortlessly, if not so traditionally, in an electric blender. Prepare all of the ingredients, except the garlic, as for Mayonnaise Made in an Electric Blender (page 156). Force the garlic through a garlic press into a bowl, and beat the blended sauce into it, a little at a time. Let blender-prepared aïoli sauce season, in a covered container in the refrigerator, for at least 1 hour before using it.

Chive Sauce | Sauce aux Ciboulettes

1 cup Beef Broth (page 52 or canned)
1 tsp cornstarch
1 Tbl cool water
1 cup Mayonnaise (page 156)
2 Tbl finely chopped chives

In a saucepan over high heat reduce the broth to ½ cup. Reduce the heat to low, add the cornstarch dissolved in the cool water, and stir until the broth thickens. Remove pan from heat and let the broth cool. Blend the cooled broth into the prepared mayonnaise and blend in the chives. Let the sauce season in a covered container in the refrigerator for at least 1 hour before serving it with cold cooked beef, beef tongue, or duckling, or using it as required in specific recipes. This recipe provides 1½ cups of the sauce.

Rémoulade Sauce | Sauce Rémoulade

½ tsp Dijon-type mustard
½ tsp anchovy paste
½ tsp lemon juice
1 cup Mayonnaise (page 156)
2 Tbl finely chopped cornichons (French sour gherkins)
1 Tbl capers
½ tsp dried chervil, crumbled
⅛ tsp pepper

In a mixing bowl blend the mustard, anchovy paste, and lemon juice into the mayonnaise. Stir in the remaining ingredients. Let the sauce season, in a covered jar in the refrigerator, for at least 2 hours before using it as a dressing for cold cooked fish, shellfish, or vegetables.

Spinach Sauce | Sauce Verte

1 pound spinach
2 scallions, white parts only, finely chopped
2 Tbl butter
1 Tbl flour
½ cup Chicken Broth (page 53 or canned)
½ cup light cream
1 egg yolk
⅛ tsp nutmeg
Salt & pepper

Trim the spinach of any heavy stems, wash it well, and drain thoroughly. Cook it in a saucepan, uncovered, over moderate heat for 3 minutes in just the water that clings to the leaves. Stir frequently. Drain the spinach completely and force it through a fine sieve or purée it in an electric blender.

Cook the scallions in 1 tablespoon of the butter, heated in a deep skillet, until they are soft but not brown. Blend in the flour and cook for 2 minutes, stirring to prevent browning. Add the chicken broth, stirring it in gradually to produce a smooth sauce. Stir in the puréed spinach. In a small bowl combine the cream and egg yolk. Add to them just enough of the spinach sauce to heat them through. Combine the mixture with the remaining spinach sauce. Add the nutmeg and season with salt and pepper to taste. Heat the sauce, without further boiling, and stir in the remaining butter. This recipe provides about 2 cups of spinach sauce to serve with sautéed veal, broiled, sautéed, or poached fish, or poached eggs, or for use as required for specific recipes.

Fresh-Tomato Purée | Coulis de Tomates

3 pounds ripe tomatoes **¼ cup water**

Core the tomatoes and cut them into quarters. Combine the tomatoes and water in a saucepan, and cook them, covered, over low heat for 20 minutes or until the tomatoes are very soft. Force them, along with any remaining liquid, through a fine sieve. Discard the tomato seeds

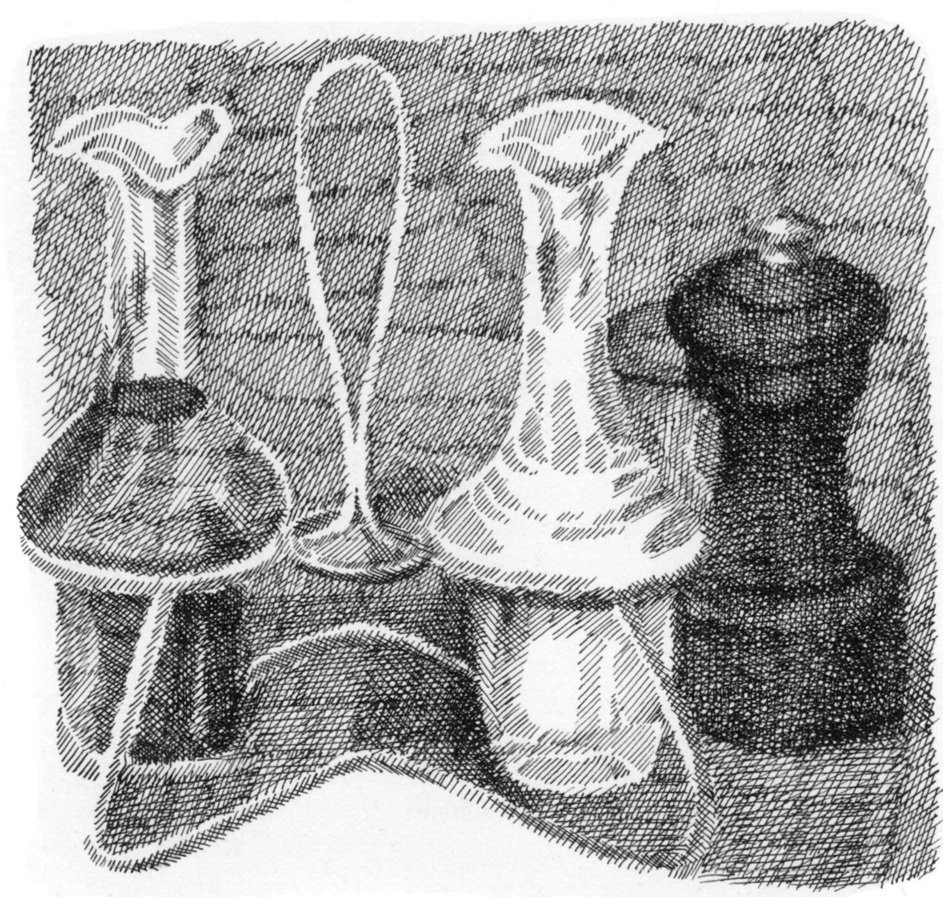

and peel. Return the sieved tomatoes to the saucepan and cook, uncovered, over moderate heat until the purée is reduced to the consistency of lightly whipped cream. This recipe provides about 2 cups of purée for use as designated in specific recipes or as desired. The purée may be kept, in a covered container under refrigeration, but only for 3 or 4 days. Thereafter the flavor begins to deteriorate. Frozen, the purée may be kept in the freezer for 1 month or longer.

Tomato-Mushroom Purée | Coulis de Tomates et Champignons

3 Tbl butter
½ pound fresh mushrooms
1½ pounds ripe tomatoes, peeled, seeded & coarsely chopped
⅛ tsp nutmeg
¼ tsp salt
⅛ tsp white pepper

Heat the butter in a skillet and in it sauté the mushrooms over moderate heat until they begin to brown. Add tomatoes and seasonings, and cook, covered, for 30 minutes or until the vegetables are soft. Force them through a fine sieve, along with any remaining liquid, or purée them, with the liquid, in an electric blender. Return the purée to the saucepan and cook, uncovered, over low heat until the purée is reduced to about 1½ cups, a quantity sufficient for 6 servings with baked, roasted, grilled, or sautéed meats, poultry, game, or fish.

Tomato Sauce | Sauce Tomate

3 pounds tomatoes, fresh or drained canned
2 Tbl butter
1 medium onion
2 cups Chicken Broth (page 53 or canned)
1 clove garlic
Bouquet Garni (see Glossary)
⅛ tsp ground allspice
Salt & pepper

Peel, seed, and coarsely chop fresh tomatoes. If drained canned tomatoes are used, remove the seeds. In a saucepan heat the butter and in it lightly brown the onion. Add the tomatoes and broth, and cook covered for 15 minutes. Add the remaining ingredients, including salt and pepper to taste, and continue cooking, with pan again covered, for 45 minutes or until the tomatoes are soft and the liquid is reduced somewhat. Remove and discard the garlic and the bouquet garni. Force the remainder through a fine sieve or purée it in an electric blender. Return the purée to the saucepan and reduce it over low heat to 3 cups. Use the sauce as directed in specific recipes or as desired.

Mushroom Flavoring | Duxelles

½ pound fresh mushrooms, very finely chopped
3 Tbl Clarified Butter (page 166)
1 small onion, finely chopped
1 large shallot, finely chopped
½ cup dry white wine
Salt & white pepper

Twist the mushrooms, a quarter at a time, in several thicknesses of cheesecloth to extract as much of their juice as possible. Heat the butter in a skillet and in it cook the onion over moderate heat until it is soft but not brown. Add the mushrooms and continue the cooking until they and the onion begin to brown. Add the shallot and, when it is soft, stir in the wine. Season with salt and white pepper to taste. Cover the pan, reduce heat to low, and cook until all the liquid evaporates. Let the mixture cool and store it in a covered container in the refrigerator where it will keep for several weeks or in a freezer for a much longer time. This recipe gives approximately 1 cup of duxelles; use to enhance the flavor of soups, stews, sauces, or as required.

Mushroom Sauce | Sauce Duxelles

3 Tbl butter
2 Tbl flour
1½ cups Beef Broth (page 52 or canned)
1 medium tomato, peeled, seeded & finely chopped
3 Tbl Mushroom Flavoring (above)
2 Tbl dry white wine
Salt & pepper
1 tsp finely chopped parsley

In a saucepan gently heat 2 tablespoons of the butter. Blend in the flour and cook for 2 minutes, stirring to prevent its browning excessively. Add the broth, stirring it in gradually to produce a smooth sauce. Stir in the tomato and cook the mixture, covered, over moderate heat until it is reduced to about 1 cup. In a small bowl moisten the mushroom flavoring with the wine, and add the mixture to the reduced sauce. Season with salt and pepper to taste, and cook, covered, over low heat for 10 minutes to blend the flavors. Stir in the parsley and remaining butter. This recipe provides about 1 cup of mushroom sauce for use with roast, grilled, or sautéed meats, poultry, or game, or as required for specific recipes.

Madeira Mushroom Sauce:

Reduce the broth ingredient to 1¼ cups and continue as directed for Mushroom Sauce, substituting ¼ cup of Madeira wine for the white wine in the recipe. Use as for Mushroom Sauce.

French Dressing | Sauce Vinaigrette

¼ tsp salt
⅛ tsp dry mustard (optional)
2 Tbl wine vinegar
⅛ tsp pepper
6 Tbl olive oil (or 3 Tbl each of olive oil and peanut oil combined)

Prepare the dressing at the table in the salad bowl or in the kitchen and take it to table in a cruet. In the salad bowl or in a mixing bowl, dissolve the salt and the mustard, if it is used, in the vinegar. Add the pepper and, with a fork, beat in the oil a little at a time until an emulsion is formed. This quantity of dressing (about ½ cup) is sufficient to provide dressing for 6 to 8 servings of salad greens.

French Dressing with Chives | Sauce Vinaigrette aux Ciboulettes

¼ tsp salt
¼ tsp dry mustard
2 Tbl white wine vinegar
1 Tbl tomato juice
⅛ tsp pepper
1 Tbl finely chopped chives
6 Tbl olive oil

In a mixing bowl dissolve the salt and mustard in the vinegar. Stir in the tomato juice and add the pepper and chives. Beat in the oil, a little at a time, until the mixture emulsifies. This recipe provides slightly more than ½ cup of chive dressing, sufficient for 3 large tomatoes, sliced; 6 servings of salad greens; or as required for specific recipes. Make only as much as may be required each time. Stored for more than 1 day, the dressing develops a bitter flavor.

Roquefort Cheese Dipping Sauce | Sauce au Roquefort

6 ounces Roquefort cheese
2 Tbl heavy cream
½ tsp finely grated orange rind
½ tsp Dijon-type mustard
2 Tbl orange juice
2 Tbl white wine vinegar
⅔ cup olive oil
Tabasco

Force the cheese through a fine sieve into a mixing bowl. Blend the cream into it. Add the orange rind and mustard, and, slowly but vigorously, beat in consecutively the orange juice, vinegar, and oil. Add a dash or two of Tabasco. Let the sauce season for 1 hour before using it as a dipping sauce for raw vegetables. This recipe provides about 2 cups of the sauce.

butters

Kneaded Butter | Beurre Manié

2 Tbl flour
2 Tbl firm unsalted butter

Unlike the other butters (recipes for which follow), kneaded butter is not a flavoring agent; nor is it a sauce, but it is so closely akin to both that it is best included here. Butters used for flavoring are compounded; so is kneaded butter, it being a composite of butter and flour. Kneaded butter is for thickening, particularly of preparations of solids and liquids cooked together, such as stews, when the sauce cannot be thickened before the cooking is completed and it is inconvenient to remove the solids before doing so. Kneaded butter makes it possible

to thicken the sauce without removing the solids. The ingredients above are usually sufficient to thicken 1 cup of completely thin sauce to proper consistency. Sauces that have thickened somewhat through reduction during the cooking need less, of course.

Incorporate the flour with the butter by literally kneading it in completely. Roll the kneaded butter between the palms of your hands into little pellets about the size of peas, and chill them thoroughly in the refrigerator. The butter can be prepared in larger quantities and stored under refrigeration or in a freezer to be used as needed. Add the pellets, a few at a time, to barely simmering liquid, and stir gently until they dissolve and the liquid begins to thicken. Continue to add small quantities of the kneaded butter until the liquid has thickened to the desired consistency. If the solids are such that stirring might tear them apart, as can happen to fish in such preparations as matelotes or bourrides, shake the pan gently over the heat until the sauce thickens. The liquid must not actually boil or the kneaded butter will cook hard. If that should happen, the solids will have to be removed, the sauce strained, and the thickening process begun again.

Clarified Butter | Beurre Clarifié

Cut a quantity of butter into small pieces and melt it in a saucepan over low heat. A white substance will rise to the top. Skim it off. Carefully pour the clear melted liquid below into a bowl, rejecting the sediment which has settled to the bottom of the pan.

Being slow to burn, clarified butter is invaluable in sautéing, and, since its moisture is greatly removed, it provides added enrichment for fine baking. Clarified butter can be kept under normal refrigeration for several weeks without deteriorating. Stored in a freezer, it can be kept almost indefinitely.

Anchovy Butter | Beurre d'Anchois

8 Tbl unsalted butter
8 canned anchovy fillets, drained

In a mixing bowl soften the butter by mashing and beating it with a wooden spoon. In another bowl mash the anchovies and force them through a very fine sieve to eliminate any remaining thread-like bones. Blend the sieved anchovies into the softened butter. Chill until firm. This recipe provides slightly more than ½ cup of anchovy butter for use mainly with broiled or poached fish.

Garlic Butter | Beurre d'Ail

8 Tbl unsalted butter
2 cloves garlic
Salt & white pepper

Let the butter soften in a mixing bowl at room temperature until it is the consistency of whipped cream. Finely chop the garlic and blend it into the butter. Season with salt and pepper. Force the mixture through a fine sieve. Chill until firm. This recipe provides ½ cup of garlic butter.

Herb Butter | Beurre de Fines Herbes

8 Tbl unsalted butter
2 Tbl fresh (or ½ tsp dried) basil, chervil, or tarragon
1 tsp strained lemon juice
Salt & pepper

In a mixing bowl soften the butter by mashing and beating it with a wooden spoon. Finely chop the desired fresh herb (or crumble the dried herb) and blend it along with the lemon juice into the softened butter. Season with salt and pepper to taste. Two herbs, or all 3, may be used in combination to provide the required amount. Chill the prepared butter until it is firm. This recipe provides ½ cup herb butter for use with broiled meats or fish or as required in specific recipes.

Lemon Butter | Beurre au Citron

10 Tbl unsalted butter
Finely grated rind of 1 lemon
½ tsp strained lemon juice
Salt & white pepper

In a mixing bowl soften the butter by mashing and beating it with a wooden spoon. Blend in the lemon rind and juice, and season with salt and white pepper to taste. Let the butter ripen for an hour or so in the refrigerator before using it. This recipe provides about ⅔ cup.

Shallot Butter | Beurre d'Echalotes

8 Tbl unsalted butter
4 shallots
2 cups boiling water
¼ tsp lemon juice
Salt

Let the butter soften in a bowl at room temperature until it is the consistency of whipped cream. Peel the shallots and blanch them in the boiling water for 1 minute. Drain them, chop them very finely, and work to a paste in a mortar with a pestle or in a bowl with a wooden spoon. Blend the paste into the softened butter along with the lemon juice and salt to taste. Chill until firm. This recipe provides ½ cup of shallot butter for use with broiled meats or fish or as required in specific recipes.

Parsley Butter | Beurre Maître d'Hôtel

8 Tbl unsalted butter
2 Tbl finely chopped parsley
½ tsp strained lemon juice
Salt & pepper

In a mixing bowl soften the butter by mashing and beating it with a wooden spoon. Blend in the parsley and lemon juice, and season with salt and pepper to taste. Chill until firm. This recipe provides ½ cup parsley butter for use with broiled meats; broiled, sautéed, or fried fish; cooked vegetables; or as required for specific recipes.

Shrimp Butter | Beurre de Crevettes

8 Tbl unsalted butter
6 ounces small cooked shrimp
¼ tsp strained lemon juice
Salt & white pepper

Let the butter soften in a mixing bowl at room temperature to the consistency of frothily whipped cream. Very finely chop the shrimp and combine them with the soft butter. Add the lemon juice, and season with salt and white pepper to taste. Force the mixture through a fine sieve or reduce it to a paste in an electric blender. Chill until firm. This recipe provides about ¾ cup of shrimp butter for use on toast as a base for canapés, to enrich sauces and soups, or as required in specific recipes.

Snail Butter | Beurre pour Escargots

1½ cups unsalted butter
1 large shallot, very finely chopped
1 medium clove garlic, pounded to paste
3 Tbl finely chopped parsley
½ tsp finely grated lemon rind
Salt & pepper to taste

In a mixing bowl soften the butter by mashing and beating it with a wooden spoon. Work the remaining ingredients into it. Keep in mind when adding salt that snails and mussels, for which this preparation is mainly intended, may themselves provide sufficient such seasoning.

This quantity of snail butter, about 1¾ cups, is sufficient for 3 dozen snails or 4 to 5 dozen (about 2 quarts) mussels.

marinades

Cooked Marinade | Marinade Cuite

6 shallots, sliced
1 medium onion, coarsely chopped
2 carrots, thinly sliced
1 clove garlic, sliced
⅓ cup bland cooking oil
2 Tbl olive oil
2 sprigs parsley
6 peppercorns
4 juniper berries
2 whole cloves
¼ tsp dried thyme
1 small bay leaf
1½ cups dry white wine
½ cup water
¼ cup cognac
½ tsp salt

Cook the shallots, onion, carrots, and garlic in the combined oils heated in a saucepan until they are soft but not brown. Add all of the remaining ingredients except the cognac and salt. Cook the marinade, covered, over moderate heat for 30 minutes. Add the cognac and salt. Pour the hot marinade over meats, poultry, or fish.

Marinade for Game | Marinade pour Gibier

6 shallots, sliced
1 medium onion, coarsely chopped
2 carrots, thinly sliced
1 clove garlic, sliced
2 sprigs parsley
6 peppercorns, crushed
4 juniper berries, crushed
2 whole cloves
¼ tsp dried thyme
1 bay leaf
1 cup red wine
¼ cup cognac
2 Tbl olive oil
⅓ cup bland cooking oil
½ tsp salt

Thoroughly combine all ingredients in a mixing bowl to provide a marinade for game and hearty meats.

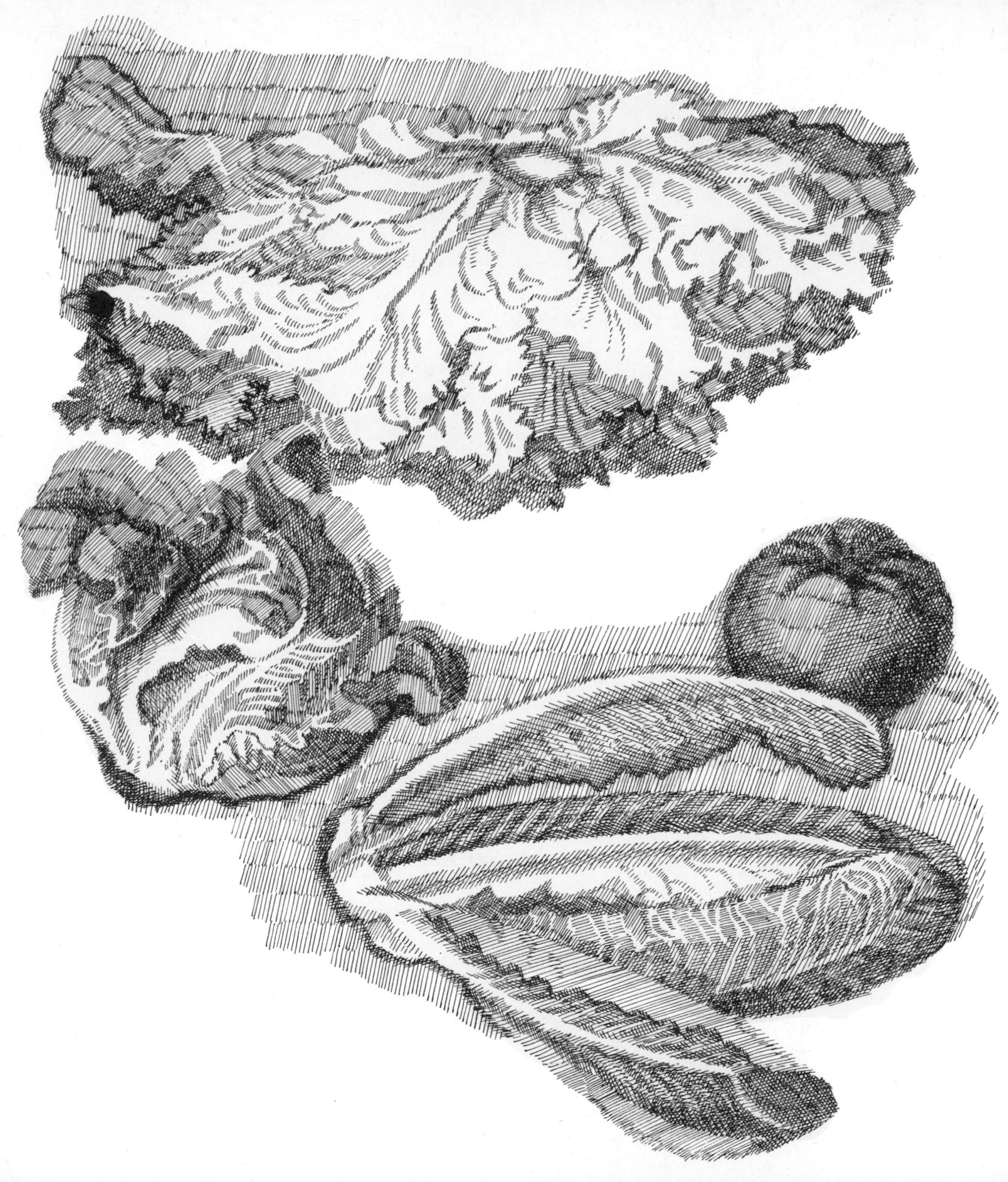

5 | main-course accompaniments

Many of the preparations in this category could themselves be considered main courses. Such, for example, are the Mediterranean-Style Combination Salad (or Salade Niçoise), the Parisian-Style Vegetable Salad, and possibly the Potato and Green Bean Salad (Salade Russe) when it is made with red caviar. The vegetables here, too, may stand by themselves as separate courses in the meal's order of service, and it is even fitting to present them so.

On the whole, these recipes incorporate simplified methods that will ease the work of the cook. An attempt has been made to present lesser-known vegetables in intriguing preparations (as salsify in cream), and glamorous but simple preparations of unglamorous vegetables, such as cabbage cooked as French pancakes. The mystery of making noodles is dispelled by presenting the recipe as the simple process it is. Many people have never tasted homemade noodles, and they need no longer deny themselves the revelation.

vegetables

Artichokes | Artichauts

To prepare artichokes for cooking, first pull off the little clinging leaves around the lower part of the artichokes. With a sharp knife trim off the stems flush with the bottoms to provide steady bases. Cut off the tops of the artichokes to a depth of about 1 inch and, with a scissors, snip off the thorny tips of the remaining leaves. Rub all of the cut surfaces, including the tips of the leaves, with lemon juice to prevent their discoloring. Fill a deep basin with cool water and add 2 tablespoons of vinegar to each 4 cups of water used to preserve the color of the artichokes. Plunge the artichokes, leaf tops down, several times into the water to free any bits of soil. The artichokes are now ready to cook.

Fill a deep kettle with enough water to submerge the artichokes, season each 2 cups with 1 teaspoon salt, and bring the water to a boil. Add the artichokes and cook them, uncovered, for 30 minutes or until they are tender, turning them frequently to keep them submerged. The artichokes are tender when a leaf can be pulled off easily and the stem ends are easily pierced with a cooking fork. Remove the artichokes and plunge them in cold water to freshen them. Set them in a colander to drain completely before serving them hot with melted butter, melted Lemon Butter (page 167), or Hollandaise Sauce (page 150); or cold with French Dressing (page 163) or Mayonnaise (page 156).

The feathery choke, midway down the center of the artichoke enclosed within the leaves, need not be removed before the artichoke is served, but it is inedible and must be removed before the heart of the artichoke, which it covers, can be eaten. If you wish to serve artichokes with the chokes removed, first pull out the little cone of light green leaves at the center of the artichoke. (Reserve it if you wish to replace it for appearance's sake when serving.) Separate the remaining leaves, carefully so as not to pull them off, and with a spoon scrape the "feathers" off the bottom, exposing the edible heart. Dispose of the feathers. You may replace the innermost cone of green leaves (many artichoke enthusiasts don't bother), and proceed with what the artichoke is all about—the eating thereof.

Enjoy the artichoke leaf by leaf first, pulling off each one at a time, dipping the bottom in the accompanying sauce and scraping off the tender pulp with your teeth. The last leaf enjoyed and the choke removed, the heart is yours. A knife and fork are now necessary. Trim any leaf ends from the rim of the heart. Cut the heart and dip the pieces in the sauce for the delectable finale.

Artichoke Hearts | Fonds d'Artichauts

6 large artichokes
1 lemon
2 tsp salt
¼ cup lemon juice, or 2 Tbl white wine vinegar

Break off the stem of each artichoke and scrape the bottom evenly. Trim the globe of all leaves, breaking off the outer dark green ones and pulling out the inner cone of lighter green leaves. Rub all cut parts immediately with the lemon, cut in half.

Cook the artichoke hearts in a saucepan in 6 cups boiling water, seasoned with the salt and lemon juice or vinegar, for 30 minutes or until they are tender. If the bottoms can be pierced easily with a sharp knife, the hearts are properly cooked. Drain them and pull out and discard the feathery chokes. Scrape the hollows of the hearts clean and trim the sides of the leaf ends. Use the hearts as required in specific recipes.

The artichoke hearts may be kept warm in the cooking liquid or cooled in it. They may also be stored in the liquid in a covered container under refrigeration. So stored they will keep for 3 to 4 days.

Artichoke Hearts with Purée of Fresh Peas | Fonds d'Artichauts Farcis

6 large cooked Artichoke Hearts (above)
1 cup Chicken Broth (page 53 or canned)
4 Tbl butter
Salt & white pepper
1½ cups shelled fresh peas (1½ pounds unshelled)
¼ tsp dried mint leaves, pulverized

Cook the artichoke hearts as directed in the recipe and keep them warm in the cooking liquid. In a saucepan heat the broth to boiling with 2 tablespoons of the butter and salt and white pepper to taste. Add the peas and cook them for 10 minutes or until they are tender. Drain the peas, reserving the broth to enrich future preparations of soups or sauces. Force the peas through a fine sieve or purée them in an electric blender, using a little of the remaining broth, if needed, to facilitate the blending. Return the purée to the saucepan and heat it gently. Season it with salt and white pepper to taste and stir in the remaining butter, melted, and the pulverized mint.

Drain the artichoke hearts, dry them well, and fill them with the purée. Place the filled hearts on a lightly buttered baking sheet and keep them warm until serving time. Serve hot to provide 6 servings.

Asparagus | Asperges

4 pounds asparagus, about 30 thick stalks

Salt

Select asparagus stalks of uniform thickness so that they will all cook tender at the same time. Snap off the bottoms of the stalks (the tough white parts) and trim off just enough of the green to even the lengths. Peel the green spears, exposing the lighter green pulp somewhat, to within 1 inch of the tips and trim off any scales within that 1-inch border. Wash the spears thoroughly by swishing them (with emphasis on the tips) in a large basin of cool water. Divide into 3 or 4 bunches and tie each in 2 places with twine. Lay the bunches flat in a kettle large enough to accommodate them, and cover them with boiling water. Add 1 teaspoon salt for each quart used. Cook the asparagus, uncovered, at boil for 10 minutes or until the spears can be pierced easily midway along the length with a gently pressed sharp, pointed knife. Remove the bunches 1 at a time with 2 forks, 1 hooked under each tie, and let the spears drain over the pan. Place the bunches on a cloth, remove the ties, and fold the cloth over the spears to keep them warm until they are to be served. They will keep warm for about 30 minutes, but if they must be kept for that long, they should be cooked for only about 8 minutes. Steaming in the cloth will make them tender.

Serve cooked asparagus, hot or cooled and chilled, as its own course, either to begin the meal or to follow the main course. Serve it hot with Lemon Butter (page 167), plain melted butter, Hollandaise Sauce (page 150), Creamed Hollandaise Sauce (page 152), or with Cream Sauce (page 144). Serve chilled asparagus with French Dressing (page 163) or with Roquefort Cheese Dipping Sauce (page 164) thinned with a little light cream, or with Mayonnaise (page 156) as is or blended with a little Fresh-Tomato Purée (page 160) and/or whipped cream. This recipe provides 6 servings.

Buttered Flageolets | Haricots Flageolets au Beurre

1 pound dried flageolets (see Note)
6 Tbl butter
1 small onion
2 whole cloves
2 tsp salt

Soak the beans overnight in enough cool water to cover them. Do not drain. Add 2 tablespoons of the butter, the onion stuck with the cloves, and the salt. Bring the liquid to a boil and cook the beans, covered, at simmer for 1½ hours or just until they are tender. Drain the beans, discarding the onion and cloves. Melt the remaining butter and blend it into the beans. This recipe provides 6 servings of flageolets, the traditional accompaniment to lamb or mutton.

NOTE: Fresh flageolets are not available commercially in the United States. The dried beans used in this preparation are obtainable in shops specializing in spices and dried fruits and legumes.

Purée of Green Beans | Purée de Haricots Verts

2 pounds green string beans
4 Tbl butter
2 Tbl finely chopped scallions, white parts only
1½ cups Chicken Broth (page 53 or canned)
Salt & pepper
1 tsp white wine vinegar
1 tsp finely chopped fresh dill (or ½ tsp dried dill weed, crumbled)

Wash the beans, trim them, and cut them into 2-inch lengths. In a saucepan gently heat 2 tablespoons of the butter and in it cook the scallions until they are soft but not brown. Stir in the broth, season it with salt and pepper to taste, and bring it to a boil. Add the beans and cook them, uncovered, for 20 minutes or until they are tender. Drain them, reserving the broth for other uses. Force the beans through a sieve, or purée them in an electric blender using as little of the cooking liquid as possible to facilitate the blending. (If the purée seems thin, cook it over low heat until it is sufficiently reduced and thick.) Return the purée to the saucepan and stir in the vinegar and dill. Reheat it gently and blend in the remaining butter. Serve the purée hot to provide 6 servings.

Cabbage Pancakes | Crêpes au Chou

3 cups shredded cabbage
9 Tbl butter
Salt & pepper
1 cup sifted flour
½ cup milk
2 eggs
1 egg yolk
4 tsp vegetable shortening
2 tsp lemon juice
1 Tbl finely chopped parsley

Blanch the cabbage in lightly salted boiling water for 5 minutes. Drain the cabbage, dry it completely, and brown it lightly in 2 tablespoons of the butter heated in a skillet. Season the cabbage with salt and pepper to taste and let it cool. In a mixing bowl combine the flour, milk, whole eggs, egg yolk, 3 tablespoons of the butter, melted and cooled, and salt to taste. Beat with a rotary beater to produce a smooth batter. Blend in the cooled cabbage.

In a skillet heat together 1 tablespoon of the remaining butter and 1 teaspoon of the vegetable shortening, adding more in the same proportion as needed to cook as many of the pancakes at a time as the pan can accommodate. Use 2 tablespoons of the batter for each of the pancakes and brown them well on both sides, turning them once. Arrange the pancakes on a warm serving platter, and sprinkle them with the lemon juice and parsley. This recipe provides 8 servings of about 4 pancakes each.

Cardoons in Red Wine Sauce | Cardons Étuvés à la Sauce Vin Rouge

3 bunches cardoons (see Glossary)
Red Wine Sauce (page 150)
1 cup orange juice, strained
Salt & pepper

Trim the cardoons of coarse outside stalks and cut the rest into 1-inch pieces. Cook the cardoons in a saucepan with enough unsalted boiling-hot water to cover for 10 minutes or until the skins are slick. Drain the cardoons, quickly rub off the skins in paper toweling, and remove the celery-like strings. Freshen the cardoons in cold water and drain again.

In a saucepan heat together the wine sauce and orange juice, and season the blend with salt and pepper to taste. Add the prepared cardoons and cook, covered, over low heat for 1 hour or until they are tender. Drain them, reserving the cooking liquid, and put them in a warm serving bowl. Keep them warm. Return the cooking liquid to the saucepan and reduce it over moderate heat to 1½ cups, stirring fre-

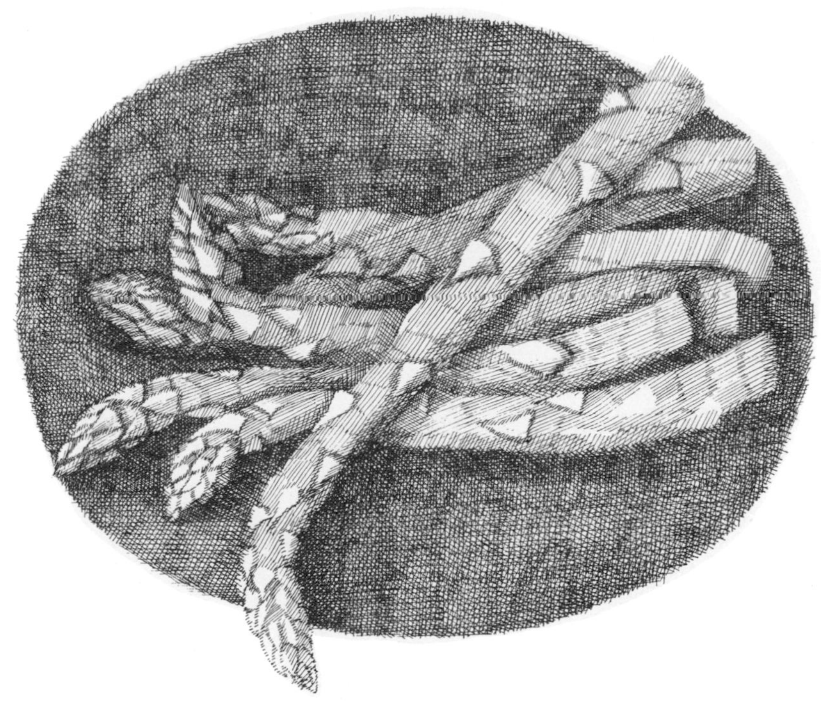

quently. Pour the sauce over the cardoons. Sprinkle, if desired, with a little additional orange juice. This recipe provides 6 servings.

Lemon Carrot Casserole | Carottes Citronnées en Casserole

24 medium carrots
¼ cup strained lemon juice
4 Tbl butter, melted
1 tsp sugar
½ tsp finely grated lemon rind
⅛ tsp dried marjoram, pulverized
Salt & pepper

Preheat oven to 350 degrees. Wash and peel the carrots, and cook them in lightly salted boiling water to cover for 15 minutes or until they are very tender. Drain them and mash them well, or put them through a ricer. In a mixing bowl combine the mashed carrots with the lemon juice, 3 tablespoons of the butter, the sugar, lemon rind, marjoram, and salt and pepper to taste. Transfer the mixture to a well-buttered 4-cup casserole and float the remaining butter over the top. Cook, uncovered, in the preheated oven for 15 minutes or until the top is nicely browned. Serve hot to provide 6 servings.

Carrots Vichy | Carottes Vichy

4 cups thinly sliced carrots
2 cups Vichy or sparkling water (see Note)
4 Tbl butter
4 tsp sugar
¼ tsp salt
⅛ tsp white pepper
2 Tbl finely chopped parsley

In a saucepan combine the carrots, Vichy or sparkling water, butter, sugar, and salt and white pepper. Cook, covered, at simmer for 20 minutes or until the carrots are almost tender. Remove cover and continue cooking for 10 minutes by which time the carrots should be properly tender and the liquid reduced to a thick syrup. Cook for a few minutes longer, if necessary, to achieve proper consistency. Transfer the carrots to a warm serving dish. Pour the syrup over them and sprinkle with the chopped parsley. This recipe provides 6 servings. NOTE: Plain water with ¼ teaspoon of baking soda dissolved in it may also be used.

Carrots with White Grapes | Carottes Véronique

2 cups Chicken Broth (page 53 or canned)
1 cup medium-dry white wine, such as Graves
3 Tbl butter
¼ tsp dried basil, crumbled
Salt & white pepper
4 cups julienne-cut carrots
1 cup seedless white grapes
½ tsp lemon juice

In a saucepan combine the broth, wine, butter, basil, and salt and white pepper to taste. Bring the liquid to a boil over moderate heat. Add the carrots and cook them for 10 minutes. Add the grapes and cook for 5 minutes longer or just until they are heated through. The carrots should still be slightly crisp. Remove the carrots and grapes, and put them in a warm serving dish. Keep them warm. Leave the cooking liquid in the pan and quickly reduce it over high heat to ½ cup. Add the lemon juice and pour the syrup over the carrots and grapes. Serve hot. This recipe provides 6 servings.

Braised Celery | Céleris Braisés

3 large bunches celery
4 Tbl butter
⅓ cup finely chopped scallions, white parts only
⅓ cup very finely chopped carrots
1½ cups Beef Broth (page 52 or canned)
½ cup dry white wine
2 sprigs parsley
Salt & white pepper
1 tsp lemon juice
1 Tbl finely chopped parsley

Preheat oven to 350 degrees. Trim the bunches of celery of leaves and roots, taking care not to separate the stalks. Wash the bunches by running cold water forcefully down through the stalks and drain them. Blanch the bunches in lightly salted boiling water for 10 minutes. Drain them and dry thoroughly, squeezing the bunches in paper toweling or a cloth to remove as much of the liquid as possible. Secure the stalks by tying the bunches at each end and at 2 equally spaced intervals between. Cut the bunches between the 2 center ties.

In a large skillet gently heat 3 tablespoons of the butter and in

it cook the scallions and carrots until they are soft but not brown. Stir in the broth and wine, and add the parsley sprigs and salt and white pepper to taste. Cook the mixture at simmer for 5 minutes. Arrange the celery halves in a lightly buttered heavy casserole and pour the liquid and vegetables over them. Cover the casserole, set it in the preheated oven, and let the celery cook for 1 hour or until the stalks are tender. Transfer the tied bunches to a warm serving platter and remove the ties. Keep the celery warm. Strain the cooking liquid, discarding the solids, and return it to the casserole. Reduce it over high heat to about ⅔ cup. Stir in the lemon juice and the remaining butter. Pour the sauce over the celery and garnish with parsley. Apportion for 6 servings.

Celeriac with Brown Butter | Céleri-Rave au Beurre Noisette

4 large celeriac (see Note)
8 Tbl butter
½ tsp salt
Juice of 3 lemons
Chopped parsley

Peel the roots and cut them into thick slices. Put them in a saucepan with 2 tablespoons of the butter and cover them with boiling-hot water. Add the salt and lemon juice. Cook the roots at simmer for 15 minutes or just until they are tender. Remove and drain the slices. In a skillet heat 3 tablespoons of the remaining butter and in it brown the slices lightly on both sides, as many pieces at a time as the pan can accommodate. Add more butter as needed to complete the sautéing. Transfer the celeriac to a serving dish and keep warm. Add any remaining butter to that in the pan and let it brown. Do not let it burn. Pour the brown butter over the celeriac and serve at once. This recipe provides 6 servings.

NOTE: Celeriac is also known as celery root and knob celery.

Purée of Chestnuts | Purée de Marrons

1½ pounds chestnuts
2 stalks celery with leaves
1 medium onion, peeled & halved
Bouquet Garni (see Glossary)
3 cups Beef Broth (page 52), or more as needed
⅓ cup dry vermouth
Salt & white pepper
2 Tbl butter
2 Tbl heavy cream

With a small, sharp, pointed knife, cut off a thin strip half way around the edge of the flat side of the chestnuts. Place the nuts in a saucepan, cover them with cool water, and bring the liquid to a boil. Cook over moderate heat for 2 minutes, or until the shells begin to curl open. Drain the nuts, pull off the shells, and with a cloth or paper toweling rub off the skins. Return the peeled chestnuts to the drained saucepan along with the celery, onion, and bouquet garni. Pour over them the beef broth (or more as needed to cover the nuts completely). Stir in the vermouth and season with salt and pepper to taste. Bring the liquid to a boil and cook the chestnuts, uncovered, at simmer for 30 minutes, or until they are soft but not mushy. Drain them, reserving the liquid. Discard the other solids. Force the chestnuts through a sieve or purée them in an electric blender, adding a little of the remaining cooking liquid to facilitate the blending. Reheat the purée and blend into it the butter, cream, and 1 tablespoon of the remaining broth. Omit the additional broth if the chestnuts were puréed in a blender. Correct the seasoning with additional salt and white pepper if needed. Serve the puréed chestnuts with lustily flavored preparations of meat, poultry, and game. This quantity of chestnut purée is sufficient for 6 servings.

Braised Endive | Endives Braisées

18 medium heads Belgian endive
6 Tbl butter
1 cup Beef Broth (page 52 or canned)
¼ cup strained grapefruit juice
Salt & pepper
1 Tbl finely chopped parsley

Trim the root ends of the endive, if necessary, and soak the heads in ice-cold water for 15 minutes. Drain them and dry with paper toweling, squeezing gently to remove any remaining water. In a skillet heat the butter and in it brown the endive on all sides, as many heads at a time as the pan can accommodate. Reassemble all endive in the skillet.

In a saucepan over high heat reduce the broth to ½ cup. Add the grapefruit juice, heat the mixture through, and pour it over the heads of endive in the skillet. Cover pan and cook over moderate heat for 10 minutes. Turn the endive, season lightly with salt and pepper, and continue cooking, uncovered, for 10 minutes longer, or until the heads are tender and the cooking liquid is almost entirely absorbed. Transfer the endive to a warm serving platter and pour the remaining cooking liquid over them. Sprinkle with the chopped parsley and serve hot. This recipe provides 6 servings.

Braised Leeks and Walnuts in Cream | Poireaux et Noix Braisés à la Crème

12 large leeks
3 Tbl butter
2 cups Chicken Broth (page 53 or canned), heated
1 Tbl flour
1½ cups light cream, heated
Salt & white pepper
⅓ cup coarsely chopped walnuts

Trim the leeks of roots and dark green leaves, and wash the stalks by running cool water from the tap forcefully down through the leaf ends.

Drain the leeks well and dry them. Arrange them in 2 layers in a skillet. Melt 2 tablespoons of the butter in the hot chicken broth, and pour the liquid over the leeks in the skillet. The liquid should barely cover the leeks. Cook them, partially covered, over moderate heat until almost tender, about 10 minutes. Transfer them to a gratin dish or shallow baking dish, leaving the remaining cooking liquid in the skillet. Continue cooking the liquid until it is reduced to a thick golden syrup.

Preheat oven to 375 degrees. In a saucepan gently heat the remaining butter and blend in the flour. Cook over low heat for 2 minutes, stirring to prevent excessive browning. Gradually stir in the hot cream to produce a smooth sauce. Blend the sauce into the syrup in the skillet. Season with salt and white pepper to taste. Pour the mixture over the leeks in the gratin dish and sprinkle with the chopped walnuts. Complete the cooking in the preheated oven for 15 minutes or until the sauce bubbles and the walnuts begin to brown. Serve hot. This recipe provides 6 servings.

Sautéed Fennel with Mustard Sauce |
Fenouil Sauté, Sauce Moutarde

6 stalks fennel (about 2 pounds)
3 cups boiling water
5 Tbl butter
½ cup dry white wine
2 Tbl flour
2 tsp dry mustard
Salt & pepper
1 Tbl chopped fresh dill (or ½ tsp dried dill weed, crushed)
2 Tbl heavy cream
3 Tbl grated Parmesan cheese

Trim the fennel and cut the stalks into halves. Cook them in the boiling water for 10 minutes. Drain them well, reserving 1 cup of the cooking liquid. In a large skillet heat 3 tablespoons of the butter and arrange the drained fennel in it, cut sides down. Cook, covered, over low heat for 20 minutes or until the halves are tender.

In a saucepan reduce the reserved cup of cooking liquid over high heat to ½ cup. Add the wine and heat it. In another saucepan gently heat the remaining butter. Blend in the flour and cook for 2 minutes, stirring constantly to prevent browning. Add the mustard and blend it in. Stir in the hot wine combination gradually to produce a smooth sauce. Season with salt and pepper to taste. Blend in the dill and heavy cream. Transfer the cooked fennel to a heat-proof serving platter and pour the sauce over the halves. Sprinkle with the grated cheese and brown lightly under a hot broiler. Serve at once to provide 6 servings.

Braised Lettuce | Laitues Braisées

3 medium heads Boston lettuce
4 Tbl butter
⅓ cup finely chopped scallions (omit darker green parts)
⅓ cup very finely chopped carrots
1 medium tomato, peeled, seeded & finely chopped
1½ cups Beef Broth (page 52 or canned)
½ cup dry white wine
2 sprigs parsley
1 small bay leaf
¼ tsp dried thyme
Salt & white pepper
½ tsp lemon juice
2 tsp finely chopped parsley

Preheat oven to 350 degrees. Remove any tough outer leaves of the lettuce and trim the root ends. Plunge the heads vigorously several times, leaf tops down, in cool water until all soil has been removed. Blanch the heads for 3 minutes in a saucepan in enough lightly salted boiling-hot water to cover them. Drain the heads and dip them immediately in cold water. Drain them again, thoroughly, and cut them down through the root ends into halves. Wrap the halves individually in several thicknesses of paper toweling and gently squeeze out any remaining water. In a skillet heat 3 tablespoons of the butter and in it cook the scallions and carrots until they are tender but not brown. Add the tomato and continue cooking until it is reduced to a paste. Stir in the broth and white wine, and add the parsley, bay leaf, and thyme. Cook the mixture at simmer for 5 minutes.

In a heavy casserole arrange the drained halves of lettuce cut sides down and pressed closely together. Pour the prepared broth mixture over them and season with salt and white pepper to taste. Cover the casserole, set it in the preheated oven, and let the lettuce

cook so for 45 minutes, or until the halves are tender but not mushy. Transfer them to a warm serving dish and keep them warm. Strain the cooking liquid, discarding the solids, return it to the casserole, and reduce it over high heat to about ⅔ cup. Stir in the lemon juice and remaining butter. Pour the sauce over the braised lettuce and sprinkle the halves with chopped parsley. This recipe provides 6 servings.

Fried Parsley | Brins de Persil Frits

Sprigs of firm fresh parsley
Salt
Bland cooking oil for deep frying

Wash the parsley in cool water and shake the sprigs dry. Wrap them very loosely in paper toweling and shake them in the wrapping to remove the remaining water. Do not pat the sprigs or press them.

In a fryer or deep saucepan heat the oil for deep frying to 350 degrees. Place a few sprigs at a time in a frying basket and lower them gently into the hot oil. Fry for just a few seconds until the sprigs are crisp. Drain them on paper toweling and sprinkle them with salt. Cook as many as required to decorate a serving platter of roast meats or poultry and the individual servings of them.

Boiled or Steamed Potatoes | Pommes de Terre Bouillies ou à la Vapeur

6 medium potatoes (about 2 pounds)
Salt

To boil potatoes:

Scrub the potatoes clean and cover them in a saucepan with boiling water seasoned with 1 teaspoon salt for each quart used. Cook them over moderate heat for 20 minutes or until they are tender but firm. Drain off the water, and dry the potatoes by shaking them in the pan over the heat for a few seconds. Serve them unpeeled, or peel the potatoes and roll them in melted butter. Either way you may serve them with plain melted butter or melted Garlic Butter (page 166) passed separately. Peeled boiled potatoes may also be sprinkled with chopped parsley. This quantity of potatoes will provide 6 servings.

To steam potatoes:

Put scrubbed unpeeled potatoes in a deep fry basket or colander over, but not touching, boiling water in a saucepan. Cover the potatoes with a napkin or towel and let them steam for 30 minutes or until they are tender. Steamed potatoes and boiled potatoes are served interchangeably.

Whipped Potatoes | Purée de Pommes de Terre

5 large potatoes (about 2 pounds)
8 Tbl butter
¼ cup milk, scalded
Salt & white pepper

For the utmost flavor, choose produce that is firm, crisp, and at the height of its color.

Peel the potatoes, cut them into eighths, and cover them in a saucepan with lightly salted boiling water. Cook them, covered, over moderate heat for 15 minutes or until they are tender but not mushy. Drain off the water, and dry the potatoes by shaking the pan over the heat for a few seconds. Mash the potatoes well or force them through a ricer or sieve. Blend the butter into the potatoes in the saucepan. Add the hot milk and beat the potatoes vigorously until they are white and fluffy. Season with salt and white pepper to taste, and serve at once to provide 6 servings. If serving is delayed for a short time, the potatoes may be kept in the top pan of a double-boiler over hot water. In that case, a tablespoon or two of heated light cream should be beaten into the whipped potatoes before they are served.

Potatoes Anna | Pommes de Terre Anna

8 large potatoes (about 3½ pounds)

1 cup butter, clarified (page 166)

Salt & pepper

Preheat oven to 425 degrees. Select potatoes of uniform size and shape. Peel the potatoes and cut them into round slices ⅛-inch thick and of as nearly the same diameter as possible. Dry the slices immediately they are cut between sheets of paper toweling. Use a 2- to 3-inch-deep straight-sided heavy metal or earthenware casserole or skillet, about 7 inches in diameter, and set it over moderate heat. Pour in ⅓ cup of the clarified butter. When the butter is hot fill the pan with the potato slices, arranging them, well overlapped, in neat layers spiraled out from the center of the pan. Float a tablespoon of the remaining butter over each layer and season each lightly with salt and pepper. Compress the layers by setting a heavy pan bottom side down on top of the potatoes and pressing them gently.

Let the butter bubble up around the sides of the potatoes. If it rises higher than ¼-inch below the surface of the potatoes, drain off the excess. If the level is lower, add more of the butter as needed. Cover the pan securely, transfer it to the preheated oven, and let the potatoes bake for 30 minutes. Remove cover and continue baking for

Beguiling harmonies of taste: Raw Asparagus Salad (page 204), Spiced Sautéed Tomatoes (page 194), and Eggs Carême in a Ring of Rice and Peas (page 76).

30 minutes longer, or until the molded slices are encased in a crisp and handsomely browned crust.

Remove pan from oven and jiggle it to make certain the potato mold is not stuck to the bottom. If it is, loosen it by gently sliding a spatula under it. Drain off the remaining clarified butter. The easiest way to do that is to siphon it off with a baster. Lacking a baster, hold a plate firmly over the potatoes and pour off the butter. Strain the butter and reserve it; it is reusable. If the potatoes are dislodged from the sides of the mold, press them back into place and return pan to oven for a few minutes until they are secured again. To serve, unmold the potato cake by inverting a serving platter over it. Reverse pan and platter together and the mold will automatically be transferred to the platter right side up: Serve at once or keep warm in the slackening oven, with the door ajar, until serving time. The mold will remain crisp and warm for half an hour or longer. Serve the potatoes cut in wedges to provide 6 servings.

Duchess Potatoes | Pommes de Terre Duchesse

2 egg yolks
Whipped Potatoes (page 186)

Preheat oven to 350 degrees. In a mixing bowl beat the egg yolks into the warm whipped potatoes. Using a pastry bag fitted with a large fluted tube, pipe 12 rosettes of equal size onto a buttered baking sheet. Brown the potatoes lightly in the preheated oven, and serve them on a platter surrounding the meat which they are to accompany. The 12 rosettes provide 6 servings.

Oven-Browned Potato Balls | Pommes de Terre Noisette

2½ pounds potatoes
2 Tbl bland cooking oil
Salt

Preheat oven to 375 degrees. Peel the potatoes and, with a potato baller, cut them into ¾-inch spheres. The potato remnants, covered with water in a bowl, can be refrigerated and used within a day or two for other preparations. Dry the potato balls thoroughly. Spread the oil in a shallow baking pan and roll the potatoes in it, coating them well. Bake them in the preheated oven for 40 minutes or until they are well browned and tender. Stir them occasionally. Serve the potatoes immediately they are done to provide 6 servings.

Oven-Browned Matchstick Potatoes:

Cut the peeled potatoes into slices about ⅛-inch thick, and cut the slices into strips of the same thickness. Dry them well and cook them as directed for the potato balls.

Sautéed Shredded Potatoes | Pommes de Terre en Lambeaux Sautées

5 large potatoes (about 2 pounds)
½ cup bland cooking oil
Salt

Peel the potatoes and shred them on the side of a grater intended for that purpose. (Cutting the potatoes with a knife will not produce fine enough shreds. Grating them will make them too fine.) Put the shreds in a bowl, cover with ice-cold water, and let them remain for 30 minutes. Drain the shreds in a strainer and dry them well. In a deep skillet heat the oil. When it is hot enough, sprinkle in the potato shreds and cook them over moderate heat until they are lightly browned and crisp. Stir frequently to keep the shreds separated and to brown them evenly. Drain them thoroughly, sprinkle them with salt to taste, and serve them immediately. They may be kept crisp and warm for a short while in a very slow oven. This recipe provides 6 servings.

Potato Puffs | Pommes de Terre Dauphine

2 medium potatoes (about ½ pound)
2 Tbl butter
1 Tbl light cream
⅛ tsp salt
⅛ tsp white pepper
½ recipe Cream Puff Paste for Hors-d'Oeuvres (page 227)
Flour for dredging
Bland cooking oil for deep frying

Peel the potatoes, quarter them, place in a saucepan, and cover with lightly salted boiling water. Cook them, covered, over moderate heat for 15 minutes or until they are tender but not mushy. Drain off the water, and dry the potatoes by shaking the pan over the heat for a few seconds. Mash the potatoes well or force them through a ricer or sieve. Blend the butter into the potatoes in the saucepan. Add the cream and beat vigorously until the potatoes are very white and fluffy. Season with the salt and white pepper.

Prepare the cream puff paste as directed in the recipe and, while the paste is still warm, blend it into the potatoes. Let the mixture cool and mold it into cylindrical shapes of equal size. Dredge them lightly with flour. In a deep fryer or saucepan, heat cooking oil for deep frying to 375 degrees and in it fry the potatoes, as many at a time as the pan can accommodate without crowding, until they are well puffed and golden brown. Drain them quickly on paper toweling and serve them at once with roast meats or poultry. This recipe provides 6 servings.

Puffed Potatoes | Pommes de Terre Soufflées

4 large baking potatoes
Fat for deep frying (see Note)
Salt

Use potatoes that are as perfectly oval as possible and of uniform size. Trim them into equal-size oval shapes, if necessary. Peel the potatoes and cut them lengthwise into slices all ⅛-inch thick. Rinse them in ice-cold water and dry them well between sheets of paper toweling.

In a deep saucepan or fryer, heat the fat to 350 degrees. Add the potatoes, as many slices at a time as the pan can accommodate without crowding. Immediately the potatoes are added, the temperature of the fat will fall to about 300 degrees. After 7 or 8 minutes when the fat is reheated somewhat, the potatoes will rise to the surface. They should not be brown but should be rather wrinkled. Remove them with a slotted spoon, spread them on a cloth or paper toweling, and let them drain. When all of the potatoes have undergone this preliminary cooking, increase the heat of the fat to 400 degrees. Return the half-cooked potatoes to the fat, again as many at a time as can be conveniently accommodated. Immediately the slices will puff and brown

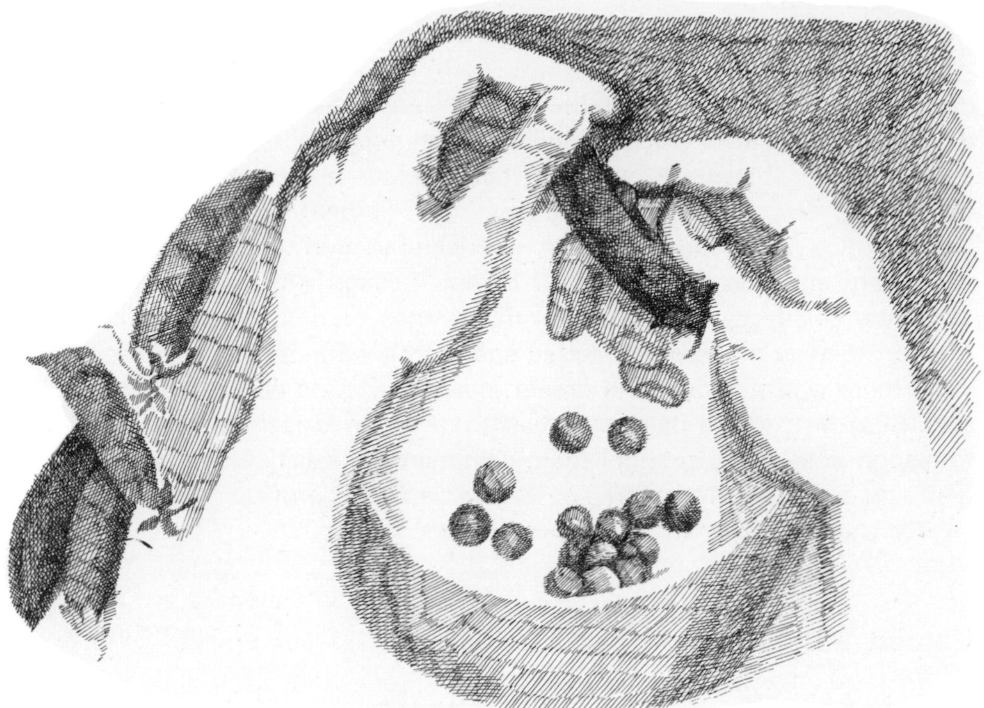

—at least, most of them will. There are always a few slices that do not. Drain them all, anyway. Remove the failures (they can be used as a snack), and sprinkle the others with salt. Serve them quickly.

Even allowing for a few failures, this recipe will provide enough puffed potatoes for 6 servings. Covered, on a cloth or paper toweling, the potatoes can be kept partially cooked for as long as 2 days before the second frying.

NOTE: Rendered beef suet is the ideal fat for this recipe; if you do not have any, use bland cooking oil.

Salsify in Cream | Salsifis à la Crème

2 pounds salsify
White wine vinegar or lemon juice
2 cups heavy cream, scalded
Salt
Dash of Tabasco
½ tsp lemon juice
Paprika

Scrub the salsify and wash it. Immediately each root is cleaned, drop it into a bowl of cool water acidulated with 1 tablespoon white wine vinegar or 2 tablespoons strained lemon juice per quart to prevent discoloring. Drain the roots, 1 at a time, and cut them into slices about ¼-inch thick. Rinse them, place in an enamel-coated or stainless steel saucepan, and cover with the hot cream. Season with salt to taste. Cook the salsify over low heat for 15 minutes or until the slices are tender. Remove them with a slotted spoon to a warm serving dish and keep them warm. Reduce the cream remaining in the pan to about ¾ cup. Season it with a dash of Tabasco, or more to taste, and the ½ teaspoon of lemon juice. Pour the cream over the salsify in the serving dish and sprinkle lightly with paprika. Serve hot to provide 6 servings. NOTE: Salsify is also known as oyster plant.

Spiced Sautéed Tomatoes | Tomates Sautées aux Épices

6 medium tomatoes (about 2 pounds)
4 Tbl Clarified Butter (page 166)
4 scallions, white parts only, thinly sliced
2 Tbl brown sugar
1 tsp red wine vinegar
½ tsp salt
¼ tsp paprika
1 small bay leaf, crumbled
4 peppercorns
2 cloves
½-inch length stick cinnamon, crushed
1 Tbl finely chopped parsley

Peel the tomatoes carefully, taking care not to pierce them. Leave the tomatoes whole and the stem ends intact. Heat the butter gently in a skillet and cook the scallions in it until they are soft but not brown. Blend in all of the remaining ingredients except the parsley. Arrange the tomatoes stem sides down over the seasonings, and cook them, uncovered, over low heat for 1 hour. Baste the tomatoes occasionally, but be careful not to pierce them. Don't move them around in the pan or they will collapse. At the end of the cooking time, remove the tomatoes to a warm serving platter and sprinkle them with the chopped parsley. Serve them hot to provide 6 servings. The tomatoes may also be served slightly chilled to accompany cold poached chicken, cold roast meats, or chilled seafood salads. (*See photograph, page 188.*)

Creamed Spinach | Épinards à la Crème

2 pounds young spinach
2 Tbl thinly sliced scallions, white parts only
2 Tbl butter
1 Tbl flour
1 cup heavy cream
Salt & white pepper
½ tsp finely grated lemon rind
¼ tsp nutmeg

Trim the spinach of any very heavy stems and wash the leaves thoroughly. Drain the greens, shaking off as much water as possible, and cook them in a saucepan over low heat, with just the water that clings to the leaves, for 3 minutes, turning the leaves frequently until they are all well wilted. Drain them in a colander, gently pressing out a little more liquid. Chop the spinach finely.

In another saucepan cook the scallions in the butter, browning them very lightly. Blend in the flour and continue cooking for 2 minutes, stirring to prevent excessive browning. Stir in the cream gradually to produce a smooth sauce. Season with salt and white pepper to taste, and add the lemon rind and nutmeg. Add the chopped spinach and let it heat through without boiling. Serve hot to provide 6 servings.

Turnip Soufflé | Soufflé de Navets

3 cups peeled & cubed white turnips
5 Tbl butter
1 Tbl finely chopped parsley
½ tsp finely grated lemon rind
Salt & white pepper
4 tsp flour
½ cup strained orange juice
3 eggs, separated
1 extra egg white

Cook the turnips in a saucepan in lightly salted water to cover for 15 minutes or until they are tender. Drain the cooked turnips and force them through a ricer or a sieve. Return this purée to the saucepan and dry it out by shaking the pan over moderate heat. Remove pan from heat and blend into the purée 3 tablespoons of the butter, the parsley, lemon rind, and salt and white pepper to taste. In another saucepan gently heat the remaining butter and blend in the flour. Add the orange juice gradually, stirring constantly until the mixture is smooth. Blend in the turnip purée and cook, stirring, for 1 minute or until it is heated through. Blend in the egg yolks. Remove pan from heat and let the mixture cool somewhat. Preheat oven to 350 degrees.

Beat the 4 egg whites until they are stiff but not dry. Stir ¼ of them into the purée. Fold in the remainder. Pour the mixture into a buttered 6-cup soufflé dish and bake it in the preheated oven for 25 minutes, or until it is well puffed, firm on top, and nicely browned. This soufflé is sufficient for 6 servings as a main-course accompaniment with roast beef or game.

Vegetable Stew Provençale | Ratatouille Niçoise

1 large eggplant (about 1 pound)
6 small zucchini (about ¾ pound)
1 tsp salt
3 medium onions (about ½ pound)
2 green peppers (about ½ pound)
1 clove garlic
4 medium tomatoes (about 1½ pounds)
½ cup olive oil
⅛ tsp ground coriander seeds
¼ tsp dried basil
Salt & pepper

Trim and peel the eggplant. Trim the zucchini, but do not peel it. Cut both into ½-inch cubes and combine them in a bowl. Sprinkle them with the teaspoon of salt and let steep for 30 minutes. Drain them and, between several thicknesses of paper toweling, press out as much more liquid as possible. Cut the onions into thin slices and the peppers into halves. Trim out the stems and the white pulp of the peppers, and cut the halves into thin strips. Finely chop the garlic, and peel, seed, and coarsely chop the tomatoes.

Heat the olive oil in a large skillet and in it cook the onions, peppers, and garlic over low heat until they are tender but not brown. Add the eggplant and zucchini, and blend in the coriander and basil.

Spread the tomatoes on top. Cover the skillet and cook for 30 minutes, or until the tomatoes have rendered much of their juice. Remove cover. Stir to combine the vegetables, season with salt and pepper to taste, and continue cooking for 20 minutes longer, or until the vegetables are soft, but not mushy, and the cooking liquid is reduced to just a little olive oil. It may be drained off, if desired. Transfer the ratatouille to a serving bowl and let it cool. Serve slightly chilled, apportioned for 6 to 8 servings as hors-d'oeuvres or hot to provide 8 to 12 servings as accompaniment to a main course.

rice

Braised Rice | Pilaf

4 Tbl butter
¼ cup finely chopped onion
1½ cups long-grain rice
2½ cups Chicken Broth (page 53 or canned), heated to boiling
Salt & white pepper

Preheat oven to 325 degrees. In a heat-proof casserole gently melt the butter. Add the onion and let it just heat through. Stir in the rice and cook it, stirring constantly until the grains whiten. Do not let the rice or onion brown. Stir in the hot chicken broth and let it bubble (it will, violently) for just a few seconds without further stirring. Season the broth with salt and white pepper to taste and cover the casserole securely. Better still, seal the casserole with heavy foil and fit the lid over it. Transfer the casserole to the preheated oven and let the rice braise for 30 minutes, or until all of the liquid is absorbed and grains are tender. Add a little more boiling-hot broth, if needed, to complete the cooking. Toss the rice lightly with a fork to separate the grains. Serve hot to provide 6 servings.

Braised Rice with Saffron | Pilaf au Safran

Braised Rice (above)
½ tsp powdered saffron

Prepare the rice as directed in the recipe, but dissolve the saffron in the chicken broth before adding the broth to the rice. Serve with curried or other well-spiced preparations.

Steamed Rice | Riz à la Vapeur

3 quarts water
2 Tbl salt
1½ cups long-grain rice

Bring the water to a full boil and add the salt. Sprinkle in the rice, a little at a time so as not to retard the boiling, and stir once, briefly. Cook, uncovered, for 12 minutes. Drain the rice and rinse it with running hot water. Drain it again, thoroughly. Wring out a large napkin or towel in cold water and with it line a colander or deep-fry basket, allowing the ends to overhang. Put the rice in the center and fold the cloth over it. Set the container over but not touching boiling water in a saucepan and let the rice steam for 30 minutes or until the grains are dry and tender. Add boiling water to the saucepan, if necessary, to complete the cooking. This recipe provides a little more than 4 cups of steamed rice, enough for 6 servings as a main-course accompaniment.

A Ring of Rice and Peas | Riz et Pois en Couronne

3 Tbl butter
1 cup long-grain rice
1 scallion, white part only, thinly sliced
2½ cups Chicken Broth (page 53 or canned)
½ cup strained orange juice
Salt & white pepper
1 cup shelled fresh peas

Preheat oven to 325 degrees. In a heat-proof casserole gently melt the butter. Add the rice and cook it over low heat, stirring constantly until the grains whiten. Stir in the scallion and heat it through. Do not let either the rice or scallion brown at all. Have ready 2 cups of the broth and the orange juice, heated together and seasoned with salt and white pepper to taste. Stir the mixture into the rice and let the liquid bubble (it will immediately and violently). Remove casserole from heat, seal the top with foil, and fit the casserole cover over it. Set casserole in the preheated oven and let the rice braise for 20 minutes.

In a saucepan cook the peas in the remaining chicken broth at simmer for 5 minutes. Drain the peas, reserving the broth under refrigeration to enrich future soups or sauces. Combine the partially cooked peas and rice in the casserole, tossing them together lightly with a fork. Do not stir the rice. Re-cover the casserole and continue the cooking for 10 minutes, or until the liquid is completely absorbed and the rice and peas are tender. Remove casserole and increase oven heat to 350 degrees. Butter a 6-cup ring mold and lightly press the rice and peas into it, filling the mold to the top. Set the mold in a pan of hot water in the newly preheated oven and cover the casserole with a heavy cloth wrung out in cold water. Let the rice and peas steam so for 10 minutes. Unmold the ring onto a round serving platter and fill the center as desired. (*See photograph, page 188.*)

noodles

Homemade Fine Noodles | Cheveux d'Ange

3 cups flour **4 eggs**

Sift the flour onto a large pastry board. Make a well in the center of the flour and break the eggs into it. Beat them lightly with a fork, at the same time working them gradually into the flour to produce a stiff but malleable dough. Knead 5 minutes or until the eggs and flour are thoroughly blended and the dough is somewhat elastic. Let it rest for 5 minutes.

Roll out the dough to tissue-paper thinness, dusting it lightly with flour as needed to prevent its sticking to the board, and turning it frequently to obtain a circular sheet. Let the sheet dry for 10 minutes. With your fingers roll it into a multi-layered cylinder about 2½ inches in diameter. With a very sharp knife cut the cylinder across the width into strips even thinner than 1/32 of an inch—so thin that they will merit the designation "angel's hair," as the French call them. Shake the strips loose onto the pastry board and let the noodles dry for 30 minutes before using them. These are primarily used as a garnish for consommés. When so used, the noodles should be precooked for 2 minutes only (no longer) in lightly salted boiling water before being cooked for an additional minute or two in the broth. To store the noodles, completely dry them and place in an airtight container. The recipe provides about 6 cups of noodles.

Homemade Noodles with Sautéed Bread Crumbs | Nouilles Fraîches à la Polonaise

Dough for Homemade Fine Noodles (above), ½ recipe
6 cups water
2 tsp salt
4 Tbl butter
1½ cups coarse fresh white bread crumbs

Prepare the noodle dough as directed in the recipe, but cut it into wider strips. The noodles should be about ⅛-inch wide.

In a deep saucepan season the water with the salt and bring it to a rolling boil. Add the noodles, a few at a time so as not to retard the boiling, and cook them for 8 minutes or just until they are tender. Drain them thoroughly, put them in a warm serving dish, and gently stir 2 tablespoons of the butter, melted, into them. Keep them warm.

Heat the remaining butter in a skillet. Add the crumbs and stir them over moderate heat until they are well browned and crisp. Sprinkle the crumbs, along with any remaining butter in the pan, over the noodles. Toss gently with 2 forks to blend, and serve at once. The noodles and bread crumbs may be kept separately for about half an hour before serving. Combine them at the last moment. Left too long after tossing, the crumbs will soften. This recipe provides 6 servings.

salads

French Green Salad | Salade à la Française

2 medium heads lettuce
French Dressing (page 163)
1 tsp chopped fresh herbs (or ½ tsp crumbled dried herbs) of choice (optional)

Use just one kind of greens such as Boston, leaf, or romaine lettuce. Separate the leaves and wash them thoroughly but gently by swishing them around in a basin of cool water. Pick up the lettuce in both hands, a few leaves at a time so as not to crush them, and shake off the water. Arrange a layer of leaves on a length of paper toweling. Cover with another length of toweling, and arrange another layer of leaves over it. Continue so with the remaining leaves. Roll the layers together gently in the toweling and wrap the roll in a cloth. The double wrapping will soak up any remaining moisture. Chill, wrapped, in the refrigerator for 2 hours or more, and chill the salad bowl as well.

Whether you pour the dressing over the greens in the salad bowl or prepare the dressing in the bowl and add the leaves is a matter of preference. If herbs are used, sprinkle them over the leaves before dressing the salad. If chives, fresh or frozen chopped, are used, the quantity may be increased to 1 tablespoon and should be blended into the dressing. Tear the leaves into convenient-sized pieces and roll in the dressing, gently so as not to crush them, but sufficiently to coat the leaves uniformly. Serve at once.

Mediterranean-Style Combination Salad | Salade Niçoise

3 large potatoes
3 large tomatoes, peeled
1 cup cooked green beans, cooled
12 lettuce leaves
8 anchovy fillets
½ cup pitted black olives
1 7-ounce can tuna fish in oil, drained
¾ cup French Dressing (page 163)

Cook the potatoes, unpeeled, until they are tender but firm, in a covered saucepan with enough lightly salted boiling water to cover them. Drain the potatoes well. Peel them, when they are cool enough to handle, and cut them into ½-inch cubes. Cut the peeled tomatoes into eighths. Leave young slender beans whole; cut mature ones into 2-inch lengths. Tear the lettuce leaves into strips (do not cut them). Coarsely chop the anchovies and slice the olives. Combine the vegetables, olives, and fish in a salad bowl, pour the dressing over them, and toss the salad gently to blend. Chill briefly. Serve the salad as one of the items of a buffet, or to provide 6 servings as a light luncheon main course or 8 as a first course.

Parisian-Style Vegetable Salad | Salade Parisienne

1 medium celeriac
¼ tsp salt
Juice of 1 lemon
1 cup thin julienne of cooked beets
1 cup diced cooked potatoes
½ cup French Dressing (page 163)
4 Hard-Cooked Eggs (page 75)
2 tsp anchovy paste
¼ tsp Dijon-type mustard
1 Tbl tomato juice
¼ cup finely flaked tuna fish
2 Tbl coarsely chopped cornichons (see Glossary)
1 tsp finely chopped fresh tarragon (or ¼ tsp dried tarragon, crumbled)
Salt & pepper
Crisp lettuce leaves

Peel the celeriac and cut it into thin slices. Put them in a saucepan and cover with boiling-hot water. Add the salt and lemon juice. Cook the slices at simmer for 8 minutes or just until they are tender. Remove and drain the slices.

In a mixing bowl gently combine the celeriac, beets, and potatoes. Pour the French dressing over them and let them marinate in it in the refrigerator for 30 minutes, stirring them occasionally so that they become uniformly seasoned. Drain off the marinade and reserve it. Set the vegetables aside for the moment.

Shell the eggs and separate the whites and yolks. Put the yolks in a mixing bowl and, with a wooden spoon, work the reserved marinade into them, a little at a time, to produce a smooth paste. Blend in the anchovy paste, mustard, and tomato juice. Coarsely chop the egg whites and stir them into the sauce along with the tuna fish, cornichons, tarragon, and salt and pepper to taste. Add the marinated vegetables and combine gently but well. Serve chilled on a bed of crisp lettuce leaves to provide 6 servings with, if desired, Herbed Bread (page 225).

Potato and Green Bean Salad | Salade Russe

3 large potatoes
3 cups green beans, trimmed
Few grains cayenne pepper
Salt & white pepper
1 cup Mayonnaise (page 156)
1 Tbl tomato paste
¼ cup red caviar (optional)

Cook the potatoes, unpeeled, until they are tender but firm, in a covered saucepan with enough lightly salted boiling water to cover them. Drain the potatoes well. Peel them, when they are cool enough to handle, and slice them. If the beans are very young and slender, leave them whole; otherwise, cut them into 2-inch lengths. Cook them, uncovered, also in lightly salted boiling water in a separate saucepan, the whole beans for about 10 minutes, the cut mature ones for about 15 minutes, or until they are tender but still slightly resistant to the bite. Drain them well, let them cool, and combine them in a bowl with the potatoes. Season the potatoes and beans with the cayenne and white pepper, and with additional salt, if needed. In another bowl combine the mayonnaise and tomato paste, and fold in the red caviar, if used. Dress the vegetables with the mixture. Serve chilled, enveloped in crisp lettuce leaves in a salad bowl to provide 6 servings as accompaniment to chilled cooked fish or shellfish or such salads, or as desired. Classically, this salad is molded in a dome-shaped bowl lined with fish or chicken aspic and presented at table unmolded, with a decoration of leaves of fresh herbs.

Raw Asparagus Salad | Salade d'Asperges Crues

3 pounds asparagus, medium stalks
French Dressing (page 163)

Trim and wash the asparagus as directed in the recipe for cooked Asparagus (page 174), and soak the spears in ice water for 30 minutes. Drain them well. Cut off the tips and reserve them. Cut the remaining part of the stalks on the bias into slices ¼-inch thick, and place them in a chilled salad bowl. Distribute the asparagus tips over the top. The asparagus may be kept so, covered, in the refrigerator for an hour or longer if it is not to be served at once. Blend in the dressing at the table. This recipe provides 6 servings. (*See photograph, page 188.*)

Red Rice Salad | Salade de Riz Rouge

2 scallions
2½ cups Steamed Rice (page 198)
1½ cups cooked beets, cut in julienne
¾ cup French Dressing (page 163)
Salt & pepper
⅓ cup sour cream
¼ cup Mayonnaise (page 156)
1 medium cucumber, peeled, seeded & coarsely chopped
6–8 cup-shaped lettuce leaves
1 medium sweet onion, thinly sliced

Trim the scallions of any bruised green ends and cut the stalks into thin slices. Combine them in a mixing bowl with the rice and beets, and blend in ½ cup of the dressing. Add salt and pepper to taste. Let the mixture season, covered, in the refrigerator for 8 hours or overnight. Shortly before serving, combine the remaining French dressing, sour cream, and mayonnaise, and blend the mixture into the red rice along with the cucumbers. Chill the salad again. At serving time arrange the lettuce leaves on a chilled serving platter and fill them equally with the salad. Sprinkle the 6 to 8 portions with the slices of onion separated into rings.

White Rice and Mushroom Salad | Salade de Riz Blanc et Champignons

½ tsp salt
¼ cup strained lemon juice
¼ tsp white pepper
¾ cup olive oil
3 cups warm Steamed Rice (page 198)
4 scallions, white parts only, thinly sliced
4 cups trimmed & sliced mushrooms (about ¾ pound)
Lettuce leaves

In a mixing bowl dissolve the salt in the lemon juice. Add the pepper, and beat in the olive oil, a little at a time, until an emulsion is formed. In another bowl combine the warm rice and the scallions, and blend into them ½ cup of the prepared dressing. Let the mixture cool, and chill it. Gently combine the mushrooms and chilled rice, and blend in the remaining dressing. Chill briefly and transfer the salad to a chilled serving bowl lined with lettuce leaves. This salad is sufficient for 6 servings.

Rice and Truffle Salad | Salade Sybarite

4 cups Chicken Broth (page 53 or canned)
½ cup strained lemon juice
Salt & white pepper
2 cups long-grain rice
1 cup French Dressing (page 163)
⅓ cup thinly sliced truffles

Put the chicken broth and lemon juice in a saucepan and season them with salt and white pepper to taste. Bring the liquid to a rolling boil.

Add the rice, a little at a time so as not to retard the boiling, and stir once, briefly. Cook, uncovered, for 12 minutes. Drain the rice, reserving the broth for other uses, and rinse the grains with hot running water. Drain again, thoroughly. Line a deep-fry basket or colander with a large napkin or towel wrung out in cold water, letting the ends overhang. Put the drained rice in the center and fold the ends of the cloth over it. Set the container over, but not touching, boiling water in a saucepan, and let the rice steam for 30 minutes or until the grains are dry and tender. Transfer the rice to a bowl, pour ½ cup of the dressing over it, and let it cool. Add the truffles and the remaining dressing. Toss the salad with 2 forks to distribute the truffles evenly and to blend in the dressing. Serve slightly chilled to provide 6 portions.

Raw Spinach and Tomato Salad | Salade d'Épinards Crus aux Tomates

1½ pounds young spinach
4 Hard-Cooked Eggs (page 75)
½ tsp anchovy paste
1 Tbl tomato juice
2 Tbl white wine vinegar
6 Tbl olive oil
Salt & pepper
3 medium tomatoes, peeled, cored & chilled

Trim off the roots and heavy stems of the spinach, and thoroughly wash and drain the leaves. Wrap them loosely in several thicknesses of paper toweling to soak up any remaining moisture, and chill the greens in the wrapping. Shell the eggs and separate the whites and yolks. Force the yolks through a sieve into a mixing bowl and blend into them the anchovy paste, tomato juice, and vinegar. Beat in the olive oil, a little at a time, until the mixture is smooth and creamy. Stir in salt and pepper to taste.

Unwrap the spinach leaves and tear them into halves. Cut the tomatoes into large cubes and combine them with the spinach in a chilled salad bowl. Pour over them the prepared dressing and toss the salad gently but sufficiently to coat the pieces evenly with the dressing. Chop the egg whites finely and sprinkle them over the top. Serve the salad well chilled to provide 6 portions.

Sliced Tomato Salad | Salade de Tomates

4 large tomatoes (about 2 pounds)
French Dressing with Chives (page 163)

Put the tomatoes in a large heat-proof bowl, cover them with boiling-hot water, and let them remain for 30 seconds. Drain the tomatoes, peel them, and trim out the stem ends. Cut the tomatoes into slices ¾-inch thick and arrange them, slightly overlapping, in a deep serving platter. Pour the chive dressing over them and chill thoroughly in the refrigerator, basting the tomatoes several times with the dressing Serve these 6 portions of tomatoes with grilled or roasted beef, lamb, pork, or chicken.

6 | cheese

"Dessert without cheese," Brillat-Savarin once noted, "is like a pretty girl with one eye." Cheese does not supplant the sweet. It is brought to the table as a separate course, following the salad, but preceding dessert. It may originally have been required to temper the lingering acidity of the salad dressing and thereby make more palatable the last glass of the dinner's wine. But that is only conjecture. After all, cheese at dinner is important to nondrinkers as well.

Cheese is not always presented in its natural state. It can take its place in the meal in a variety of forms, such as cheese balls or fondue. Brillat-Savarin included a recipe for fondue in his *Physiology of Taste.* It resembles the one presented here only in that its cheese is Gruyère. It calls for a quantity of eggs three times the weight of the cheese, and butter half the weight of the cheese. Even granting the promised marvelous effect, the dish would seem to be less the lovely wine- and kirsch-flavored melted cheese we know today, than a marvelously rich Gruyère omelette.

Cheese: How to Buy It and How to Serve It

Cheese, the most universally popular of all foods, is also the most versatile. Not only does it maintain its own place in the course of the meal, it contributes handsomely to a great variety of other delights of the table from hors-d'oeuvres to desserts.

The purveyor of cheese who can or will provide a taste before you buy is a rarity these days, and the buyer must in great measure rely on what he sees. Fortunately, seeing can be believing. For cheese more frequently than not is as good as it looks. It is, of course, important to know how it should look.

Of the French cheeses which are the happy preoccupation of this chapter, Roquefort, for example, should appear as regal as its designation as the king of cheeses suggests. The curd should be of almost ermine whiteness, contrasting sharply with the bright blue-green marbling which sets it apart from lesser blue-veined cheeses. If the "ermine" appears to have yellowed and the streaks of marbling look dry and gray, that Roquefort is past its prime.

Brie, considered to be the queen of all cheeses, should look, uncut, like a large, white, satin-covered disc averaging about 12 inches in diameter and 1 inch thick. The crusts should be evenly parallel throughout, but a little swelling at the center does not necessarily indicate deterioration—possibly just pride. Collapse at the center, however, is an almost certain indication of overripeness already arrived or rapidly approaching. Pass that cheese by. Cut Brie should display delicately yellow, shimmeringly beautiful curd. It should appear to be easily spreadable, but look always to be on the verge of flowing.

A perfect Brie is a complete joy; an imperfect one can be heartbreaking. Imperfection is most frequently evidenced by a thin, hard-looking streak running horizontally through the center of the curd. The cheese may look encouragingly unripe, but it is undependable. Even wrapped in a damp cloth and left at room temperature for a few days, as is frequently recommended, such Brie will not often ripen properly. The hard-looking streak will remain adamant.

Camembert, third in the line of ascendancy to the cheese throne, is a small cheese, about 4½ inches in diameter and 1½ inches thick.

Usually more cooperative than Brie, Camembert may on occasion progress from youth to old age without seemingly ever having ripened at all. Since most Camembert nowadays comes packed in round boxes of chipped wood and well wrapped, it is not possible to examine the crust, which, properly, should be a light amber color. The crust darkens considerably as it becomes overripe. It is possible to determine the ripeness of a Camembert by its size. If it appears to be too small for the box, it has dried and shrunk. Pass it by. The round should just fit the box and be just soft enough to give slightly when pressed. When cut, it should be a very pale yellow, and be soft but not runny.

There are, of course, a great many other French cheeses available in the United States. Most of these are small cheeses, among them several of the goat cheeses, and these are never sold cut. Therefore it is impossible to determine their ripeness simply by looking at them.

Gruyère cheese, indicated for several of the recipes, is preferably French-made. It is somewhat less sweet than the Swiss-made.

Cheese is best served simply, preferably on a cheese board without decoration or garniture. Serve no more than three different kinds of cheese (don't try to out-French the French Line). They should be in convenient sizes arranged on the board with enough room between them to permit them to be cut easily. Provide each cheese with a knife of its own. Serve the cheese, just before dessert, with fresh fruit if desired, but always with good crusty French bread. Wine, the wine of dinner, is requisite. Some of the cheese recipes which follow may be served instead of cheese alone.

Fried Cheese Balls | Boulettes au Fromage

4 Tbl butter
5 Tbl flour
2 cups milk
Salt & white pepper
3 cups grated Gruyère cheese (about ½ pound)
¼ tsp dried chervil, pulverized
3 egg yolks
1 whole egg
1 Tbl bland cooking oil
Flour for dredging
Fine dry bread crumbs
Bland cooking oil for deep frying

In a saucepan melt the butter over low heat. Blend in the flour and cook, stirring, over low heat until the flour is lightly browned. Add gradually 1¾ cups of the milk, scalded, stirring constantly to produce a very thick, smooth paste. Season with salt and white pepper to taste. Add the grated cheese and the chervil, stirring until the cheese melts and is incorporated in the paste. Remove pan from heat and beat in the egg yolks, 1 at a time. Spread the paste ½-inch deep in a buttered platter and let it cool. Cover it with waxed paper and chill it in the refrigerator for at least 2 hours. Cut the chilled paste into 1-inch squares and roll them into balls between the palms of your hands.

In a mixing bowl beat together the whole egg, the tablespoon of cooking oil, and the remaining milk. Dredge the balls with flour, dip them in the egg mixture, and coat them completely with bread crumbs.

In a deep saucepan or fryer heat sufficient bland cooking oil for deep frying to 375 degrees, and in it fry the cheese balls, as many at a time as the pan can accommodate without crowding, for 1 minute or until they are golden brown. Remove them with a slotted spoon, drain them quickly on paper toweling, and serve them at once, with toothpicks, as a cocktail snack, or cool them somewhat and serve as accompaniment to the salad course. This recipe provides about 36 pieces.

Roquefort Mousse | Mousse au Roquefort

2 envelopes (2 Tbl) unflavored gelatine
⅓ cup cool water
6 egg yolks
2 cups heavy cream
¾ pound Roquefort cheese, smoothly sieved
1 Tbl cognac
2 egg whites
Finely chopped parsley

Soften the gelatine in the cool water. In the top pan of a double-boiler beat together the egg yolks and ½ cup of the cream, and add the softened gelatine. Set the pan over barely simmering water and cook, stirring constantly, until the gelatine dissolves and the mixture thickens into a creamy custard. Blend in the sieved cheese and the cognac. Remove pan from over water and let the mixture cool completely.

In a mixing bowl beat the egg whites until they are stiff but not dry. In another bowl stiffly whip the remaining cream and fold in the beaten egg whites. Fold that mixture into the cooled cheese custard.

Increase the height of a 4-cup-capacity soufflé dish by tying a 4-inch collar of waxed paper around the rim. Fill the soufflé dish with the mousse mixture and chill it for 2 hours or until it is completely set. Remove the paper collar and press finely chopped parsley into the exposed sides of the mousse. Serve from the soufflé dish to provide 6 to 8 servings as a cheese course.

Cheese Fondue | Fondue de Fromage

1 clove garlic, cut
1½ cups dry white wine, such as a Riesling
1 pound Gruyère cheese, shredded
2 tsp cornstarch
3 Tbl kirsch
Black pepper
Cubes of French Bread

Rub the inside of a chafing-dish pan or heat-proof earthenware casserole with the cut clove of garlic. Discard the garlic. Set pan over a moderately hot chafing-dish burner at the table, and pour in the wine. Bring the liquid to the boiling point, but do not let it actually boil. Add the cheese, a little at a time, stirring until it melts and the mixture is smooth. Dissolve the cornstarch in the kirsch and blend it into the fondue. Season with freshly ground black pepper to taste. Serve with cubes of crusty French bread to be dipped into the cheese on long-handled forks. Each person serves himself, at the same time stirring the fondue to prevent its becoming lumpy. If the fondue thickens excessively, it may be thinned with a little more heated wine and, if desired, additional kirsch.

Cheese Soufflés | Soufflés au Fromage

5 Tbl butter
2 tsp fine dry bread crumbs
2 tsp grated Parmesan cheese
¼ cup flour
1¼ cups milk, scalded
½ tsp salt
2 dashes Tabasco
3–4 drops lemon juice
5 eggs, separated
1 extra egg white
1 cup shredded Gruyère cheese
6 paper-thin slices Gruyère cheese, about 2 inches square

Butter 6 individual, 1⅓-cup-capacity soufflé dishes (or one 8-cup soufflé dish) with 1 tablespoon of the butter and coat them lightly with the bread crumbs and grated cheese combined. Set them aside for the moment. Preheat oven to 375 degrees.

In a saucepan over low heat melt the remaining butter and blend the flour into it. Cook this roux for 2 minutes, stirring constantly so that it does not brown. Add the hot milk and beat vigorously with a whisk to produce a smooth, very thick sauce. Season it with the salt, Tabasco, and lemon juice. Beat in the egg yolks, 1 at a time, and let the batter cool to lukewarm. In a mixing bowl beat the 6 egg whites until they are stiff but not dry. Stir ¼ of them and the shredded cheese into the yolk mixture. Fold in the remaining whites. Pour equal amounts of the mixture into the prepared soufflé dishes and smooth the tops evenly. The dishes should be only about ⅔ full. Gently place a square of the thinly sliced cheese on top of each filling. Set the dishes in the preheated oven and bake for 20 minutes, or until the fillings are puffed over the tops of the dishes and are golden brown and firm. Serve them at once.

Cheese Custard Tart | Quiche de Campagne

Short Plain Pastry (page 236)
7 ounces French goat cheese (see Note)
4 ounces ripe Camembert cheese
4 eggs
1¼ cups milk
2 Tbl chopped fresh dill (or 1 tsp dried dill weed)
1 Tbl chopped chives
¼ tsp white pepper
Few grains cayenne pepper

Preheat oven to 400 degrees. Prepare pastry as directed in the recipe and with it line a 9-inch pie pan. Line the pastry shell with buttered foil and fill it with dried beans to keep the pastry in place during the preliminary baking. Bake in the preheated oven 5 minutes. Remove the filling and foil, and bake 3 minutes longer.

Trim the cheeses of rind. This is best done with a vegetable peeler

while the cheeses are cold. Let the cheeses soften completely, at room temperature, in a mixing bowl. Vigorously beat in the eggs. Stir in the milk and blend in the herbs and seasonings. This filling may also be combined in an electric blender. Pour the mixture into the partially baked pastry shell, and bake in the still preheated oven 40 minutes, or until a knife inserted in the center of the custard can be withdrawn clean. Serve hot, cut in wedges to provide 6 servings.
NOTE: Goat cheeses of Valençay and Banon brands may be used in this recipe.

Savory Cheese Roll | Roulade de Fromage Piquante

6 ounces Gervais cheese, softened
1 tsp finely chopped chives
¼ tsp finely grated lemon rind
2 tsp sour cream
1 tsp heavy cream
4 Tbl butter
5 Tbl flour
1 tsp sugar
¼ tsp salt
⅛ tsp white pepper
2 cups milk, scalded
4 eggs, separated

In a mixing bowl thoroughly combine the cheese, chives, lemon rind, and sour and heavy creams. Let the mixture season at room temperature until needed.

Preheat oven to 325 degrees. In a saucepan melt the butter over low heat. Blend in the flour, sugar, salt, and pepper, and cook for 2 minutes, stirring constantly to prevent browning. Add the milk, stirring it in gradually to produce a smooth, thick sauce. Remove pan from heat and beat in the egg yolks. Let the sauce cool somewhat. Beat the egg whites until they are stiff but not dry, and stir ¼ of them into the yolk mixture. Fold in the remainder.

Rub a 11 x 15 x 1-inch jelly-roll pan lightly with bland cooking oil. (Do not use butter; it will burn.) Cover the bottom with waxed paper and oil the paper. Spread the prepared batter evenly in the pan and bake it in the preheated oven 40 minutes, or until it is well browned. Invert it onto a buttered sheet of waxed paper and peel off the baking paper. Spread the exposed surface with the prepared cheese mixture, and roll down the length, enclosing the filling in the roll. Serve, warm or cooled, as a light-luncheon main course, sliced to serve 6.

Sweet Cheese Roll | Roulade de Fromage Douce

Savory Cheese Roll (above)
3 Tbl seedless raspberry preserves

Prepare as for Savory Cheese Roll, but omit the chives and instead blend the raspberry preserves into the cheese filling. Roll and slice as indicated. Serve as a tea accompaniment to provide 6 to 8 servings.

Roquefort Cheese Shortbread | Gâteau Croustillant au Roquefort

¼ pound Roquefort cheese
½ cup unsalted butter
1 Tbl sugar
1 egg, well beaten
2 Tbl cream
1¾ cups flour
¼ cup cornstarch

Preheat oven to 300 degrees. In a mixing bowl thoroughly cream together the cheese, butter, and sugar. Beat in the egg and cream. Sift the flour with the cornstarch, and blend them into the creamed mixture to produce a smooth semisoft dough. Pat it out, between sheets of waxed paper, into a rectangle ¼-inch thick, and prick the surface all over with the tines of a fork. Cut the dough into 1½-inch squares and arrange them on a baking sheet. Bake in the preheated oven 45 minutes, or until the squares are lightly browned. Cool them on a rack. This recipe provides 3 dozen squares of shortbread, which may be served as a salad accompaniment or as cocktail snacks.

Camembert Cheese Shortbread:

Prepare the shortbread for baking as directed for Roquefort Cheese Shortbread (above) but substitute ripe Camembert cheese, trimmed of crust, for the Roquefort, increase the eggs to 2, and add ¼ teaspoon salt. Pat the dough on a lightly floured baking sheet into a round ¼-inch thick, cut it into 16 wedges, and bake it in a preheated 350-degree oven 30 minutes, or until the wedges are lightly browned. Cool on a rack and serve as for Roquefort shortbread.

BIJOUT
BOULANGERIE

7 | breads and pastries

There is no reason why the family kitchen cannot produce loaves of crusty, good-tasting French bread. It makes all the more sense for Americans, who—unlike the French—rarely have the convenience of a local bakery to provide daily fresh-baked loaves of every description.

The molding of a French loaf is usually done by one of two methods. The first uses a piece of accordion-pleated canvas, with the ropes of dough nested in the hollows. The other uses long, narrow baskets, called *bannetons,* in which the dough rises in the traditional shapes. Neither method suits the amateur. The first requires much dexterity, acquired through practice, to unmold the loaves, and the *bannetons* required for the second are practically unavailable in the United States.

Determined to find another way, I petitioned the mother of invention and was answered with the mailing-tube method described in the recipe for Sour-Dough White Bread (page 220). It makes the unmolding of the loaves practically foolproof and is offered in hopes of encouraging a revival in the art of French-bread baking.

Sour-Dough Starter | Levure pour Pain Français

1 cake fresh yeast (or 1 envelope activated dry yeast)
1 cup warm water (105-115 degrees)
1 cup flour
½ tsp salt
½ tsp sugar

Use a large crock or other large container of at least 4-quart capacity. The starter rises to great heights as it seasons and you will need a receptacle of the indicated size to contain it. Soften the yeast in the warm water. Blend in the flour, salt, and sugar. Cover the crock and set it in a warm place in the kitchen. Every day for the next 4 days, stir into the mixture an additional ¼ cup each of warm water and flour combined, and re-cover the crock. After the sixth day the pungent aroma rising from the crock will tell you that the starter is ready. Transfer it to a container with a tightly fitting cover and keep it under refrigeration until it is needed.

The starter will keep indefinitely, provided it is replenished as directed in the recipes here. If it is not used frequently, it should be bolstered every week or so with ¼ cup of flour blended with ¼ cup of warm water. The starter will separate and needs only to be stirred to reblend the ingredients before using.

Sour-Dough White Bread | Pain Français

½ cup Sour-Dough Starter (above)
1 cup lukewarm water (80-85 degrees)
1¼ cups flour

The daily bread of France is rarely baked in home ovens. Bread in France comes from the neighborhood bakery. As for sour dough, it is not French at all. It is purely an American creation, the result of trying to duplicate the flavor of the French loaf, which it does, if not exactly, quite happily enough. The flavor of the bread made by the American method given here is derived from a "starter"—a fermented mixture which provides the leavening as well as the special flavor.

Allow 2 days for preparing this bread and proceed as follows:

First Day:

Prepare the batter: Remove the starter from the refrigerator and stir it well. Transfer ½ cup of it to a warm 3-quart mixing bowl. Return the remainder, covered again, to the refrigerator. Stir the lukewarm water into the starter in the bowl and thoroughly blend in the flour. Stir for 5 minutes or until the mixture is completely smooth. Cover the bowl with plastic wrap and let the batter season in a warm, draft-free place overnight for 12 hours.

Second Day:

Prepared Batter (above)
3–3½ cups flour
1 tsp sugar
1 tsp salt
½ cup buttermilk
¼ cup milk
1 Tbl butter
Additional butter, melted

Replace the ½ cup of sour-dough starter, taken from the container in the refrigerator, with ½ cup of the prepared batter. Blend into the remaining batter ½ cup of the flour sifted with the sugar and salt. In a saucepan combine the buttermilk and milk, and heat to lukewarm (80 to 85 degrees). Add the butter and let it melt. Stir the mixture into the batter and add 2 cups more of the flour until the dough becomes too stiff to work with a spoon. Turn the dough out onto a lightly floured pastry board and knead in enough of the remaining ½ to 1 cup flour for 10 minutes to produce a smooth, soft (but not sticky), elastic dough. Butter a large glass mixing bowl. Form the dough into a ball, set it in the bowl, and brush it with melted butter. Cover the bowl with plastic wrap, set it in a warm, draft-free place, and let the dough rise for 2 hours or until it doubles in bulk. Mark the height of the dough with a strip of adhesive tape on the outside of the bowl and check the rise against that mark. Deflate the risen dough by punching it down. Reshape it and let it rise again, covered with the plastic wrap, for 1 hour. Deflate it again and turn it out onto the floured pastry board. Let it rest for a few minutes.

Pat the dough into a rectangle and fold it in half. Press the seal gently to secure the seam. Pat the dough again into a rectangle and fold it again, securing the edges as before. Cut the dough into 6 equal-size pieces and let them rest for a few minutes. With your hands roll each piece of the prepared dough into a rope about ¾-inch in diameter and 12 inches long, and fit each gently into a buttered mold of the same length, 1⅜ inches wide and 1 inch deep (see Note). Cover the molds lightly with a cloth and let the ropes of dough rise until they fill the molds. Sprinkle 2 baking sheets lightly with white cornmeal and invert 3 of the risen loaves onto each sheet spacing them about 3 inches apart. Preheat oven to 400 degrees.

With a very sharp knife or a razor blade, slash each loaf slightly on the diagonal in 3 places down the length, cutting into the loaves horizontally about ¼-inch deep. Brush them with cold water and let them rest for 5 minutes. Bake the loaves in the preheated oven 30 minutes or until they are nicely browned and sound hollow when thumped. Brush the loaves twice with melted butter, after the first 5 minutes of baking and again 15 minutes later. Cool the loaves on a rack.

Since most home ovens can accommodate only 1 large baking sheet at a time, chill the loaves on the second sheet in the refrigerator until they can be baked. The 6 loaves provided by this recipe are approximately the size of those known in France as *ficelles.* Using other molds of proper size, the recipe may be adapted to provide 4 *bâtards,* loaves about 3 x 16 inches. The recipe also will supply 4 *pains de ménage* (round loaves about 8 inches in diameter, shaped by hand and made without molds) or 18 *petits pains* (rolls, shaped by hand into 3-inch lengths and also made without molds). The familiar *baguettes,* about 24 inches long and 2 inches wide, are too large to be baked in most home ovens. *(See photographs, page 237.)*

NOTE: To make molds for sour-dough white bread use heavy cardboard mailing tubes, 1½ inches in diameter. These are available in stationery shops. Cut the tubes into 6 pieces, each 12 inches long. With a very sharp knife or a razor blade trim off ⅓ of each tube straight down the length, leaving a trough 1 inch deep with an opening 1⅜ inches wide. Cover each mold completely with foil.

Sour-Dough Brown Bread | Pain Bis

1 cup Sour-Dough Starter (page 220)

2 cups lukewarm water (80–85 degrees)

2½ cups flour

Allow 2 days for preparing this bread and proceed as follows:

First Day:

Remove the starter from the refrigerator and stir it well. Transfer 1 cup of it to a warm 3-quart mixing bowl. Return the remainder, covered again, to the refrigerator. Stir the lukewarm water into the starter in the bowl and thoroughly blend in the flour. Stir for 5 minutes or until the mixture is completely smooth. Cover the bowl with plastic wrap and let the batter season in a warm, draft-free place overnight for 12 hours.

Second Day:

Prepared Batter (above)
3 cups sifted white flour
2 tsp sugar
2 tsp salt
¼ cup unsweetened dark cocoa
1 cup buttermilk
½ cup water
2 Tbl butter
3–3½ cups rye flour
1 Tbl caraway seeds (optional)

Replace the 1 cup of sour-dough starter, taken from the container in the refrigerator, with 1 cup of the prepared batter. Blend into the remaining batter 1 cup of the white flour sifted with the sugar, salt, and cocoa. In a saucepan combine the buttermilk and water, and heat to lukewarm (80 to 85 degrees). Add the butter and let it melt. Stir the mixture into the batter and add the remaining white flour and 2 cups of the rye flour until the dough becomes too stiff to work with a spoon. Turn the dough out onto a lightly floured pastry board and knead in enough of the remaining 1 to 1½ cups rye flour for 10 minutes to produce a smooth, soft (but not sticky) dough. Butter a large glass mixing bowl. Form the dough into a ball, set it in the bowl, and brush it with melted butter. Cover the bowl lightly with a cloth, set it in a warm, draft-free place, and let the dough rise for 2 hours or until it doubles in bulk. Mark the height of the dough with a strip of adhesive tape on the outside of the bowl and check the rise against that mark. Deflate the risen dough by punching it down. Transfer it to a pastry board dusted with rye flour and let it rest for a few minutes. Cut the dough into 6 equal parts and shape each into a round loaf about 2 inches high. Arrange the loaves on lightly greased baking sheets and let them rise in a warm, draft-free place for 1 hour or until they double in bulk. Preheat oven to 375 degrees.

With a very sharp knife or a razor blade, slash a cross about ⅛-inch deep in the tops of the loaves and brush them with melted butter. Bake the loaves in the preheated oven, as many at a time as can be accommodated, for 30 minutes, or until they are well browned and sound hollow when thumped. Cool the loaves on a rack.

Brioche | Brioche

1 cake fresh yeast (or 1 envelope activated dry yeast)
1 Tbl sugar
¼ cup warm water (105–115 degrees)
2 cups flour
1 tsp salt
4 eggs
¾ cup unsalted butter
1 tsp cool water

Soften the yeast, with 1 teaspoon of the sugar, in the warm water. Into a mixing bowl sift the flour with the salt and remaining sugar. Blend in 3 of the eggs and the softened yeast to produce a smooth, soft, and sticky dough. Turn the dough out onto a lightly floured pastry board and let it rest for a few minutes. In a mixing bowl work the butter with a wooden spoon until it is about the same consistency as the dough. Knead the butter into the dough, about 2 tablespoons at a time, until the mixture is firmer and springs back into shape when gently stretched. Transfer the dough to a buttered glass bowl and cover it with plastic wrap. Set the bowl in a moderately warm place, and let the dough rise for 3 hours or until it almost triples in bulk. Mark the original height of the dough with a strip of adhesive tape on the outside of the bowl, and check the rise against the mark.

Turn the dough out onto the lightly floured pastry board again and beat it with the palm of your hand into a rectangle. Fold the rectangle in thirds along the length and return it to the bowl. Chill, covered, for several hours or overnight.

Divide the dough into 12 pieces of equal size. Cut a piece about the size of 2 teaspoons from each of the 12 pieces and roll each into a small ball. Roll the large pieces also into balls. Place each large ball in a well-buttered ½-cup-capacity brioche mold or baking cup. Cut a cross into the top of each ball and set a small ball into it. Set the pans in a warm place, free from drafts, and let the molded dough rise until it doubles in bulk, about 1 hour. Preheat oven to 425 degrees.

Brush the tops of the dough with the remaining egg beaten with the cool water, and bake in the preheated oven 15 minutes, or until the brioches begin to shrink from the sides of the pans and a cake tester inserted in the centers of the brioches can be withdrawn clean. Unmold the brioches and cool them completely on a rack, or serve them slightly warm. Brioche paste can be kept under normal refrigeration for several days, to be used as needed.

Herbed Bread | Pain aux Herbes

8 Tbl butter
¼ cup finely chopped parsley
2 scallions, white and lighter green parts, finely chopped
¼ cup grated Parmesan cheese
2 Tbl sesame seeds, toasted
Salt & pepper
1 loaf Sour-Dough White Bread (page 220)
1 clove garlic, cut

In a mixing bowl soften the butter with a wooden spoon and thoroughly blend into it all ingredients except the bread and garlic, seasoning the mixture with salt and pepper to taste. Cover the bowl and let the mixture season in the refrigerator for 30 minutes.

Cut the bread into halves lengthwise and brown it lightly under a hot broiler. Rub the browned surfaces with the cut clove of garlic and spread them equally with the herb butter. Return the bread to the hot broiler and heat the halves until the butter bubbles. Serve the bread hot, cut to provide 6 to 8 servings.

Baba and Savarin Paste | Pâte à Baba et Savarin

1 cake fresh yeast (or 1 envelope activated dry yeast)
2 Tbl warm water (105–115 degrees)
2 Tbl lukewarm milk
2 Tbl sugar
¼ tsp salt
2 eggs, lightly beaten
2 cups flour
5 Tbl butter, melted & cooled

In a warm bowl soften the yeast in the warm water, and stir into it the lukewarm milk, the sugar, and the salt. Thoroughly blend in the eggs, flour, and melted butter. Beat with a wooden spoon for 5 minutes or until the paste is smooth and very elastic. Transfer it to a buttered glass bowl and cover it with a light cloth thoroughly wrung out in warm water. Set the bowl in a warm place, free from drafts, to let the dough rise for 1½ hours or until it doubles in bulk. Mark the height of the unrisen dough with a strip of adhesive tape on the outside of the bowl and check the rise against that mark. Deflate the risen dough and proceed as directed in the recipes for Rum Babas (page 247) or Savarin (page 248).

Cream Puff Paste for Hors-d'Oeuvres and Garnitures | Pâte à Choux pour Hors-d'Oeuvre et Garnitures

1 cup water
1 tsp salt
⅛ tsp white pepper
7 Tbl butter, cut into small pieces
1¼ cups sifted flour
4 eggs

In a saucepan season the water with the salt and white pepper and bring it to a boil. Add the butter and, when it melts, add the flour all at once, stirring until the resulting paste frees the sides of the pan and is formed into a ball. Remove pan from heat and thoroughly beat in the eggs, 1 at a time. Using a pastry bag, pipe the paste onto an ungreased baking sheet in the size and shape required. Bake as directed for the particular size (see recipes following through page 228).

Cream Puff Paste for Desserts | Pâte à Choux Sucrée

1 cup water
⅛ tsp salt
1 tsp sugar
7 Tbl butter, cut into small pieces
1¼ cups sifted flour
4 eggs

Proceed as for Cream Puff Paste for Hors-d'Oeuvres and Garnitures (above), adding the sugar with the salt.

How to Shape Cream Puff Paste

Tiny Puffs | Petits Choux

Using a pastry bag fitted with a ¼-inch tube, pipe onto an ungreased baking sheet mounds of the paste about ¼-inch in diameter and ¼-inch high, spacing the mounds about 1 inch apart. Bake in a preheated 375-degree oven 10 minutes, or until the mounds are well puffed, nicely browned, and crisply firm. Cool the puffs in 1 layer on a piece of cheesecloth on a rack. Use as garniture for clear soups.

Small Puffs | Profiteroles

Using a pastry bag fitted with a ½-inch tube, pipe onto an ungreased baking sheet mounds of the paste ¾-inch to 1 inch in diameter, as desired, and ½-inch high. Brush the tops with egg beaten with cool water and bake in a preheated 425-degree oven 20 minutes, or until the mounds are nicely browned, well puffed, and firm. Pierce the sides of the puffs in several places with the tines of a fork and let them remain in the oven, with the heat off and the oven door ajar, for 10 minutes longer to dry thoroughly. Cool the puffs on a rack and use as required for specific recipes. The puffs will be 1 inch to 1½ inches in diameter. The recipe provides about 3 dozen such puffs.

Large Puffs | Grands Choux

Using a pastry bag fitted with a ¾-inch tube, pipe onto an ungreased baking sheet mounds about 2 inches in diameter, rounded to a height of 1 inch at the center and spaced 2 inches apart. Brush the tops with egg beaten with cool water. Bake in a 425-degree preheated oven 20 minutes, or until the mounds have doubled in size and are lightly browned. Reduce the heat to 375 degrees and continue baking for 10 minutes longer or until the puffs are well browned and firm. Pierce the sides in several places with the tines of a fork and let the puffs remain in the oven, with the heat turned off and the oven door ajar, for 10 minutes longer to dry thoroughly. Cool the puffs on a rack, and fill as required for specific recipes. One dozen puffs are provided.

Éclairs | Éclairs

Using a pastry bag fitted with a ½-inch flat tube, pipe the paste onto an ungreased baking sheet in 3-inch lengths, 1 inch wide and ¾-inch high, spacing them 2 inches apart. Bake as for Large Puffs. Cool on a rack and use as required. This recipe provides about 1 dozen éclairs.

Cream Puff Ring | Couronne de Pâte à Choux

Using a pastry bag fitted with a very large tube, pipe the paste onto an ungreased baking sheet in a ring 7 inches in diameter, with the ring itself 1¼ inches wide and 1 inch high. Brush the top with egg beaten with cool water. Bake in a preheated 375-degree oven 45 minutes, or until the ring is puffed to twice its original size and is well browned and firm. Pierce the sides in several places with the tines of a fork and let it remain in the oven, with the heat off and the oven door ajar, for 10 minutes longer to dry out. Cool the ring on a rack and use as required for specific recipes.

Puff Pastry | Pâte Feuilletée

4 cups flour
2 tsp salt
1 pound firm unsalted butter (4 sticks)
1¼ cups ice-cold water (approximate)

Into a mixing bowl sift the flour with the salt. Remove and reserve ½ cup of it. Into the remainder blend ¼ pound of the butter (1 stick) to produce a mixture the texture of coarse meal. Beat in just enough of the water to produce a dough that is firm but pliable. Form the dough into a brick shape, wrap it in waxed paper, and chill it in the refrigerator for 30 minutes.

In another mixing bowl work the reserved flour into the remaining butter, chopping it in with a wooden spoon. Knead it quickly on a lightly floured board until the flour is completely incorporated and the mixture is smooth. The butter must remain as firm as possible. Shape it into a square about 1 inch thick.

On a lightly floured pastry board roll the chilled dough into a round about 10 inches in diameter. Place the brick of butter in the center and fold the dough over it, enclosing it completely. Secure the edges by pressing them together. Dust the dough with flour and roll it into a rectangle about ½-inch thick and twice as long as it is wide. Fold ⅓ of the length in toward the center and fold the opposite end over it to produce 3 layers.

Roll the dough across the folds, again into a rectangle ½-inch thick and twice as long as it is wide. Fold it into thirds as before. Wrap the dough in waxed paper and in foil, and chill it for 30 minutes.

Roll the dough again across the folds into a rectangle ½-inch thick and twice as long as it is wide. Fold into thirds, and roll and fold again. Wrap and chill for another 30 minutes.

Roll, fold, and roll the dough as before. Fold it once more, wrap it, and chill it for at least 2 hours until it is needed. Roll, shape, and bake as required for specific recipes. Puff pastry may be kept under normal refrigeration for a week or so. Frozen and stored in the freezer, it will keep for several months.

How to Shape Puff Pastry

Large Patty Shells | Vol-au-Vent

Puff Pastry (page 229)
1 egg
1 tsp cool water

Roll chilled puff pastry into a rectangle slightly thicker than ½-inch and, using a salad plate as a pattern, cut from the dough 2 rounds, each about 8 inches in diameter. Reserve all trimmings. Cut a round 5 inches in diameter from the center of 1 of the large rounds, leaving a ring 1½ inches wide. Set the small round aside in the refrigerator for the moment. Score a 5-inch circle ¼-inch deep in the center of the second round, taking care not to cut through the round. Brush the border of that round with cold water and fit the 1½-inch ring over it. Press it gently to secure it. Rinse a baking sheet in ice-cold water and leave it damp. Place the shell on the sheet and chill it so in the refrigerator for 1 hour. Preheat oven to 425 degrees.

Remove the baking sheet from the refrigerator and with a skewer or a sharply pointed knife pierce down through the 2 layers of pastry at 2-inch intervals all around the ring. Pierce the lower round in several places also. Brush the top of the ring with the egg beaten with the cool water, taking care not to let any dribble over the sides of the shell, which will prevent the shell from rising properly. Bake in the preheated oven for 20 minutes, or until the shell almost triples in height and begins to brown. Reduce the heat to 350 degrees. Slide a second chilled baking sheet under the one in the oven, to prevent the shell from burning, and continue the baking for 30 minutes longer or until the shell is well browned and crisp. If it browns too quickly, lay a sheet of foil lightly over the top.

Remove the baking sheets from the oven and scoop out any unbaked pastry from the center of the shell. Return the shell on the baking sheet to the oven and let it remain, with the oven heat off and the door ajar, for a few minutes until the center of the shell dries. Cool the shell on a rack and fill as directed for specific recipes or as desired.

The reserved round in the refrigerator may be baked as a cover for the patty shell. Roll the round to a diameter of 8 inches. Decorate the top with shapes cut from the pastry trimmings, securing them with some of the beaten egg. Place the cover on a chilled baking sheet and chill it so for 1 hour. Brush the top with the beaten egg and bake it in a preheated 425-degree oven for 20 minutes and at 350 degrees for 10 minutes longer, or until the disk is well puffed and nicely browned. The filled shell will provide 6 servings.

Individual Patty Shells | Bouchées

Puff Pastry (page 229)
1 egg
1 tsp cool water

These smaller shells, for individual servings, are made in the same way as the larger sizes, but are served without covers. Roll the dough ¼-inch thick and cut from it 16 rounds each 3½ inches in diameter. From the center of 8 of those rounds cut a small round 2 inches in diameter, leaving rings ¾-inch wide. Assemble the shells as for the larger size (see instructions in preceding recipe).

Arrange the 8 shells on a baking sheet rinsed in ice-cold water and still damp, and chill them so in the refrigerator for 30 minutes. Preheat oven to 425 degrees. Brush the tops of the shells with the egg beaten with the cool water and bake in the preheated oven 20 minutes, or until the shells are well puffed, nicely browned, and crisp. Remove the baking sheet from the oven and turn off the heat. Scoop out any unbaked centers from the shells and return the shells to the slackening oven for a few minutes to dry out the centers. Fill as directed in specific recipes or as desired.

Puff Pastry for Napoleons | Pâte pour Mille-Feuilles

Puff Pastry (page 229)
1 egg
1 tsp cool water

Roll the chilled pastry into sheets ⅛-inch thick. Trim the edges of the dough and cut it into equal-length strips 2 inches wide. Arrange the strips well separated on 1 or 2 baking sheets and chill them so in the refrigerator for 30 minutes. Prick them at close intervals with the tines of a fork. Preheat oven to 425 degrees.

Brush the strips with the egg beaten with the water and bake in the preheated oven 20 minutes or until the strips are well browned and crisp. Place a cool baking sheet on top of the strips to keep them from

curling and let them cool on the sheets on which they baked. This recipe provides sufficient puff pastry strips for 10 to 12 Napoleons each 2 inches wide and 3 inches long.

Miniature Patty Shells | Petites Bouchées

Puff Pastry Trimmings (see Note of following recipe)
1 egg
1 tsp cool water

These tiny shells are made from a single thickness of the pastry. Roll the dough ¼-inch thick and cut from it as many rounds, each 1½ inches in diameter, as required. With a 1-inch cookie cutter press down to make a circle ⅛-inch deep in the center of each round. Arrange the rounds on a chilled baking sheet and chill them in the refrigerator for 30 minutes. Preheat oven to 425 degrees.

Brush the tops of the rounds with the egg beaten with the cool water and bake in the preheated oven 10 minutes, or until the shells are well puffed, brown, and crisp. Scoop out any unbaked centers and return the shells to the oven, with the heat off and the oven door ajar, to dry the centers. Fill as directed for specific recipes or as desired. Reheat briefly before serving as cocktail snacks.

Puff Pastry Garnitures | Fleurons

Puff Pastry Trimmings (see Note)
1 egg
1 tsp cool water

Roll the dough ¼-inch thick and cut from it a variety of shapes as required: rounds 1½ inches in diameter, crescents, ovals—fluted or plain edged. Bake as for Miniature Patty Shells (above) and use as garnish for serving platters and individual portions of, particularly, fish and creamed preparations.

NOTE: There are always great quantities of puff pastry scraps and these can and should be salvaged. The trick is to recombine them so that the layers run in the same direction as they were when the dough was rolled and cut into shapes. However, even if that is not possible, the trimmings will still provide adequate pastry. Press them lightly together, roll them into a rectangle, and spread it with a little soft butter. Fold the rectangle in thirds; chill, roll, and fold twice more; and wrap and refrigerate until needed.

Croissants | Croissants

1 cake fresh yeast (or 1 envelope activated dry yeast)
¼ cup warm water (105–115 degrees)
2½ tsp sugar
½ tsp salt
¾ cup lukewarm milk (80–85 degrees)
½ cup firm unsalted butter
2 cups flour
1 egg
1 tsp cool water

Soften the yeast in the water and stir in 1 teaspoon of the sugar. Dissolve the remaining sugar and the salt in the lukewarm milk. Melt 2 tablespoons of the butter and let cool to lukewarm. Sift the flour into a glass mixing bowl and blend in the softened yeast, the milk mixture, and the 2 tablespoons of butter. Beat lightly with a wooden spoon 6 to 8 strokes or just until the dough is smooth and slightly resilient. Do not overbeat or the dough will be difficult to roll. Cover the bowl lightly with a cloth and set it in a warm place, free from drafts, to let the dough rise for 2 hours or until it triples in bulk. Mark the original height of the dough with a strip of adhesive tape on the outside of the bowl and check the rise against that mark. Deflate the risen dough by pressing it down. Turn it out onto a lightly floured pastry board and let it rest for a few minutes. Roll it into a rectangle about ½-inch thick and twice as long as it is wide. Soften the remaining butter just enough to make it pliable and, beginning at 1 end of the dough spread it to cover ⅔ of the rectangle, leaving a ¼-inch border around the edges. Fold the unbuttered ⅓ of the rectangle in toward the center and fold the opposite end over it to produce 3 layers. Roll the dough across the folds again into a rectangle ½-inch thick and twice as long as it is wide. Again fold ⅓ in toward the center and fold the opposite ⅓ over it. Dust the dough with flour, wrap it in a double thickness of waxed paper and chill it in the refrigerator for several hours or overnight.

Unwrap the dough and deflate it. Divide it into halves and roll each into a round ¼-inch thick and 10 inches in diameter. Cut each round into 6 pie-shaped wedges of equal size. Beginning at the rounded edge, roll each of the 12 wedges to the point. Do not roll too tightly. Bend the rolls inward slightly to form crescents with the points inside the curves. Arrange the crescents on a baking sheet, cover them lightly with a cloth, and let them rise in a warm place, free from drafts, for 1 hour or until they almost double in size. Preheat oven to 450 degrees.

Brush the crescents with the egg beaten with the teaspoon of cool water and bake in the preheated oven 5 minutes. Reduce heat to 400 degrees and continue the baking 10 minutes or until the crescents are golden brown. Cool them on a rack. Serve them slightly warm.

Flaky Pastry | Demi-Feuilletée

2 cups flour
½ tsp salt
8 Tbl butter
3 Tbl ice-cold water
¼ tsp lemon juice

Sift the flour and salt together into a mixing bowl and work in the butter to the size of large peas. Combine the water and lemon juice, and blend just enough of the mixture into the flour to produce firm but pliable dough. Shape it into a ball, wrap it in waxed paper, and chill it for 15 minutes.

Roll the dough on a lightly floured pastry board into a rectangle 1 inch thick. With your thumb mark off the rectangle into thirds along the length. Fold an end third over the middle third. Fold the opposite third over the first, making 3 layers of the dough. Roll the dough across the folds into a rectangle ¾-inch thick. Fold as before into thirds. Wrap the folded dough in waxed paper and chill it for 15 minutes.

Roll, fold, and roll the dough again, reducing the thickness of the rectangle to ½-inch. Fold it into thirds, wrap it in waxed paper, and chill it again for 15 minutes.

Once again roll, fold, and roll the dough, reducing the thickness of the rectangle this time to ¼-inch. Fold as before. Wrap the dough and chill it for 1 hour before using it as directed in specific recipes.

Short Plain Pastry | Pâte Brisée

1½ cups flour
¼ tsp salt
5 Tbl butter
1 Tbl vegetable shortening
2 Tbl ice-cold water, or more as needed

Into a mixing bowl sift the flour with the salt. Quickly but thoroughly rub into it the butter and shortening combined, and blend in only enough water to produce a dough that will just hold together and is not sticky. Set the dough on a lightly floured pastry board and with the outer side of your hand press the dough forward in one sweeping motion to form a strip about 8 inches long. This is the French method of making certain that the flour and fat are properly combined. Form the dough into a ball, wrap it in waxed paper, and chill it for 30 minutes in the refrigerator (not in the freezing compartment). Quickly roll the dough to a thickness of about ⅛-inch and of a size to fit a 9-inch pan about 1½ inches deep, allowing for an overhang about ½-inch all around. Use as required for specific recipes.

Short Sweet Pastry | Pâte Brisée Sucrée

Add 1 tablespoon sugar to the ingredients of Short Plain Pastry (above), sifting it into the mixing bowl along with the flour and salt. Prepare exactly as for the plain short pastry. This pastry is used principally for dessert tarts. Rolled out to a thickness of ⅛-inch the paste is sufficient for a 9-inch tart shell about 1½ inches deep with an overhang of about ½-inch all around to provide a plain or decorative edge.

Beer Batter | Pâte à la Bière

1 cup flour
½ tsp baking powder
½ tsp salt
1 egg
⅔ cup light beer, or more as needed

In a mixing bowl sift together the flour, baking powder, and salt. Blend in the egg, well beaten, and the beer to produce a batter the consistency of frothily whipped cream. Add more beer, if needed. Use for coating fish, shellfish, or vegetables to be deep fried.

When series of precise—but not difficult—steps is followed, crusty Sour-Dough White Bread (page 220) is the reward.

et dough rise until it doubles.

2. Deflate dough by punching it.

3. Reshape, let rise, deflate again.

4. Turn it out onto floured board.

Pat dough into rectangle.

6. Fold rectangle in half.

7. Press gently to secure seam.

8. Pat, fold, and seal again.

. Cut dough into 6 pieces.

10. Roll each piece into a rope.

11. Fit each rope into buttered mold.

12. Let rise in molds.

vert loaves onto baking sheets.

14. Slash the loaves.

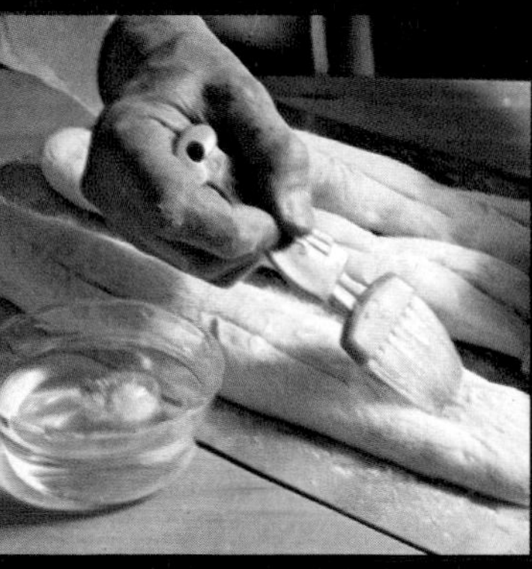

15. Brush them with cold water.

16. Baked bread is golden brown.

Quick Beer Batter | Pâte à la Bière

1 cup flour
½ tsp salt
⅔ cup beer

In a mixing bowl beat all ingredients with a rotary beater until smooth. This batter makes for a light and very crisp coating. Use for marinated or partially cooked fish, shellfish, or vegetables to be deep fried.

French Pancakes | Crêpes

2 whole eggs
2 eggs yolks
1½ cups milk
⅓ cup cool water
3 Tbl cognac
2 Tbl bland cooking oil
1 cup sifted flour
½ tsp salt
Additional milk
Additional cool water

In a mixing bowl combine the eggs, yolks, milk, water, cognac, and cooking oil. Add the flour and salt, and beat the mixture until it is completely smooth. Chill it for at least 1 hour. The batter will thicken somewhat as it chills. Before using it, thin it with equal quantities of additional milk and water to the consistency of light cream.

Heat a 7-inch crêpe pan or skillet and grease it very lightly with butter. Pour in ¼ cup of the batter and tilt the pan immediately, swirling the batter evenly over the bottom. Cook the crêpe over moderate heat, browning it lightly on both sides. Proceed in the same way with the remaining batter. This recipe provides 18 crêpes for 6 servings for main-course preparations to be filled as directed in specific recipes.

Cooled and separated with sheets of waxed paper, crêpes will keep under normal refrigeration for 2 weeks or longer. Frozen and stored in the freezer they will keep for 2 months.

Dessert French Pancakes | Crêpes Sucrées

Add 1 tablespoon sugar to the ingredients for French Pancakes (above), and combine and cook as directed in the recipe. Use as required in specific recipes.

Perfect companions at table
or *al fresco:* bread
and wine, fruit and cheese.

8 | desserts

The best any dictionary of cookery seems able to do for dessert is to describe it as the last course of a meal. One such lexicon dismisses dessert by calling it the remains of a meal. Webster manages "a course of fruit, pastry, pudding, ice cream, or cheese served at the close of the meal," but even that is insufficient homage to the greatest of all the riches of cookery. No other course can compare with it. Desserts are the most delicate, the most beautiful, the most romantic, the most exciting, the most inventive, the most tempting, and the most satisfying of all the delicacies of the table.

France is largely responsible for the greatness of desserts. They came from all parts of the world to receive the refinement that is the French touch. Creams came from Bavaria and England, and confections made their way from Greece and Turkey. Meringues crossed the border from Italy, and almonds crossed over from Spain.

The recipes which follow are in the tradition of France. Others, created in homes here, reflect the French influence, despite necessary substitutions of ingredients and simplified methods of preparation.

Almond Meringue Layer Cake | Gâteau Dacquoise

3 eggs, separated
1/8 tsp cream of tartar
Few grains salt
1 cup fine granulated sugar
1 tsp vanilla extract
1/2 cup finely ground blanched almonds
3 Tbl cornstarch
1/2 cup milk, scalded
1/2 ounce (1/2 square) unsweetened chocolate, melted & cooled
1/4 tsp powdered coffee
1 tsp hot water
3/4 cup unsalted butter, softened
1/8 tsp almond extract
1 cup toasted blanched almonds, finely crushed

In a mixing bowl beat together the egg whites, cream of tartar, and salt, until the whites begin to stiffen. Add 1/2 cup of the sugar, 1 tablespoon at a time, continuing to beat until the meringue is completely smooth and very thick. Beat in the vanilla. Combine the ground almonds, cornstarch, and 1/4 cup of the sugar, and fold the mixture carefully, but thoroughly, into the meringue.

Preheat oven to 250 degrees. Butter and flour a baking sheet and trace in the flour 2 rounds, each 8 inches in diameter. Using a pastry bag fitted with a large plain tube, pipe 1/2 the meringue in a spiral over each of the rounds, covering them completely. Smooth the tops with a spatula. Bake in the preheated oven 30 minutes, or until the meringues are crisp to the touch and can be easily dislodged from their positions on the baking sheet. Remove the rounds carefully with a spatula to a rack, and let them cool.

In the top pan of a double-boiler beat the egg yolks with the remaining sugar until the mixture is thick and lemon-colored. Blend in the hot milk, a little at a time. Set pan over, but not touching, barely simmering water and cook, stirring constantly, until the custard is thick enough to coat the spoon thickly. Remove pan from over water and thoroughly blend in the melted chocolate, the powdered coffee dissolved in the hot water, the softened butter, and the almond flavoring. Reserve 1/2 of this butter cream and spread the remainder evenly over 1 of the cooled meringue layers. Fit the second layer over it and coat the entire cake with the reserved butter cream. Sprinkle the top of the cake with part of the crushed toasted almonds and press the remainder into the sides. Chill the cake for at least 2 hours before cutting it into wedges to provide 6 servings.

Apricot Confection Bars | Calissons d'Aix

2 Tbl butter
3 cups fine granulated sugar
1 egg, beaten
¼ cup sifted cake flour
3 cups almonds
3 cups apricot purée (see Note)
1 egg white
1 cup confectioners' sugar
¼ tsp almond extract

Preheat oven to 425 degrees. In a mixing bowl thoroughly cream the butter with 2 tablespoons of the sugar. Blend in 2 tablespoons only of the beaten egg. Reserve the remainder. Gently, but thoroughly, stir in the flour. Lightly butter and flour the bottom of a shallow 10 x 15-inch baking pan and spread the batter evenly over it. Bake in the preheated oven 6 minutes or just until the edges of the pastry begin to brown. Remove pan from oven and let the tissue-thin pastry cool in the pan. Reduce oven heat to 300 degrees.

Roll the almonds into a powder with a rolling pin, or pulverize them in an electric blender. Combine them in a saucepan with the apricot purée and the remaining sugar. Set pan over very low heat and cook, stirring constantly, until the mixture is firm enough to hold a shape but still spreadable. Remove pan from heat and beat into the mixture the reserved portion of beaten egg. Spread the paste smoothly over the pastry in the baking pan.

Beat the egg white into soft peaks. Add the confectioners' sugar, a little at a time, continuing to beat until the mixture is very thick. Stir in the almond flavoring and spread the mixture evenly over the almond

apricot paste. Set the pan in the newly preheated oven and let it remain for 5 minutes or until the glaze is set. Cool the cake and cut it into 24 bars, each about 2 inches by 3 inches.

NOTE: This quantity of apricot purée is derived by forcing 24 large, peeled and pitted cooked apricots through a fine sieve or by reducing them to a purée in an electric blender.

Little Chocolate Cakes | Délices de Divonne

4 ounces (4 squares) unsweetened chocolate
½ cup sugar
2 Tbl flour
6 Tbl butter, softened
3 eggs, separated
3 ounces (3 squares) semisweet chocolate, melted
3 Tbl cognac

Preheat oven to 350 degrees. Melt the unsweetened chocolate in a saucepan over simmering water. Let it cool slightly and combine it in a mixing bowl with the sugar, flour, softened butter, and the egg yolks, beaten. Fold in the egg whites, beaten until stiff but not dry.

Pour the batter into sets of cupcake pans with cups 1½ inches in diameter, filling the cups to ⅔ their capacity. Bake in the preheated oven 12 minutes. Partially cool the cakes in the pans and remove them to a rack to complete the cooling. The centers of the cakes will be slightly underdone when the cakes are removed from the oven. That is as they should be. They will become firm as they cool. When they are completely cool, coat them with the melted semisweet chocolate blended with the cognac. This recipe provides about 2½ dozen little cakes.

Chocolate Leaves | Feuilles au Chocolat

4 Tbl butter
4 Tbl sugar
1 egg
⅓ cup finely ground almonds
¼ tsp rum
¾ cup flour, sifted
6 ounces (6 squares) semisweet chocolate, melted

Preheat oven to 300 degrees. In a mixing bowl thoroughly cream together the butter and sugar. Beat in the egg and blend in the almonds and rum. Lightly but thoroughly stir in the flour.

Press the batter into leaf shapes through a leaf stencil onto a lightly buttered and floured baking sheet (see Note). Bake in the preheated oven 6 minutes or just until the edges of the leaves are lightly browned. Remove the cookies immediately and cool them on a rack. Invert the cookies so that the smooth sides are upright and brush them with the melted chocolate, coating them well. Before the chocolate sets, trace lines in the coating with a pointed knife to simulate the veins of a leaf. This recipe provides about 5 dozen small leaf cookies. NOTE: Metal leaf stencils of various sizes are available in shops specializing in kitchenwares.

Jelly Roll | Roulade à la Confiture de Groseilles

3 eggs, separated
6 Tbl sugar
½ cup sifted flour
1 Tbl additional sugar
¾ cup red currant jelly

Preheat oven to 375 degrees. In a mixing bowl beat the egg whites into soft peaks. Add 3 tablespoons of the sugar, a tablespoon at a time, continuing to beat until the whites are stiff and glossy. In a separate bowl beat the yolks with the remaining sugar until they are thick, and stir into them 2 tablespoons of the flour. Fold in ¼ of the egg whites. Fold in the remaining flour, 2 tablespoons at a time, alternating those additions with thirds of the remaining beaten egg whites.

Butter an 8 x 12-inch baking pan, cover the bottom with waxed paper, and butter the paper. Spread the prepared batter evenly in the pan and bake it in the preheated oven 10 minutes or until the cake begins to shrink from the sides of the pan. Sprinkle a sheet of waxed paper with the additional sugar and invert the sponge cake onto it. Peel off the baking paper. Spread the cake with the jelly and using the under paper as a guide, roll it across the width for a slender roll or down the length for a thicker one. This jelly roll provides 8 to 12 slices, depending upon the thickness of the roll.

Sheet Sponge Cake | Feuille de Biscuit de Savoie

2 eggs, separated	**¼ tsp vanilla extract**
2 Tbl sugar	**½ cup cake flour, sifted**

Preheat oven to 375 degrees. In a mixing bowl beat the egg whites into soft peaks. Add the sugar a little at a time, continuing to beat until the whites are stiff and glossy. Beat in the vanilla. In another bowl beat the egg yolks until they are thick, and fold them into the whites, a part at a time, alternately with similar additions of the flour.

Butter an 8 x 12-inch baking pan, cover the bottom with waxed paper, and butter the paper. Spread the prepared batter in the pan and bake it in the preheated oven 10 minutes or until the cake begins to shrink from the sides of the pan. Invert the cake onto a rack to cool. Peel off the baking paper. Cut the cake into small squares and serve with berries or other fruit, custards, or ice cream.

Rum Babas | Babas au Rhum

Baba and Savarin Paste (page 225)
1½ cups water
1 cup sugar
Juice of 1 lemon, strained
⅔ cup full-bodied rum
½ cup Apricot Glaze (page 274)
6 glazed cherries, halved
Thin slice candied angelica, about 2 inches square (see Glossary)

Prepare the paste and let it rise as directed in the recipe. Deflate it and divide it into 12 equal parts. Roll them between the palms of your hands into balls. Thoroughly butter 12 individual baba molds, each 2 inches high and 2 inches in diameter, and place a ball of dough in each. The dough should fill each mold to only ⅓ its capacity. Set the molds in a warm place, free from drafts, cover them lightly with a cloth, and let the dough rise to ¼-inch above the rims of the molds. This will take about 45·minutes. Preheat oven to 375 degrees.

Set the filled molds on a cookie sheet in the preheated oven and bake 12 minutes, or until the tops are nicely browned and a cake tester inserted in the center of each cake can be withdrawn clean. Unmold the babas onto a cake rack and let them cool until they are slightly warm.

In a saucepan heat together the water, sugar, and lemon juice, stirring only until the sugar dissolves. Cook at simmer for 2 minutes. Remove pan from heat and stir in the rum. Cool to lukewarm. Transfer the slightly warm babas to a deep platter that can accommodate them in a single layer. Pour the lukewarm syrup over them and let them absorb it for 30 minutes, turning them frequently so that they become evenly saturated. Drain the babas on a rack set over a baking pan. Brush them with the apricot glaze and arrange them upright in a serving dish. Decorate the tops with the halves of glazed cherries and small leaves cut from the slice of angelica. Serve, if desired, with slightly sweetened whipped cream flavored with a little rum.

Savarin | Savarin

Baba and Savarin Paste (page 225)
1½ cups water
1 cup sugar
⅔ cup kirsch
½ cup Apricot Glaze (page 274)
Glazed fruits
Toasted blanched almonds
1 cup Custard Cream (page 257)
½ cup heavy cream, whipped

Prepare the paste and let it rise as directed in the recipe. Deflate it and divide it into 12 equal parts. Roll the pieces of dough between the palms of your hands into balls and press them gently, one touching the other, around the bottom of a well-buttered 5-cup-capacity savarin or ring mold (see Note). Cover the mold lightly with a cloth wrung out in warm water. Set it in a warm place, free from drafts, and let the dough rise for about 1 hour, or until it reaches the rim of the mold. Preheat oven to 375 degrees.

Bake in the preheated oven 30 minutes, or until the savarin is well browned and a cake tester inserted in the center can be withdrawn clean. If the top shows signs of browning too quickly, cover it lightly with buttered foil. When the baking is completed, remove pan from oven and let the savarin rest for 5 minutes, by which time it will have shrunk somewhat from the sides of the mold. Unmold the cake onto a rack and let it cool to just slightly warm.

In a saucepan cook together the water and sugar at simmer for 2 minutes, stirring just until the sugar dissolves. Remove pan from heat, add the kirsch, and let the syrup cool to lukewarm. Fit the ring mold back over the slightly warm savarin, and invert the rack and mold together, thereby returning the savarin to its baking position in the mold. Reserve 2 tablespoons of the kirsch syrup and pour ½ of the remainder over the savarin. After 10 minutes pour the second ½ and let the cake absorb it for 15 minutes. Drain off any remaining syrup.

Unmold the savarin again, onto the rack over a baking pan, and let it drain. Brush it with the apricot glaze, and decorate the top with glazed fruits and toasted blanched almonds. Fill the center with the custard cream flavored with the reserved 2 tablespoons kirsch syrup and combined with the whipped cream. This recipe provides 8 generous servings.

NOTE: Molds of either ¼-cup or ½-cup capacity may be used to provide respectively about 24 or 12 individual savarins. Bake the smaller savarins about 12 minutes and the larger ones about 18 minutes in a preheated 375-degree oven.

Napoleons | Mille-Feuilles

Puff Pastry for Napoleons (page 232)
Apricot Glaze (page 274)
4 cups Pastry Cream (page 274), well chilled
Confectioners' sugar

Prepare the pastry strips as directed in the recipe and brush them lightly, on 1 side only, with the apricot glaze. Arrange them in sets of 3 strips each, interspersing the strips with layers of pastry cream. Chill well. Sift confectioners' sugar over the tops and cut each set of mounded strips into 3-inch lengths to provide 10 to 12 servings.

The napoleons may alternately be filled with 4 cups each of either pastry cream blended with 3 squares (3 ounces) melted semisweet

chocolate, or Chantilly Cream (page 274), plain or combined with ½ cup Praline Powder (page 273) or pulverized almonds.

Cheese Mousse Tart | Tarte Zéphirienne

12 Tbl butter (1½ sticks)
14 Tbl sugar
⅛ tsp salt
2 tsp vanilla extract
2 cups sifted all-purpose flour
1 whole egg, beaten
3 Tbl cake flour (approximate)
2 cups (1 pound) cream cheese
3 eggs, separated
1 tsp grated lemon rind
⅛ tsp lemon juice
2 envelopes (2 Tbl) unflavored gelatine
⅓ cup cool water
¾ cup heavy cream, whipped
Additional butter
Additional all-purpose flour

Prepare a bottom crust by creaming together in a mixing bowl until light and fluffy 10 tablespoons (1¼ sticks) of the butter, 3 tablespoons of the sugar, and the salt. Stir in 1½ teaspoons of the vanilla and the all-purpose flour. Pat the dough evenly in the bottom of a shallow 8 x 12-inch baking pan and chill it in the refrigerator for 30 minutes. Preheat oven to 350 degrees, and bake the crust in it for 8 minutes or until the pastry is lightly browned.

In a small mixing bowl cream the remaining butter with 2 tablespoons of the sugar. Blend in 2 tablespoons only of the beaten whole egg and stir in just enough of the cake flour to produce a batter that can be thinly spread without running. Set the batter aside for the moment.

In another mixing bowl cream the cheese with 5 tablespoons of the sugar. Beat in the 3 egg yolks and the remaining beaten whole egg along with the remaining vanilla, the grated lemon rind, and lemon juice. Soften the gelatine in the water in the top pan of a double-boiler. Set pan over simmering water and let the gelatine dissolve. Blend it into the cheese mixture. In a separate bowl beat the 3 egg whites into soft peaks. Add the remaining sugar, a little at a time, continuing to beat until the whites are stiff and glossy. Fold them into the whipped cream, and fold that into the cheese mixture. Spread this filling evenly over the cooled crust in the baking pan and chill it in the refrigerator until it is set.

Preheat oven to 425 degrees. Invert a second 8 x 12-inch baking pan and butter and lightly flour the bottom (the outside, that is). Spread that surface very, very thinly with as much of the prepared cake flour batter as needed. The coating should be less than 1/16-inch thick. Bake it in the preheated oven (coated side of the pan up) for 6 minutes or until the pastry is lightly and evenly browned. Remove pan from oven and very carefully loosen the sheet of pastry by sliding a long metal spatula under it. Slide the pastry onto the set cheese filling in the baking pan. Chill again, briefly. Cut the tart, in the pan, lengthwise into 3 strips of equal width. Cut the strips into 4 equal-size pieces to provide 12 squares.

Fruit and Nut Tartlets | Tartelettes aux Fruits et aux Noix

1 cup sifted flour
⅛ tsp salt
4 Tbl unsalted butter
½ cup Almond Paste (page 273 or see Note)
2 egg yolks
1½ tsp cornstarch
⅓ cup milk
2 Tbl sugar
⅛ tsp vanilla extract
1 cup Praline Powder (page 273)
2 squares (2 ounces) semisweet chocolate, melted
Assorted small fruit (cherries, grapes, strawberries, blueberries, banana slices, etc.)
Walnut halves
⅓ cup Apricot Glaze (page 274)

Sift the flour and salt into a mixing bowl. Work in the butter to produce a mixture resembling coarse cornmeal. Blend in the almond paste and 1 egg yolk. Form the dough into a ball, wrap it in waxed paper, and chill it in the refrigerator for 1 hour.

In the top pan of a double-boiler dissolve the cornstarch in the milk. Add the sugar and beat in the remaining egg yolk. Cook over barely simmering water, stirring constantly until the mixture thickens. Remove pan from over water and stir in the vanilla. Let this pastry cream cool completely.

On a lightly floured pastry board roll out the chilled dough slightly less than ¼-inch thick, and cut from it rounds about 2 inches in diameter. Fit the rounds into very small fluted pans 1½ inches in diameter and ½-inch deep (see Note). Prick the bottoms of the shells with the tines of a fork. Set the pans on a baking sheet and chill them so in the refrigerator for 30 minutes. Preheat oven to 350 degrees. Bake the chilled tartlet shells in the preheated oven, in the pans on the baking sheet, for 10 minutes or until they are light golden in color. Remove them from the oven and let them cool for 5 minutes before removing them from the pans. Cool completely.

In a small bowl combine the praline powder and melted chocolate. Spread each pastry shell with ¼ teaspoon of the mixture and cover with ¼ teaspoon of the pastry cream. Set fruit and walnut halves in the cream and brush them with apricot glaze. This recipe provides sufficient pastry, chocolate praline paste, pastry cream, and apricot glaze for about 4 dozen tartlets. (*See photograph, page 256.*)

NOTE: Commercial almond paste is available in specialty food shops. Small fluted tartlet pans are available in stores specializing in housewares.

Strawberry Flutes | Flutes aux Fraises

1 egg
⅓ cup sugar
3 drops almond extract
5 Tbl butter, melted & cooled
½ cup sifted flour
½ cup ripe strawberries
1 cup heavy cream
¼ cup confectioners' sugar
8 small whole ripe strawberries

Preheat oven to 450 degrees. In a mixing bowl combine the egg, sugar, and almond flavoring, and beat the mixture until it is light in color and very thick. Add the melted butter gradually, and thoroughly stir in the sifted flour. On a well-buttered baking sheet arrange 4 mounds of the batter of 1 tablespoon each, widely separated. With a metal spatula or the back of a spoon spread the mounds into rounds about 5 inches in diameter. Bake them in the preheated oven 5 minutes or just until the edges begin to brown. Remove pan from oven, loosen the wafers with a metal spatula, and roll them while they are still warm and flexible

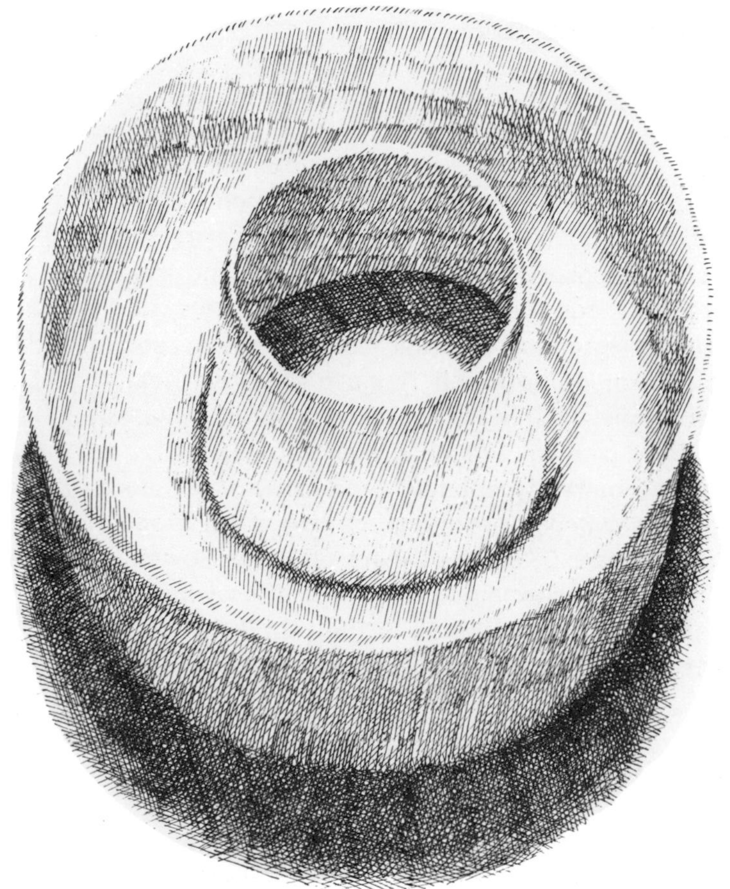

into tubes about 1 inch in diameter. If the wafers become too crisp to roll (they become crisp as they cool), return pan to oven and let them warm through for a moment. Bake and roll the remaining batter in the same way.

Wash and hull the ½ cup of strawberries and mash them. Stiffly beat the cream with the confectioners' sugar, and fold in the mashed berries. Pipe the cream into the cooled flutes, using a pastry bag fitted with a large plain tube. Place a small whole strawberry in the top. This recipe provides 8 flutes.

Brasserie Fritters | Beignets Brasserie

¾ cup water
½ tsp salt
2 Tbl sugar
½ cup unsalted butter
1 cup flour
4 eggs
Bland cooking oil for deep frying
Jam or marmalade
Cinnamon
Confectioners' sugar

In a saucepan season the water with the salt and sugar, and bring the liquid to a boil. Add the butter and, when it melts, add the flour all at once, beating vigorously until the resulting paste frees the sides of the pan and is formed into a ball. Remove pan from heat and beat in the eggs, 1 at a time. Chill in the refrigerator for 30 minutes.

In a fryer or deep saucepan heat cooking oil for deep frying and in it cook the batter by spoonfuls, as many at a time as the pan can accommodate without crowding, turning them frequently until they are golden brown. Drain the fritters on paper toweling, slit them, fill them with jam or marmalade, and dust them with the cinnamon and confectioners' sugar combined in the proportion of 1 part cinnamon to 4 parts of sugar. Serve hot. This recipe provides 18 large fritters.

Orange Pancakes | Crêpes à l'Orange

¼ cup sugar
2 Tbl butter
Juice of 2 oranges, strained
Juice of 1 lemon, strained
1 tsp finely grated orange rind
¼ cup orange-flavored liqueur (Grand Marnier, Cointreau, Curaçao, or such)
18 Dessert French Pancakes (page 239)
1 additional teaspoon sugar
¼ cup cognac

In a chafing-dish pan over moderate heat of the burner caramelize the sugar in the butter. Heat the orange and lemon juices, and blend them into the caramel, stirring until it dissolves. Add the orange rind and the liqueur, and continue cooking until the mixture is syrupy.

Fold the prepared pancakes into quarters and arrange them, overlapping slightly, in the sauce. Moisten them with a little of the sauce,

Fruit, nuts, chocolate, and Chantilly cream lend character to a variety of dessert pastries.

and sprinkle them with the additional sugar. Pour the cognac over them and set the spirit ablaze. Baste the pancakes with the sauce until the flame expires. Serve the pancakes hot, apportioned for 6 servings, with the sauce poured over them.

Custard Cream | Crème

4 egg yolks
½ cup sugar
1 tsp cornstarch
Few grains salt
2 cups milk, scalded
1 tsp vanilla extract

In the top pan of a double-boiler beat the egg yolks with the sugar, cornstarch, and salt until they are well blended. Add the hot milk, stirring it in gradually. Set pan over simmering water and cook, stirring constantly, until the mixture thickens sufficiently to coat the spoon lightly. Remove pan from over water and stir in vanilla. Let the custard cream cool. Flavor it as required in specific recipes.

Bavarian Cream | Bavarois à la Crème

Custard Cream (above)
1 envelope (1 Tbl) unflavored gelatine
¼ cup cool water
Flavoring (see Note)
2 egg whites
1 cup heavy cream, whipped

Prepare the custard cream as directed in the recipe and, while it is still hot, dissolve in it the gelatine softened in the water. Blend in the desired flavoring. Let the cream cool completely. Beat the egg whites until they are stiff but not dry and fold the egg whites and the whipped cream into the cool cream. Rinse a 6-cup mold in ice-cold water, drain it, and pour in the prepared cream. Chill in the refrigerator for 2 hours or until the cream is set. Unmold it onto a chilled serving platter and decorate as desired. This quantity of Bavarian cream is sufficient for 6 servings.

NOTE: Flavor Bavarian cream with one of the following: 1 cup puréed

Coffee to linger over: carefully brewed and served *en demi-tasses,* accompanied by delicate Fruit and Nut Tartlets (page 251).

fresh strawberries, raspberries, or peaches; ¼ cup almond paste dissolved in ¼ cup heated light cream; 1 tablespoon powdered coffee; ½ cup strained orange juice, 2 tablespoons orange-flavored liqueur, and 2 tablespoons Orange Sugar (page 275); ½ cup Praline Powder (page 273) and 1 ounce (1 square) each of unsweetened and semisweet chocolate, melted; 3 tablespoons maple syrup; or as desired.

Glazed Strawberry Cream | Crème Brûlée aux Fraises

1 pint fresh strawberries (see Note)
6 egg yolks
⅓ cup sugar
1 tsp cornstarch
1 Tbl milk
2 cups heavy cream
2–3 drops almond extract
3 Tbl light brown sugar
3 Tbl granulated sugar

Hull and wash the strawberries. Force them through a sieve or purée them in an electric blender. In the top pan of a double-boiler beat the egg yolks with the sugar until they are thick. Blend in the cornstarch dissolved in the milk. In another saucepan heat the cream, but do not let it boil, and stir it into the egg yolks, adding it very gradually. Blend in the strawberry purée. Set the double-boiler pan over simmering water and cook the mixture, stirring it constantly until it thickens. Remove pan from over water and stir in the almond flavoring. Apportion the cream among 6 small heat-proof dishes (such as small gratin dishes) for individual servings. Let the creams cool, and chill them in

the refrigerator until the surfaces are firm. Combine the sugars and sift 1 tablespoon over the top of each, covering the cream completely with an even layer about ⅛-inch thick. Set the dishes on a baking sheet under a hot broiler and let them remain just long enough to caramelize the sugar. Turn the dishes frequently so that the sugar browns evenly and does not burn. Let the creams cool at room temperature and chill them briefly in the freezer compartment of the refrigerator before serving them.

NOTE: Frozen strawberries, well drained, may be substituted when fresh berries are not available.

Snow Eggs with Violets | Oeufs à la Neige du Printemps

4 eggs, separated
1 cup sugar
1 tsp grated lemon rind
3 cups milk
Additional milk
2 tsp lemon juice
Few grains salt
½ cup heavy cream
2 tsp kirsch
Candied violets
Candied mint leaves

In a mixing bowl beat the egg whites into soft peaks. Add ½ cup of the sugar, a little at a time, continuing to beat until the whites are stiff and glossy. Fold in the lemon rind.

In a deep skillet over low heat bring the milk to a gentle simmer. With a large oval spoon, scoop out 6 to 8 large egg shapes of the beaten egg whites and poach them, as many at a time as the pan can accommodate without crowding, in the milk for 2 minutes. Turn them carefully and poach them for 2 minutes longer. Remove them with a slotted spoon to a cloth or paper toweling and let them drain and cool.

Strain the remaining poaching milk into a saucepan and add as much more milk as needed to provide 3 cups. Reheat it without letting it boil. In the top pan of a double-boiler beat the egg yolks and stir into them the lemon juice and salt. Reserve 2 teaspoons of the sugar and blend the remainder into the egg yolks. Gradually stir in the hot milk. Set the pan over, but not touching, simmering water in the bottom pan of the double-boiler, and cook, stirring constantly, until the mixture thickens just enough to coat the spoon. Cool this custard cream and chill it. Stir it occasionally to prevent a crust from forming.

Stiffly whip the cream, sweeten it with the reserved 2 teaspoons sugar, and flavor it with the kirsch. Cover each of the cooled meringue eggs with a ¼-inch thick coating of the cream and arrange them on a baking sheet. Chill them so in a freezer for 30 minutes or until the coatings are partially frozen. Decorate each egg with 2 or 3 candied violets and a small candied mint leaf. Transfer the eggs to a shallow serving bowl and pour the chilled custard cream around them. This recipe provides 6 to 8 servings.

Cherry Charlotte | Charlotte aux Cerises

½ cup sweet white wine, such as Sauternes
1 cup sugar
1 cup sour cherries, pitted
4 eggs, lightly beaten
¾ cup light cream
7 ounces (7 squares) semisweet chocolate, melted
1 Tbl unflavored gelatine
¼ cup cool water
¼ tsp vanilla extract
2½ cups heavy cream, whipped
1 Tbl kirsch
1 Jelly Roll (page 245)

In a saucepan combine the wine and ¼ cup of the sugar, and heat until the sugar dissolves. Add the cherries, washed, and poach them gently for 2 minutes. Let them cool in the wine.

In the top pan of a double-boiler beat the eggs with the remaining sugar. In another pan heat the light cream and stir it vigorously, a little at a time, into the eggs. Blend in the melted chocolate. Set the pan over, but not touching, simmering water and cook, stirring constantly until the mixture thickens. Remove pan from over water. Add the gelatine, softened in the water, and stir until it dissolves. Stir in the vanilla and let the mixture cool. Drain the cherries and stir them into the cooled custard. Reserve 2 cups of the whipped cream and fold the remainder into the custard. Flavor the reserved cream with the kirsch and chill it.

Prepare the jelly roll as directed in the recipe and roll it across the width. Cut the roll into slices ¼-inch thick and with them line a 6-cup-capacity bowl. Pour in the prepared custard and distribute any remaining slices of jelly roll over the top. Chill the cake for several hours until the filling is set. Unmold the cake onto a chilled serving platter. Cut it in wedges to provide 8 to 10 servings, with the kirsch-flavored whipped cream passed separately.

Chilled Praline Soufflé | Soufflé Glacé Praliné

⅔ cup sugar
¼ cup shelled almonds
¼ cup shelled filberts
4 eggs, separated
¾ cup milk
1-inch piece vanilla bean
1 envelope unflavored gelatine
¼ cup cool water
1 Tbl dark rum
2 cups heavy cream
½ cup toasted almonds, crushed

In a skillet combine ½ cup of the sugar, the almonds, and filberts, and cook over low heat until the sugar melts and becomes amber in color. Pour this praline mixture onto a lightly buttered baking sheet and let it cool and harden completely. Roll it into a powder or pulverize it in an electric blender.

In the top pan of a double-boiler combine the egg yolks, milk, vanilla bean, and remaining sugar. Set the pan over, but not touching, simmering water in the bottom of the double-boiler, and cook the mixture, stirring constantly, until it thickens. Remove and discard the vanilla bean. Soften the gelatine in the cool water and dissolve it in the hot custard. Remove pan from over hot water, and stir the rum and prepared praline powder into the custard. Let the mixture cool, stirring it from time to time to prevent its becoming set.

In a mixing bowl stiffly whip the cream. Transfer ½ cup of it to another bowl and chill it thoroughly. Into the remainder fold the egg whites, beaten until stiff but not dry. Fold this mixture into the cooled praline custard. Increase the height of a 4-cup-capacity soufflé dish by tying a heavy waxed paper collar, 4 inches wide, around the rim. Pour in the soufflé mixture and chill it in the refrigerator for 2 hours or until it is set. At serving time remove the paper collar from the soufflé dish. Press the crushed almonds into the exposed sides of the soufflé and sprinkle a few over the top. Decorate the top with rosettes of the reserved whipped cream, piping them on with a pastry bag fitted with a star tube. This recipe provides 6 servings.

Lime Soufflé | Soufflé aux Limettes

6 eggs yolks
½ cup sugar
Grated rind of 3 limes
Juice of 3 limes
7 egg whites
Confectioners' sugar

Preheat oven to 375 degrees. In a mixing bowl beat the egg yolks with the sugar, lime rind, and juice until they are very thick. Separately beat the egg whites until they are stiff but not dry, and fold them carefully but thoroughly into the yolks. Butter and lightly sugar an 8-cup soufflé dish and transfer the batter to it. Set the dish in a deep roasting pan in the preheated oven and pour boiling-hot water around it to a depth of about 1 inch. Bake for 30 minutes, or until the soufflé is well puffed and browned. Dust the soufflé with confectioners' sugar and serve it at once, apportioned for 6 servings with, if desired, chilled, lightly sweetened, vanilla-flavored whipped cream.

Madeira Jelly | Madère en Gelée

2 envelopes (2 Tbl) unflavored gelatine
½ cup cold water
3 cups sweet Madeira wine
½ cup red Bordeaux wine
½ cup strained orange juice
⅓ cup sugar

Soften the gelatine in the water. In a saucepan combine the wines, orange juice, and sugar, and heat until the sugar is dissolved. Dissolve the softened gelatine in the wine mixture. Let it cool and pour it into a 6-cup mold rinsed in ice-cold water and drained. Chill it until it is set. Unmold the jelly onto a chilled serving platter. This recipe provides 6 servings.

Prune Whip | Crème aux Pruneaux

1½ cups pitted dried prunes
½ cup sugar
Thin peel of ½ lemon
½ tsp vanilla extract
3 egg yolks
½ cup milk
½ cup heavy cream, whipped

Soak the prunes in a saucepan in boiling-hot water to cover until they're soft, about 1 hour. Cook them over low heat 30 minutes until they're very soft. Drain the prunes, and force the pulp through a fine sieve or purée it in an electric blender. Let it cool. Combine it with the sugar, lemon peel, vanilla, egg yolks, and milk in the top pan of a double-boiler. Set the pan over simmering water and cook, stirring constantly, until the mixture thickens. Remove the lemon peel and discard it. Cool the custard and fold it into the whipped cream. Chill thoroughly. This recipe provides 6 servings.

Chestnut Pudding | Pouding aux Marrons

2 pounds chestnuts
2 cups milk
3 squares (3 ounces) unsweetened chocolate
⅛ tsp salt
1½ cups sugar
⅓ cup cognac
3 eggs
1 cup heavy cream, whipped

With a sharp knife slash a cross in the flat side of the chestnuts. Put the nuts in a saucepan, cover them with cool water, and bring the liquid to a boil over moderate heat. Cook the chestnuts at boil for 30 minutes. Drain them and, when they are cool enough to handle, shell them and rub off the skins. Return the nuts to the saucepan with 1 cup of the milk and heat without boiling. Strain the milk through a fine sieve into a mixing bowl and force the chestnuts through, or purée them with the milk in an electric blender.

In a saucepan combine the chocolate, the remaining milk, the salt, and 1¼ cups of the sugar. Heat gently until the chocolate melts and the sugar dissolves. Add the chestnut purée and cook, stirring until the mixture is smooth and creamy. Remove pan from heat and stir in ¼ cup of the cognac. Preheat oven to 375 degrees.

In a mixing bowl beat the eggs until they are light and frothy. Add enough of the chestnut mixture, a little at a time, to warm the eggs through, and combine that mixture with the remaining chestnut purée. Spread this batter in a buttered 2-quart pudding mold and set the mold in a pan of hot water in the preheated oven. Bake 45 minutes or until the pudding is firm to the touch. Unmold it onto a serving platter and serve it warm, providing 6 portions with the whipped cream, sweetened with the remaining sugar and flavored with the remaining cognac, passed separately.

Rice and Apple Caramel Custard | Crème Renversée au Riz et aux Pommes

½ cup rice, washed & drained
2 cups milk
¼ tsp salt
1 large cooking apple
4 Tbl butter
¼ cup Calvados or applejack
1 cup sugar
3 egg yolks, beaten
2 Tbl water

In the top pan of a double-boiler soak the washed rice in the milk for 30 minutes. Add the salt. Set the pan over simmering water and cook the rice, covered, for 45 minutes or until it is very tender and all but about ½ cup of the milk has been absorbed. Remove pan from over water and let the rice and milk cool.

Peel and core the apple and cut it into slices across the core. In a skillet heat 2 tablespoons of the butter and in it sauté the slices of apple over moderate heat for 5 minutes or just until they are tender, turning them once. Pour the Calvados or applejack over them, set it ablaze, and shake pan until the flame expires. Let the slices cool in pan.

In a mixing bowl cream the remaining butter with ½ cup of the sugar and blend in the beaten egg yolks. Stir the mixture into the cooled rice and milk. Preheat oven to 325 degrees.

Cook the remaining sugar and the water in a 6-cup-capacity charlotte mold over moderate heat until the sugar caramelizes. Remove mold from heat and swirl the caramel around in it to coat the bottom and sides evenly. When the coating is firm, spread ½ the rice mixture in the mold. Cover with the apple slices, and cover them with the remaining rice mixture. Set mold in a pan of hot water in the preheated oven and bake for 30 minutes or until the custard is set. Remove it from the oven and let it stand for 15 minutes. Unmold it onto a serving dish and pour any remaining caramel around it. Serve warm, apportioned for 6 servings, with, if desired, chilled whipped cream, lightly sweetened and flavored with a little Calvados or applejack.

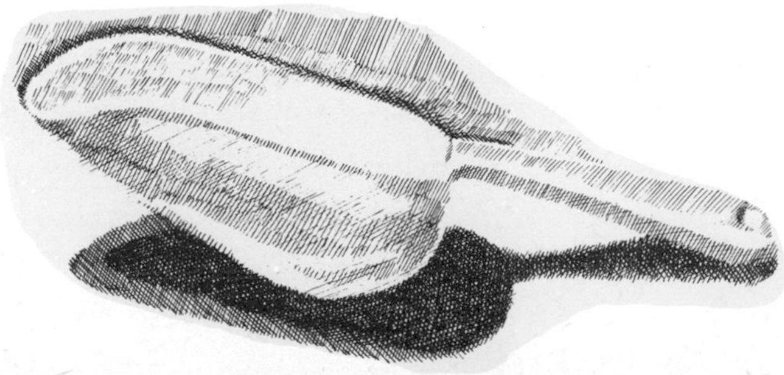

Lemon Rice Pudding | Pouding au Riz Citronné

¼ cup rice, washed & drained
2 cups milk
¼ tsp salt
2 eggs, separated
2 Tbl butter
½ cup sugar
1 Tbl lemon juice
1 Tbl finely grated lemon rind
¼ tsp nutmeg
½ cup heavy cream, whipped

Soak the rice in the milk in the top pan of a double-boiler for 30 minutes. Add the salt. Set pan over gently simmering water and cook the rice, covered, stirring it occasionally, for 45 minutes or until it is very tender and all but about ½ cup of the milk is absorbed. In a mixing bowl lightly beat the egg yolks, and stir enough of the hot rice into them to warm them through. Combine the mixture with the remaining rice and milk. Continue cooking, stirring constantly, for 2 minutes. Remove pan from over hot water. Cream the butter with the sugar, lemon juice and rind, and nutmeg, and stir the mixture into the rice custard. Set the mixture aside to cool. Preheat oven to 325 degrees.

Stiffly whip the cream and stir it into the cooled rice custard. In a mixing bowl beat the egg whites just to the soft-peak stage and fold them into the rice. Transfer the mixture to a buttered 1-quart casserole and bake it in the preheated oven 30 minutes or until the pudding is set and the top is lightly browned. Cool the pudding slightly. Serve warm with, if desired, sweetened whipped cream flavored with vanilla.

Blushing Peaches | Pêches Rougissantes

6 large ripe peaches
1 cup sugar
6 Tbl butter
Juice of 1 orange
Juice of 1 lemon
Thin peel of 1 lemon
2 cups raspberry purée (see Note)
⅓ cup cognac
Toasted blanched almonds, crushed (optional)

In a saucepan cover the peaches with boiling water and let them remain so for 2 minutes. Drain the peaches, plunge them into cold water, and drain them again. Carefully, with your fingers, pull off the peel, beginning at the stem ends of the fruit. Set the peeled peaches aside.

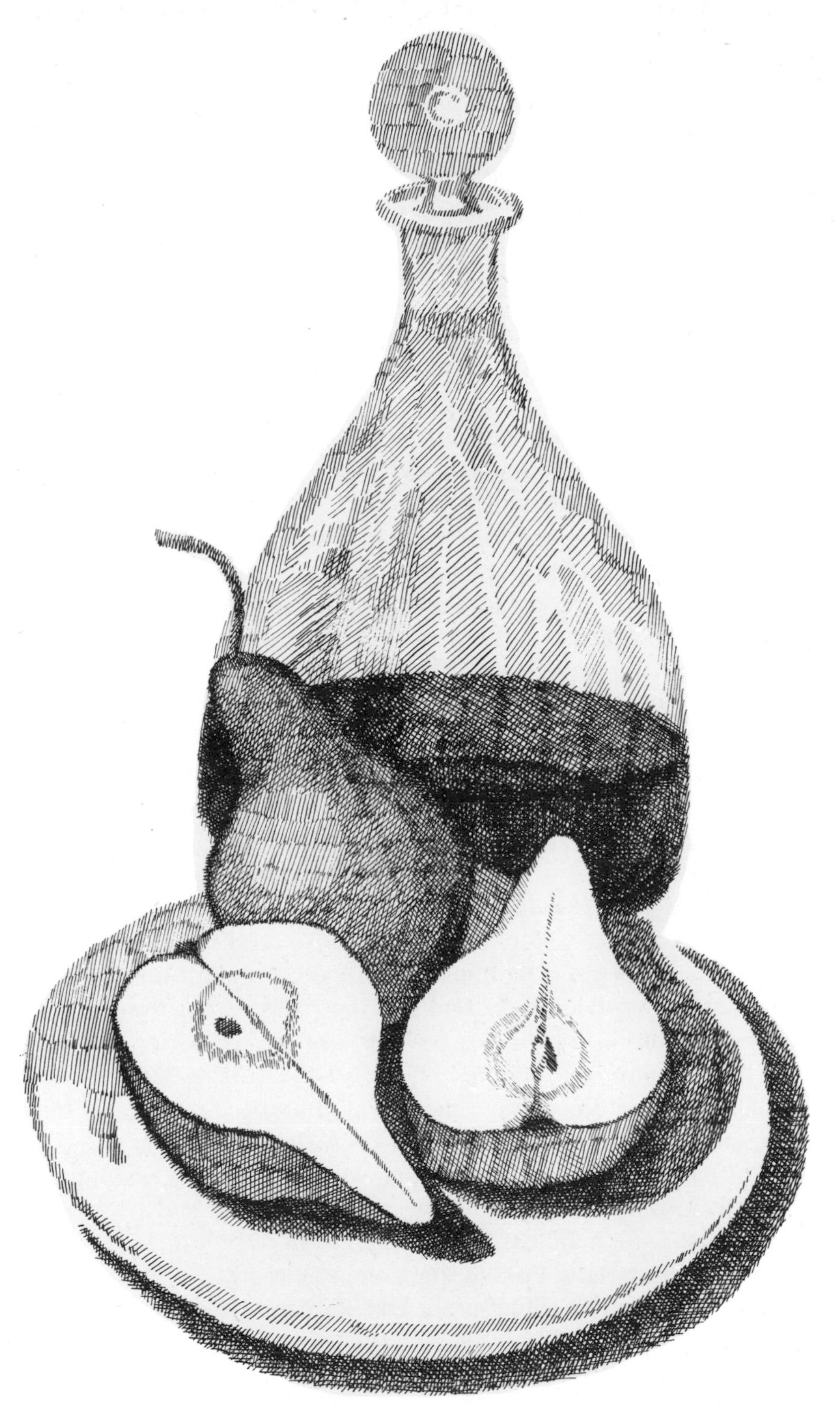

In a skillet over moderate heat caramelize the sugar in the butter. Pour in the juices, heated, stirring until the caramel dissolves. Add the lemon peel and stir in the raspberry purée. Bring the liquid to a gentle simmer. Add the peaches and roll them around in the sauce until they are heated through and acquire a blush. Gently warm the cognac, set it ablaze, and pour it over the fruit and into the sauce. Baste the peaches with the sauce until the flame expires. Serve the peaches, individually, with a quantity of the sauce poured over them and, if desired, a sprinkling of crushed toasted blanched almonds. The sauce may be prepared in advance and the peaches poached in it in a chafing dish at the table. Or the peaches and sauce may be served cool with the solidified butter removed.

NOTE: The required quantity of raspberry purée may be obtained by forcing the contents of 2 packages frozen raspberries, defrosted, through a fine sieve, or by puréeing them in an electric blender and straining out the seeds.

Praline-Glazed Pears in White Port |
Poires Pralinées au Porto Blanc

6 firm ripe pears
3 cups white port wine
¼ cup Vanilla Sugar (page 275)
6 egg yolks
¾ cup heavy cream, whipped
⅓ cup Praline Powder (page 273)

Peel the pears, cut them into halves lengthwise, and remove the cores. Heat the port in a deep skillet and poach the pears in it just until they are tender. Do not overcook. Remove the skillet from the heat and let the pears cool in the liquid. Drain the pears, reserving the wine.

In the top pan of a double-boiler beat the vanilla sugar into the egg yolks until it is completely incorporated and the mixture is thick. Add 1 cup of the port wine. Reserve the remainder for other uses (see Note). Set pan over hot, but not boiling, water, and cook, beating constantly with a rotary beater until the mixture is thick and frothy. This should take about 5 minutes. Remove pan from over water and let the custard cool completely. Fold in the whipped cream.

Place the pears in a heat-proof baking dish, arranging the halves core sides down. Spread the creamed custard over them and sprinkle with the praline powder. Set the dish under a hot broiler and let it remain until the powder melts and the custard is lightly browned. Watch it carefully so that it does not burn. Remove the dish from the broiler and let the pears and custard cool. Chill thoroughly in the refrigerator. This recipe provides 6 servings.

NOTE: The remaining pear-flavored port wine provides a basis for a refreshing drink. Pour ½ cup of the cooled wine in a 10-ounce highball glass. Add ice cubes and fill the glass with Vichy, Perrier, or other sparkling water. Garnish the drink with ½ slice of orange.

Pineapple Meringue Oranges | Oranges à l'Ananas Meringuées

4 large navel oranges
1 cup light cream
1 cup flaked coconut
½ cup sugar
3 eggs, separated
1½ cups crushed fresh pineapple, drained
½ cup heavy cream, whipped

Peel 1 of the oranges. Separate the segments, skin and chop them. Cut the remaining 3 oranges into halves, and squeeze out the juice. Reserve the juice for drinking. Scoop out and discard the pulp residue, taking care not to damage shells. Chill the shells in the refrigerator.

In a saucepan combine the light cream, coconut, and 2 tablespoons of the sugar. Heat gently to scald the cream and dissolve the sugar. Remove pan from heat and let the coconut steep for 30 minutes. Strain this mixture through several thicknesses of cheesecloth into a bowl, and press the coconut to extract as much more of the cream as possible. Discard the coconut. Scald the cream in the saucepan again. Beat the egg yolks in the top pan of a double-boiler and gradually stir in the hot coconut cream. Set pan over, but not touching, simmering water, and cook, stirring constantly, until the cream thickens enough to coat the spoon thickly. Remove pan from over water and let the custard cool completely, stirring it occasionally to prevent a crust from forming. Combine the pineapple and chopped orange pulp with the cooled custard, and fold in the whipped cream. Fill the chilled shells with the mixture, cover them with waxed paper, and set them in the freezer compartment of the refrigerator with the temperature control at its coldest point or in a deep freezer. Let them remain for 1 hour, stirring the fillings at 20-minute intervals in the refrigerator and at 10-minute intervals in a deep freezer. Continue the freezing, without stirring, for 1 hour longer or until the fillings are firm.

In a mixing bowl beat the egg whites into soft peaks. Add the remaining sugar, a little at a time, continuing to beat until the whites are stiff and glossy. Swirl the meringue into domes over the tops of the filled oranges, spreading it to the rims and sealing in the fillings completely. Set the oranges on a baking sheet under a hot broiler and let the meringue domes brown lightly. Serve the 6 portions immediately.

dessert sauces

Caramel Custard Sauce | Sauce Crème Caramel

½ cup sugar
3 Tbl boiling-hot water
2 cups light cream
3 egg yolks

In a skillet over moderate heat melt ⅓ cup of the sugar until it caramelizes lightly. Blend in the hot water, stirring until the caramel dissolves. Blend in the cream, and heat without boiling. Remove pan from heat.

In the top pan of a double-boiler beat the egg yolks with the remaining sugar, and stir in the hot caramel cream, very gradually. Set the pan over, but not touching, simmering water and cook, stirring constantly until the sauce coats the spoon. Transfer the sauce to a bowl and let it cool, stirring it occasionally to prevent a skin from forming. Serve cool, with puddings, cake, or ice cream. This recipe provides about 2 cups of caramel custard sauce. Refrigerated, it will keep for 3 to 4 days.

Chestnut Sauce | Sauce aux Marrons

1 cup preserved chestnuts, with syrup (see Note)
¼ tsp vanilla extract
½ cup heavy cream

Force the chestnuts along with the syrup and vanilla through a sieve into a mixing bowl. In a separate bowl whip the cream just until it begins to thicken. It should not be stiff. Blend the whipped cream into the chestnut purée. Serve the 1½ cups of sauce provided by this recipe with baked custard, fruit puddings, or ice cream.
NOTE: Preserved chestnuts are available in specialty food shops.

Spiced Chocolate Sauce | Sauce au Chocolat Epicée

4 ounces (4 squares) unsweetened chocolate
¼ cup sugar
¼ cup water
½ cup heavy cream
⅛ tsp nutmeg
⅛ tsp cinnamon
Few grains ground cloves
2 Tbl cognac
Light cream, as needed

In the top pan of a double-boiler over simmering water, heat together the chocolate, sugar, and water until the chocolate melts and the sugar is dissolved. Blend in the heavy cream and add the spices and cognac. Let the mixture heat through. Remove pan from over water and blend in light cream to produce the consistency desired. Serve hot or cooled with ice cream and custard and bread puddings.

Orange Chocolate Sauce:

Prepare as above, but substitute ½ cup strained orange juice for the water. Reduce heavy cream to ¼ cup and omit the spices. An orange-flavored liqueur, such as Grand Marnier, Cointreau, or Curaçao, may be substituted for the cognac.

Mocha Sauce:

Prepare as for Spiced Chocolate Sauce, but substitute 1½ teaspoons powdered coffee for the spices. Cognac for this sauce is optional.

Cider Sauce | Sauce Normande

3 egg yolks
¼ cup sugar
1½ cups apple cider, heated
½ cup heavy cream
2 Tbl Calvados or applejack

In the top pan of a double-boiler beat the egg yolks with the sugar. Add the hot cider gradually, stirring it in a little at a time. Set pan over simmering water and cook, stirring constantly until the mixture coats the spoon. Remove pan from over water and stir in the cream. Add the Calvados or applejack. This recipe provides about 2 cups of sauce to be served with apple desserts or fruit puddings.

Raspberry Sauce | Sauce aux Framboises

2 cups fresh raspberries
¾ cup sugar
⅓ cup water
Additional sugar
⅔ cup heavy cream, whipped

In a saucepan combine the berries, sugar, and water, and bring the liquid to a boil. Reduce the heat to low and cook, skimming once or twice, until the berries are reduced to juice. Strain out the seeds. Add additional sugar, if needed. Return the juice to the saucepan and the heat, and continue cooking for 10 minutes or until the juice is syrupy. Remove pan from heat and let syrup cool. Blend in the whipped cream. This recipe provides about 2 cups of sauce for use with ice cream, puddings, or mousses.

dessert basics

Almond Paste | Pâte d'Amandes

1 cup blanched almonds
2 egg whites
1½ cups sifted confectioners' sugar

Roll the almonds into a fine powder with a rolling pin or pulverize them in an electric blender. In a mixing bowl beat the egg whites to a froth and stir in the almond powder. Work in the sugar to produce a smooth paste. This recipe provides 1 cup of almond paste. Stored in a covered container in the refrigerator, it can be kept several weeks. Actually, the flavor improves as it ages. Use the paste as required in specific recipes or as desired.

Praline Powder | Pralin en Poudre

1 cup sugar
½ cup shelled almonds
½ cup shelled filberts

Heat the sugar gently in a skillet. As it begins to melt add the nuts and continue heating until the sugar melts completely and begins to turn amber in color. Stir to coat the nuts thoroughly. Pour this praline onto a lightly buttered baking sheet or sheet of foil, and let it cool and harden completely. Pound or roll it into a powder between sheets of waxed paper or pulverize it in an electric blender. This recipe provides slightly more than 2 cups of praline powder. Stored in a tightly covered container, the powder will remain dry, but it should be used within about 2 months. Thereafter the ground almonds may become rancid. Use the powder as required in specific recipes or as desired.

Chantilly Cream | Crème Chantilly

1 cup heavy cream
2 Tbl confectioners' sugar
Flavoring (see Note)

In a well-chilled mixing bowl whip the cream until it begins to thicken. Add the sugar and continue whipping until the cream is stiff. Stir in the desired flavoring. Take care not to overbeat the cream or it will be churned into butter. This recipe provides 2 cups of Chantilly cream. NOTE: Flavor with 1 teaspoon vanilla extract or 1 tablespoon cognac, rum, yellow Chartreuse, or orange-flavored liqueur.

Pastry Cream | Crème Pâtissière

4 egg yolks
⅓ cup sugar
2 tsp cornstarch
¼ cup milk
1 cup light cream, scalded
¼ tsp vanilla extract

In the top pan of a double-boiler beat the egg yolks with the sugar until they are thick. Dissolve the cornstarch in the milk and combine it with the yolks. Add the hot cream, stirring it in very gradually. Set the pan over, but not touching, barely simmering water and cook, stirring constantly until the mixture thickens sufficiently to coat the spoon thickly. Remove pan from over water and stir in the vanilla. Let the cream cool, stirring it occasionally to prevent a crust from forming. This recipe provides about 2 cups of pastry cream. Other flavorings, such as chocolate, spirits, praline powder, or pulverized almonds, may be substituted for the vanilla. Use the cream as filling for cakes or pastries, or as required in specific recipes. Refrigerated, pastry cream may be kept for 4 or 5 days. It should not be frozen.

Apricot Glaze | Glaçage d'Abricots

1 cup apricot preserves
1 Tbl water, liqueur, or brandy

In a saucepan bring the preserves to a gentle boil over low heat. Stir in the water and strain out the solids. Use the clear glaze while it is warm. It may be reheated. If liqueur or brandy is used, it should be stirred into the heated preserves off the heat. Store the glaze, cooled, in a covered container. It need not be refrigerated.

Chocolate Glaze | Glaçage de Chocolat

8 ounces (8 squares) unsweetened or semisweet chocolate
¼ cup water
4½ tsp cocoa butter or vegetable shortening

Grate the chocolate and combine it in the top of a double-boiler with the water and shortening or cocoa butter. Set pan over hot, but not boiling or even simmering, water. When about half of the chocolate is melted remove pan from over water and stir gently until the chocolate and shortening are completely melted and the ingredients are combined. Let the glaze cool very slightly before pouring it over the material to be glazed. The glazed material may be chilled, if necessary, to hasten the setting. This recipe provides 1 cup of chocolate glaze. It can be kept in a covered container under refrigeration, but may require additional shortening and water when it is reheated.

Orange Sugar | Sucre d'Orange

¼ cup sugar
Thin peel of 1 orange

Rub the peel into the sugar, impregnating the grains completely with the zest. Fruit sugars, such as this, do not retain flavor for any length of time. It is advisable to prepare only as much as needed at a time.

Vanilla Sugar | Sucre Vanillé

1 vanilla bean
4 cups granulated or confectioners' sugar

Slit the vanilla bean lengthwise and cut it into 2-inch pieces. Combine the pieces with the sugar in a tightly covered container and let the sugar absorb the flavor for 3 to 4 days before using it. Replenish with unflavored sugar.

9 | wine, apéritifs, and coffee

It is true that a dish can be no better than the ingredients provided for its making, but to use such an exalted wine as a Château Haut-Brion 1959—for example—in the preparation of a simple beef stew would be downright pretentious, not to say out of all proportion. By the same token, to provide for the stew a wine of meager flavor would be to demean it. In this chapter, suggestions are given for cooking wines, as well as for "little" wines to drink with everyday family meals and distinguished wines for great occasions.

Not many Frenchmen drink great or near-great wines with frequency. The French daily wine is *vin ordinaire,* and this custom holds for the United States, too. The French in this country, like the Americans themselves, have discovered American wines and know them for the fine and reasonably priced products they are.

Apéritifs and coffee—those before and after drinks—contribute their own grace to the experience of dining. Some refreshing apéritifs are offered here, as well as an appreciation of coffee in its various French moods—from the invigorating *café au lait* of breakfast, to the tiny cup of strong coffee that so delightfully rounds out dinner.

All Gaul is divided for wine production into six main regions: Alsace, Bordeaux, Burgundy, Champagne, Loire, and Rhône. Alsace provides —principally—light, fresh wines: Riesling, Traminer, Gewurztraminer. Bordeaux and Burgundy, of course, are productive of the great wines of France. The top wines of Bordeaux are now, as they were when classified in 1855, in preparation for the Paris Fair of that year, Château Lafite, Château Margaux, Château Latour, and Château Haut-Brion. Château Mouton-Rothchild, although listed somewhat below the top four, is considered by many connoisseurs to be equal if not superior to some of them. Burgundy's kings of the vineyards are, among the red wines, Chambertin, Musigny, Romanée-Conti, and Richebourg, and among the white wines Meursault and Montrachet. The most popular is probably Pouilly-Fuissé.

To taste any of these great wines is to experience one of the supreme pleasures of the table. Another spectrum of joyful tasting, infinitely less costly, is provided by the "little" French wines, those produced by lesser-known vintners and minor *châteaux*. The great wines have already been evaluated and acclaimed. The little ones are not all plentiful, and may never become famous, but they merit discovery and are well worth seeking out. They are ideally suited to the family table.

Awaiting your pleasure among these little wines are the *vins du pays,* the wines of the French countryside. Among them are such red wines as Corbières Chaintruel, Fitou, Les Baux, Cahors, Bandol, and Bouzy (the last a still wine from the Champagne district), and such whites as Côtes de Bergerac, Jurançon, Sauvignon de Saint-Bris, Blanc de Blancs de Cassis (a traditional accompaniment to bouillabaisse), Roussette de Seyssel, Crépy, and Monbazillac (a sort of country cousin, at least as far as sweetness is concerned, to light Sauternes). Somewhat better known and more readily available in the United States are the regional wines of France, labeled, according to their native regions, as Médoc, Saint-Émilion, Bourgogne Rouge or Blanc, Graves Supérieure, et cetera. (Graves Supérieure does not indicate a better wine than one simply labeled Graves. It merely designates a Graves from another area in the region.) The crisp, frequently flint-dry wines of the Loire include such as Muscadet, Sancerre, and Pouilly-

Fumé. Wines of the Rhône, sturdy and full-bodied, include the popular Chateauneuf-du-Pape. Among Americans probably the best known of all French wines is Beaujolais, a light, joyous wine from the region of the same name.

Among the bottlings of minor châteaux, the following are, with varying frequency, available in the United States: Château La Fleur Milon, Château Marbuzet, Château Loudenne (white and red), Château Hanteillan, Château Bellevue, and Château Coutelin-Merville. The wines of almost all minor châteaux are vintage (that is, designated as to year), as are many of the country and regional wines, and they are, for the most part, relatively inexpensive.

The best wines of the United States, some of which merit the designation of greatness, are produced in California and in the Finger Lakes region of New York State. The premium wines are those that bear the names of the grape varieties from which they are made. Look for such as Pinot Noir, Cabernet Sauvignon, Gamay Beaujolais among the reds—the nearest French equivalents of which are, respectively, light Burgundy, red Bordeaux, and Beaujolais. Among the fine varietal white wines, you may find Pinot Chardonnay reminiscent of the French Pouilly-Fuissé, Sauvignon Blanc somewhat similar to the French Graves, Chenin Blanc to Vouvray, Traminer to its counterpart in Alsace, Pinot Blanc to one of the light white Burgundies. A Grenache rosé may remind you of a Tavel rosé of France's Rhône region.

A word about those vintage years: Don't become obsessed with them. Some regions produce good wines even in "bad" years, and off years can and do frequently provide bargains.

You do not need a complete knowledge of wines to be able to select a proper bottle of wine for dinner. Don't be intimidated by such dogma as "red wine with red meat," "white wine with veal, poultry, and fish." The right wine to accompany any preparation is the wine that tastes best with it. Only one caution should be observed: Sweet wine is not the ideal companion for any foods other than fruit and desserts. Served with other courses, it may stifle the appetite. Otherwise, let the wine be red or white, with white meat or red, and drink hearty and enjoy it.

Experiment. Taste a variety of wines and discover those that please you. The variety of available French wines can provide a lifetime of happy tasting. The number of wines produced in Bordeaux alone is vast. There are sixty-one classified growths of red Bordeaux, and more than four hundred others produced in the region.

If you lack confidence about selecting a good wine, put your trust in a wine merchant whose shop indicates that he knows something about wines. Observe the variety of his stock and how it is displayed. If the wines are presented standing upright, you may be certain that he has little knowledge of wine and no respect for it. Table wine should be displayed, as it should be stored, with the bottles on their sides in racks. So stored the corks remain damp and firm, preventing deterioration of the wine. A knowledgeable wine merchant will want to help you. Tell him what you like or dislike about the wines he recommends to you so that he can become acquainted with your tastes and advise you properly about future choices.

Buy wine several days to a week in advance of the day it is to be served. Wine suffers from being agitated, as it is when shaken in a delivery truck or even when carried, however gently, a short distance from the wine shop. In order to provide the bouquet and flavor expected of it, the wine must be allowed to rest in a place neither too hot nor too cool, with the bottle on its side in a rack. Several hours before it is to be opened, stand the bottle upright to allow any sediment to settle to the bottom. Open a bottle of red wine a good hour before the wine is to be served and leave the cork out. This allows the wine to "breathe" and further enhances its flavor.

To open the bottle, first cut off the top of the foil capsule that encloses the cork. Use a sharp knife and cut around the capsule just above the ridge near the top of the bottle. Wipe the exposed top of the cork with a damp cloth. Insert the point of the corkscrew into the center of the cork and screw it in well. If you use a corkscrew with two levers attached to each side of the top, the levers will rise as you screw in the point. When they reach the top, press them back into position. This will draw the cork so that it need only be lifted out. With an ordinary corkscrew, exert steady pressure upward and ease out the cork.

Smell the cork. It should smell of wine. If it smells of cork the wine may also smell of it. Pour a little of the wine into a glass and taste it. If it is all right, set the bottle aside at room temperature—still with the cork out—until serving time.

Serve the wine in stemmed, thin, clear glasses. For red wine, the bowls should be large and tulip-shaped. The bowls of white-wine glasses should be smaller and straight. If space is at a premium, all-purpose glasses of medium size are suitable for all table wines except Champagne. Pour red wine to fill the glasses to no more than one-half capacity. White wine may be poured a little more fully. In no instance should the glasses be completely filled. Replenish the wine, as needed. A host serves himself first to determine—particularly in the case of white wine opened just before it is served—that the wine is as it should be. Also, if any bits of cork have dropped into the bottle, they will not be inflicted upon the guests.

Red wine is usually at its best served at room temperature, always assuming that the room is not overheated. Regardless of the tempera-

ture of the room, the temperature of the wine should not be less than 65 degrees Fahrenheit, nor ever more than 70 degrees. Light red wines such as Beaujolais taste better when they are slightly chilled, about 60 degrees. White wines, including Champagne, and rosés should be chilled.

Generally, the wine should complement the dinner, although if a wine is a very special one of rare vintage, it may well be treated as the star, and the dinner arranged in its honor. Nowadays, only one wine is customarily served with dinner and that with the main course. If more than one wine is served the best effect is created by keeping the flavors and densities in proper sequence. Thus, a light wine precedes a heavier one, a less dry precedes a drier, and a sweet wine is served last, with dessert. Dry white wines are served before red wines.

Wines are not, of course, limited to accompanying the meal. They also serve to whet the appetite for it. The most elegant of appetizer wines is considered, naturally, to be Champagne, particularly Champagne labeled *brut,* which designates the driest (note that "dry," as relates to wine, means not sweet). *Brut* Champagne is also most preferred to accompany the meal, although "extra dry," which is actually somewhat sweet, is also served. "Dry" Champagne, which is quite sweet, and *doux,* which is very sweet (and rarely available in the United States) are dessert wines.

apéritifs

The designation of *apéritifs*—appetizer wines—is most frequently applied to specifically flavored, fortified wines (those of greater alcoholic content). Included among those are the French Byrrh, Dubonnet (sweet red and drier blond), Lillet, St. Raphael, Pernod, and dry and sweet vermouths. Red and dry white table wines provide the basis for other apéritifs, as do such unflavored fortified wines as the Sercial (relatively dry) type of Madeira. Wines—red or white—as apéritifs are always served chilled. Recipes for a few of these wine appetizers are given below.

Kir

8 ounces dry white wine, well chilled
1 ounce (2 Tbl) crème de cassis liqueur

Pour the wine into a chilled 10-ounce highball glass and stir in the liqueur. Kir was named for a mayor of Dijon, which city produces the red currant liqueur and syrup called cassis.

Claret and Bitters | Clairet Amer

6 ounces chilled red Bordeaux wine
½ ounce (1 Tbl) orange bitters

Pour the wine into a chilled 8-ounce highball glass and stir in the bitters. Chilled Vichy or soda water, to fill the glass, may be added, if desired.

Vermouth Cassis

4 ice cubes
6 ounces dry vermouth
1 ounce (2 Tbl) crème de cassis liqueur
Chilled Vichy or soda water

Into a 10-ounce highball glass containing the ice cubes pour the vermouth and liqueur. Add enough Vichy or soda water to fill the glass and stir gently to blend.

Vermouth on the Rocks

4 ounces (½ cup) sweet or dry vermouth (see Note)
3 ice cubes
Strip of thin lemon peel

Pour the vermouth over the ice cubes in an Old-fashioned glass. Twist the strip of lemon peel over the drink and drop it into the glass.

NOTE: This apéritif may also be prepared with 2 ounces (¼ cup) each of sweet and dry vermouth combined.

Pernod Apéritif | Un Lait

2 ounces (4 Tbl) Pernod
4 ice cubes
1 Tbl ice-cold water

Pour the Pernod over the ice cubes in an Old-fashioned glass and blend in the water. As the Pernod and water combine the mixture turns milky white, hence the French designation, a milk.

wine in cooking

A wine for cooking should be modest, but of good quality, one that imparts rather than imposes its flavor, so as to blend with the flavors of the other ingredients of a preparation to produce a harmonious entity. (Save the great wines for drinking only. They assert themselves too strongly, and, besides, are far too expensive for this purpose.)

Wine for cooking generally means table wine, red or dry white, of 10 to 12 percent alcoholic content, but dry vermouth (about 20 percent alcohol) may be substituted for the white wine. Red vermouth, which is sweet, cannot be used as a substitute for red table wine, which is invariably dry. For general cooking use, provide yourself with such red wine as Pinot Noir, and such whites as Pinot Blanc or Pinot Chardonnay, either French or American. The Californian counterparts of those wines are excellent and are available in gallon and half-gallon sizes, as well as the usual 25-ounce bottles. Sweet white wines, such as lesser Sauternes (the Californian types of such wines are designated as sauterne) are occasionally used in cooking, primarily for desserts. Madeira, among the fortified wines, as well as port, are used in cooking, mostly for sauces. Liqueurs such as Grand Marnier, Cointreau, and Curaçao are for desserts, but cognac, almost alone of the spirits, is omnipresent in French cookery.

Unless you use wine frequently, buying it in sizes larger than the usual bottle is not advised. Once opened, table wine deteriorates, though it can be kept for a little while, perhaps a day or two, under refrigeration. When cooking, use what you require of a bottle of wine,

and serve the rest at the table. Half-bottles, although a little more expensive, can ultimately prove economical if just a small quantity is needed in cooking and a remaining two glasses or so will suffice at table. If the wine is not used, or not soon required, leave the bottle open at room temperature and let the wine turn to vinegar, which it will obligingly do. The process can be hastened with the addition of a little wine already turned.

Company dining at the family table is brought to a proper finale with dessert. Cognac or liqueurs and coffee are best served in the living room. If several after-dinner drinks are offered, let the assortment be modest: in addition to cognac, perhaps a crème de menthe, and an orange-flavored liqueur, or green or yellow Chartreuse. Cognac may be served in the balloon-shaped glasses called snifters or in small liqueur glasses. In France, particularly in the Chartreuse Massif region which is the liqueur's home, green Chartreuse is often served chilled or over ice.

coffee

When dining in the French manner, coffee is almost mandatory at midday and in the evening, but never with the meal, always after and separately, and always in small cups (*demi-tasses*). Morning coffee in France, as at the tables of French families in the United States, is strong, but tempered with hot milk and sweetened to taste. Coffee in the evening is also strong, and black. A *filtre*—a cup of filtered coffee—is made in a little drip pot with the grounds placed in a separate compartment above; the hot water is poured over them and allowed to seep through leisurely. As with all good French cooking, the making of coffee is never hurried.

Coffee for home consumption in France is usually bought in the bean and ground in the kitchen, as needed, in a little *moulin à café,* a coffee mill.

For French-style coffee to be made in an American kitchen, buy French-roast coffee beans and have them ground, or grind them finely yourself, for drip coffee. For two dinner demi-tasses, place 2 tablespoons of the ground coffee in the container of a filter or drip-coffee maker. Moisten the grounds with a little fresh boiling water and let the grounds steep for a minute. Pour in ⅔ cup of boiling-hot water in two infusions, a half at a time, adding each half only after the prior one has seeped through. The coffee maker may be set on a warmer, but the coffee should not be allowed to boil. Serve immediately it has seeped through. Make just as much as may be needed for the required number of servings. Do not reheat.

To make breakfast coffee with milk—*café au lait*—for two persons, double the ingredients and combine the brewed coffee with hot rich milk, or serve the milk separately to be added as desired. Enjoy the coffee leisurely with a little loaf of French bread and sweet butter, and you are ready to face the day.

glossary

Angelica A plant, the leafstalks and roots of which are candied by boiling them in lemon-flavored sugar syrup. Angelica is green in color and is used to decorate desserts, pastries, and confections, and to flavor preserved fruits.

Aspic Natural jellied essence of meat, poultry, or fish, or food molded in such jellies. Aspic can also be made by dissolving softened gelatine in a hot, flavored liquid.

Bard To enclose lean meat, poultry, or fish in thin sheets of fresh pork to keep it moist during cooking and to enhance flavor.

Baste To moisten meat, poultry, fish, or other foods with a liquid or melted fat at intervals during cooking.

Beat To turn a mass over and over rapidly with a fork, whisk, or rotary beater in order to aerate it, or to blend ingredients.

Blanch To scald or steam uncooked fruits, nuts, or vegetables in order to make their skins easier to remove.

Blend To combine one ingredient or mixture thoroughly with another; also the process of reducing an ingredient or mixture to a finer texture in an electric blender.

Bouquet garni Aromatic herbs, basically bay leaf, parsley, and thyme, combined in proportion to their strength and tied together or enclosed in cheesecloth, for seasoning a variety of preparations. Tying them together makes it easier to remove and discard them when the cooking is completed.

Braise To cook foods, that have been browned in fat, at low temperature in a covered casserole with a minimum of liquid.

Caramelize To heat sugar in a pan until it melts and turns amber in color, or to coat a mold or substance with such melted sugar.

Cardoons Thistle-like plants of the globe artichoke family, the edible portions of which are the stalks and the center ribs of the prickly leaves. The flavor of of cardoons is somewhat like that of both celery and artichokes.

Celeriac A variant of celery grown for its thick edible root rather than its stalk. It is known also as knob celery and celery root.

Clarify To make a fat-free stock entirely clear by simmering it with lightly beaten egg whites and straining the stock through a sieve lined with a dampened cloth.

Cornichons French designation for a type of small cucumber. Picked green and pickled in vinegar, these little gherkins are served as a condiment.

Cream To work a firm ingredient, such as butter or cream cheese (often in combination with sugar), to the consistency of lightly whipped cream, first by pressing it with a spoon or spatula against the side of a bowl to soften the substance, then by whipping it.

Deflate To release gas or air from risen dough by punching it down.

De-glaze To blend a liquid (wine, spirit, stock, or, occasionally, cream) into the concentrated cooking juices remaining in a pan after meat, poultry, or fish have been roasted or sautéed in it; done to incorporate the flavor of the juices.

De-grease To remove from soups, sauces, or stews the fat rendered during cooking, by skimming it off the surface with a spoon or by passing a sheet of paper toweling or other absorbent paper over the surface of the liquid, thereby blotting up the grease.

Demi-glaze A very thick brown sauce, derived by boiling and thereby reducing a stock. Demi-glaze is used to coat preparations of meat or poultry.

Dice To cut foods into cubes of required size.

Fillet A slice of boneless meat or fish, or the process of boning.

Flame To pour a gently warmed spirit over food and set it ablaze. The alcohol is thereby volatilized, leaving only the true flavor of the spirit with which to imbue the food.

Fry To cook in a quantity of liquid fat sufficient to cover the food to be prepared.

Glaze To give food a lustrous coating, either with a sugar substance (for desserts) or demi-glaze. Desserts, and occasionally vegetables, are glazed by sprinkling them lightly with sugar and subjecting them to heat under a broiler until the sugar melts.

Marinate To steep (as meat, poultry, fish, or vegetables) in a mixture basically of wine, spirit, or vinegar, along with oil and seasonings, to flavor the food, to reduce its flavor, or to tenderize it.

Meat glaze Extract of meat, produced by cooking stock until the essence is reduced almost to a solid. It is used for flavoring.

Mince To chop with a knife into the smallest possible bits.

Poach To cook in a liquid at simmer.

Purée Food mashed and sieved to produce a substance of near-liquid consistency.

Reduce To thicken a liquid by boiling it down, thereby also concentrating its seasoning and flavor.

Roux A blend of flour and butter or other fat, heated together, and used to provide thickening.

Sauté To cook with a small amount of fat, generally in a skillet.

Scald To heat a liquid just below the boiling point, to facilitate combining it with another substance or blending it into a mixture.

Simmer To cook gently, slightly below or just at the boiling point.

Stock Broth made by cooking meat, poultry, fish, and/or vegetables in seasoned water. Stock may be white (made with chicken, veal, or fish), or brown (made with chicken or beef).

Truss To prepare poultry for cooking by binding the legs and wings with twine, securing them close to the body of the bird.

Whip To beat, as cream, with a fork, whisk, or rotary beater or an electric device similar to it, in order to aerate a substance and thereby thicken it.

index

a

b

c

d

e

f

g

h

j

k

l

m

q

r

s

Recipe index in French

d

e

f

g

q

r

s

t

v